MW00803252

Why We Love Parades

Why We Love Parades

Their History and Enduring Appeal

DOUG MATTHEWS

McFarland & Company, Inc., Publishers
Jefferson, North Carolina

LIBRARY OF CONGRESS CATALOGUING-IN-PUBLICATION DATA

Names: Matthews, Doug, author.
Title: Why we love parades : their history and enduring appeal / Doug Matthews.
Description: Jefferson, North Carolina : McFarland & Company, Inc.,
Publishers, 2023. | Includes bibliographical references and index.
Identifiers: LCCN 2022043059 |
ISBN 9781476688794 (paperback : acid free paper) ∞
ISBN 9781476647067 (ebook)
Subjects: LCSH: Parades—Social aspects. | Parades—History. |
BISAC: SOCIAL SCIENCE / Holidays (non-religious) |
RELIGION / Holidays / General
Classification: LCC GT3980 .M37 2023 | DDC 394/.5—dc23/eng/20221103
LC record available at https://lccn.loc.gov/2022043059

BRITISH LIBRARY CATALOGUING DATA ARE AVAILABLE

ISBN (print) 978-1-4766-8879-4
ISBN (ebook) 978-1-4766-4706-7

© 2023 Doug Matthews. All rights reserved

*No part of this book may be reproduced or transmitted in any form
or by any means, electronic or mechanical, including photocopying
or recording, or by any information storage and retrieval system,
without permission in writing from the publisher.*

On the cover: Oil painting depicting the Triumph
of Archduchess Isabella in the Brussels Ommeganck
of Sunday, 31st May 1615, Denys van Alsloot, 1616.
(© Victoria and Albert Museum, London)

Printed in the United States of America

*McFarland & Company, Inc., Publishers
Box 611, Jefferson, North Carolina 28640
www.mcfarlandpub.com*

To all the talented artisans and scribes through the ages
who left us remarkable evidence of parades.

Table of Contents

Between pages 82 and 83 are 16 plates containing 32 color images

Acknowledgments

Books like this are never completed in isolation.

My sincere thanks for helping me with this project go to my long-time writing colleagues and friends, Julie Ferguson and Joyce Gram, both of whom made extensive suggestions for improvements.

Although I have not known them for long, the folks at McFarland have been friendly and knowledgeable in guiding me through the process of publication. I would especially like to thank Layla Milholen, my editor and contact through most of the process.

My wife Marimae has always encouraged me in this endeavor and has patiently tramped with me over the ruins of civilizations and through countless museums searching for clues and signs of ancient parades. Thank you, my love.

Preface

The subject of this book has been bouncing erratically around my brain for more than 15 years.

My former job as a special events producer required me to create memories for my clients and, to use a rather corny phrase, "cause applause." I often researched the history of different civilizations as a source of inspiration for new ideas. It was during this research that I first encountered some of the world's most astonishing historical special events, many of which are little known to most people today, such as ancient Egypt's Opet Festival, the Ptolemaieia in Hellenistic Alexandria, and the meeting between England's Henry VIII and France's François I at the Field of the Cloth of Gold in 1520. These encounters suggested that a history of special events might provide an intriguing subject for a book. After spending about five years struggling to write the beginning of this history, it became evident that the subject was far too broad to encapsulate in a single book. No doubt that was why nobody else had attempted it.

I had almost given up on the idea of an all-encompassing book when, about 10 years ago, the revelation struck me that almost all the influential and, indeed, spectacular historical special events incorporated a parade of some sort. In fact, for many of them, the parade *was* the event. I began to think that maybe it was the parade itself that was the key to these events being so memorable and influential. After speaking with an anthropologist who indicated that a book on the subject of parades might be of general interest as she did not think one had been written before, I made up my mind. I would write that book about parades—why we "love" them, what they mean, why we even have them. But there were challenges.

The first was how to choose specific *public* parades on which to concentrate from the literally millions that have been staged over the last 5000 years since writing was developed. I tried to narrow them down to spectacles that had sufficient evidence in the form of descriptions near their time of execution, either in actual writing or in carvings on monumental architecture, to prove they were important to the civilizations that conceived them. Those in this book are the result of using that filter. As readers, you may ask why I did not include this or that parade and I beg your indulgence in accepting my choices. I needed to keep the list short enough that I could convey certain points without extensive repetition, plus I needed to only use parades that had sufficient, credible evidence—and, more than anything, *interpretable* evidence— that they took place. In addition, I wanted to include significant parades from other cultures and took pains to avoid over-emphasizing those from western, Euro-centric societies (although there are still more than I wanted). As to be expected, there is also

1

considerable information that has been left unsaid in the actual text due to require-
ments for brevity, so I would encourage readers with sufficient interest to check my
references.

The second challenge was my own background. The substance of the book is
mostly anthropological and I am not an anthropologist. Neither am I a historian nor
a psychologist, two other disciplines that figure prominently in the book. My academic credentials go as far as a master's degree in engineering, so obviously I would
probably not be considered credible by academics in those other disciplines. I do,
however, have broad practical experience in the field of producing special events (my
second career), as I mentioned, including a few modest parades. I also spent some 10
years as a university lecturer in event production, during the course of which I wrote
five textbooks, two of which continue to be used around the world. As a result, I am
well versed in how to research a book such as this.

I consider that there are more benefits than disadvantages to this diverse background. For starters, I can imply and theorize as much as I want—based on research,
of course—without fear of censure from academic colleagues. This, hopefully, makes
the book more interesting. Also, I can write freely, without pressure to conform to
an academic style that, for the lay reader, would make a book such as this almost
unreadable.

In fact, there are numerous excellent academic books that have already been
written by anthropologists and historians that deal with *specific* parades, most not
intended for a general audience. On the other side of the coin, there are numerous
children's books about parades, a fact that implies a certain childish simplicity to the
subject. As far as I have been able to determine, this is the first book that meets these
two extremes in the middle.

As an added note, my enthusiasm for parades and historical special events has
been spurred on over the last two decades by extensive traveling to the original locations of some of the most prominent historical parades described in the book. There
is nothing like seeing in person where history was made. This has been augmented
by participation in a couple of archaeological digs, a pastime and a subject that continues to fascinate me. One was at a Mayan site in Belize and another at a Khmer site
in Thailand. There is an unforgettable thrill at being the first person in hundreds or
thousands of years to touch a long-buried object, building, or yes, even a body.

I hope that my enthusiasm for history and parades rubs off on you, the reader,
and that you will come away having a new appreciation for all that parades have contributed—and continue to contribute—to societies around the world.

Introduction: Forming Up

In advance of a recent St. Patrick's Day parade, a reporter said he hated parades. He claimed to have done an online survey in which 40 percent of respondents agreed with him and a mere 12 percent said they loved a parade.[1] That's not what we are led to believe by prevailing wisdom that tells us, "Everybody loves a parade," a notion derived from the song "I Love a Parade" written in 1931 by Harold Arlen and Ted Koehler for the Cotton Club nightclub show *Rhythmania*.

This disconnect is a testament to how western society has changed in the short time since Arlen and Koehler put pen to paper. We've gone from anticipatory excitement waiting for the razzmatazz of a parade, to a ho-hum, "been there, done that" attitude. Maybe it's too much of a good thing—after all, we've been inundated with entertainment of every imaginable form during that time—or maybe we just don't understand parades. Most of us, too, know little about the contribution of parades to human history.

Consider these six examples.

The ancient Roman Triumph was the signature spectacle of that bellicose society. Part of the triumphal procession, held to celebrate victory in war, was the exhibition of captured booty. This booty went into the coffers of the state and decreased the need for excessive taxation. No wonder the Romans thought war was a good idea. The triumph became a template through the centuries for all types of parades right up to modern sports and military victory parades and even certain religious processions.

The processions that accompany rites of passage, particularly those for royalty or celebrities, can have deep and lasting effects. The funeral procession of Alexander the Great was in part to blame for the breakup of his empire and a 40-year war among his generals that forever changed the face of the Middle East.

The rallies of the Nazi Party in 1930s Nuremberg, Germany, replete with thousands of goose-stepping soldiers and patriotic martial music, collectively became recognized as one of the most successful political marketing efforts in human history. We know what happened as a result.

Pride parades began as humble protest marches in the 1970s. Today, their powerful messages about social acceptance and tolerance have clearly shaped modern thought.

Carnival parades with their hedonistic themes bring millions of dollars into host communities, helping to improve lives.

Major thoroughfares in London, Washington, D.C., Paris, Berlin, Mexico City, New Delhi, and Beijing were designed for parades. These grand boulevards became iconic symbols recognized around the world.

There is a reason so many parades helped to shape societies throughout history—and still do. They ventured beyond mere ephemeral entertainment and connected emotionally with their audiences. I call these connections *moving encounters*. The aim of this book is to get reacquainted with the great parades of history and of modern times, and, thanks to these moving encounters, to explain how they have been so successful in conveying messages that shaped societies.

So, let's start "forming up," the military term for preparing for the parade.

What Is a Parade?

Parade as a noun can refer to different forms of the same activity.[2] The other, possibly more appropriate, noun for the activity in many cases is "procession." What is the difference?

Dictionaries offer a plethora of conflicting definitions, and the use of the words is often confusing. The two activities are related in their basic physical structure, but I believe they are distinctly different. This difference can be explained by my own personal definitions:

> *A parade is the linear and organized movement of human beings, objects, or animals between two physical locations that may or may not be the same, for the purpose of display.*
>
> *A procession is a parade with a ritually significant structure that incorporates rituals or ceremonies at the starting and/or ending location, for purposes other than simple display.*

In its basic format a parade is no more than showing off. It's "display in motion." The word itself derives from mid–17th-century French meaning a pompous show (which comes from the Greek word *pompē*). It has a beginning and an ending point, occasionally the same if the route is circuitous, but with no purposeful, linked activity at either end that immediately precedes or follows it. If one thinks about the different parades that might be witnessed in a lifetime, whether a festival parade, a pride parade, a Mardi Gras parade, or a military parade, it is likely that a choice was made to view it for no other reason than to see who and what was in it—in other words, its content. There was no intent to witness a particular ceremony at the end or the beginning. The experience was all about watching only the parade itself.

The actual elements of a parade, as mentioned in my definition, can be almost anything. Mac Reyonds, a journalist for the *Vancouver Sun* newspaper, described the 1955 parade preceding the Pacific National Exhibition, an annual summer event held in Vancouver, Canada. The parade had more than 250,000 spectators, which was significant because the city's entire population at that time was just under 600,000.

> Under a pale sun that strained through the clouds for attention, the record crowd lined the four-and-a-half-mile parade route twelve deep, jammed curbs and climbed ladders and balanced on neon signs.... There was a freshness to the parade as well as color and bigness and noise and floats and bands and marchers and clowns. There were flower peacocks, little boys in Indian turbans, mobile rock gardens, Calypso singers beating on oil drums, pastel colored toy trains, glockenspiels, Great Danes, silver helmets and saxophones.[3]

The variety of human and non-human elements possible in any parade is obvious, as shown in the above quote, with all having something unique to contribute. Their order is usually dependent on how the parade is crafted and what message is intended. More about this in Chapter One.

For a procession, the choice to view the activity would be made with the full knowledge that there is something more important going on and that the procession, although integral to the larger event, is not the focus of one's attendance. Modern processions can, for example, be part of weddings, funerals or other rites of passage, political assemblies, corporate meetings, sporting competitions, or religious gatherings. Without any evidence to the contrary, anthropologists generally believe that processions preceded parades in prehistory as unique human activities.[4]

Compared to a parade, the elements of a procession have more meaning and are generally arranged in a predetermined order. Usually, the person, group, or other entity who is either being honored or is the principal celebrant of an event that precedes or follows the procession, is placed at the end or, less often, at the beginning. Otherwise, elements may be as diverse as those in parades.

There are two more forms of linear human movement en masse that are associated with parades and those are protest marches and pilgrimages. Due to their purposes, they would best be described as sub-forms of processions since they invariably have a ceremony or ritual at their destination.[5] I define them as follows.

> *A protest march is a loosely organized parade with a simple, often ritually significant, structure, that may or may not incorporate a ceremony at the ending location. It may also be called a rally or demonstration.*
>
> *A pilgrimage is a journey, usually personal, to a specific, meaningful location to pay homage to someone or something, or to act as a form of religious devotion. A procession may take place at the destination.*

In the case of pilgrimages, their movement is not organized although it may be at the destination, and there is no significant structure. I will not be covering pilgrimages in any detail in this book.

For clarity in the rest of the book, when speaking about all these as general forms of activity, I will refer to them as parades, but when speaking specifically about a certain one, I will use the proper term, either parade, procession, protest march, or pilgrimage.

Who Are the Players?

Assuming everybody does love a parade, as we have been led to believe, who is everybody? One would first think it is only those people viewing the parade as spectators, but what about the people *in* the parade, the participants? And what about the people who have organized and subsidized the parade? They all have their own reasons for being part of the action. Something has drawn them to this particular type of public display.

Anthropologist Don Handelman has neatly summed up the general purpose of public events, also meaning public parades.

As the flow of living so often is not, public events are put together to communicate comparatively well-honed messages. If the flow of mundane living may be quite uncertain in terms of direction and outcome, the converse is true of public events. In the extreme case, they are operators of, and on, social order. Not only may they affect social order, they may also effect it.... They are culturally designed forms that select out, concentrate, and interrelate themes of existence ... lived and imagined ... that are more diffused, dissipated, and obscured in the everyday.... Their mandate is to engage in the ordering of ideas, people, and things. As phenomena, they not only are cognitively graspable, but also emotionally livable.[6]

This statement is key to understanding the entire purpose of this book. Let's take a look at it in depth. First of all, for any event, including a public parade, a message must be delivered *to* somebody *by* somebody *for* some reason. There is a simple relationship that shows how this is done in Figure I-1.

Therefore, a well-crafted parade, one that has a clear message that is delivered effectively by the participants, is one that will be met with emotional appreciation, applause and, yes, even love, by the spectators. This is where the second part of Handelman's statement comes in. It basically means that parades mirror the societies that spawn them and, through the careful manipulation of the elements of the parade, they can send a message that encourages people (spectators) to take some sort of action that will maintain or change social order. Here are two simple examples.

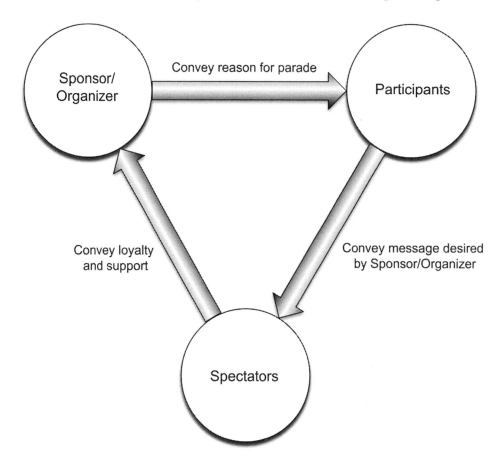

Figure I-1: Parade stakeholder relationship.

The Macy's Thanksgiving Day Parade, through the use of giant, inflatable symbols and blatant commercialism, encourages both the continuation of American pop culture and excessive holiday spending.

Coronation and commemoration parades of Britain's House of Windsor, through inordinate pageantry and a well-oiled promotional machine, validate the monarchy's continued existence and the unabated consumption of anything royal, from coffee mugs to commemorative postage stamps.

To create such spectacles is no simple task.

Sponsors

The putting together or staging of a parade falls to its sponsor. In today's world, this may be a commercial entity, a city, a non-profit organization, a church, or a host of others.[7] In the distant past, a sponsor would usually be a monarch or a chief priest. Over the last 5000 years, sponsors staged parades for religious, political, or military reasons, frequently combined. What they were seeking was loyalty: loyalty to themselves, a god, or a governing body. How well they achieved this depended on their skillful organization—usually through a subordinate organizer—of the participants in the parade. The military Roman Triumph, for example, would not have succeeded for so long had it not been a political advertisement for the governing senate and emperor.

This grounding feature of parades remained until the Long 19th Century when the impact of secular humanism, democratization, and commercialism took hold. After this, the main reasons for staging most public parades became commercial and social. Commercialism, especially, became an enticing motivation for sponsors and for participants—those people or organizations walking, marching, or moving in the parade. Within certain guidelines, their individual messages could be shaped in explicit, unambiguous ways to appeal to spectators. This became known as *target marketing*.

When it comes to loving parades from the sponsor's standpoint, the possibility of million- or billion-dollar windfalls is hard not to love. In researching the largest parades in the world since the beginning of the millennium, I found some startling statistics on parades and their economic value to host communities.

Of 17 parades in this time period with more than 10 million participants, all were religious pilgrimages. The largest had a mind-boggling 60 to 80 million participants! This was the Kumbh Mela, a Hindu pilgrimage, held in Hardwar, India, in 2010.[8] Another four Kumbh Melas also made the top 17. In general terms, the Kumbh Mela regularly contributes around $2.2 billion USD to the local economy and up to 600,000 jobs.[9] Another annual religious procession, the Arba'een Pilgrimage for Shia Muslims to the city of Karbala, Iraq, has had more than 10 million participants in nine of the last 20 years. No reliable economic value estimates are known.

Remember, these were all participants. When it comes to sheer numbers of spectators at parades since the beginning of the millennium, the largest is thought to be a religious procession of the Black Nazarene (a black version of Christ) in 2015 in Manila, Philippines, which had 5.5 million spectators. The largest secular parade in the same time period is thought to be the 2016 World Series victory parade in

Chicago, Illinois, after the Chicago Cubs won their first World Series since 1908.[10] The estimated number of live spectators was five million. At the top of the list of secular parades *not* in this time period was the April 1951 ticker tape parade in New York City to honor General Douglas MacArthur just 15 days after being relieved of duty by President Truman.[11] The estimated number of spectators was more than seven million. Because these were one-off events, the value to local economies was not recorded.

However, for other regularly held parades there are some well-measured examples. The annual Muslim Hajj pilgrimage to Mecca, Saudi Arabia, rakes in about $12 billion USD, making it the most lucrative.[12] In fact, it alone is responsible for 20 percent of the country's non-oil revenue. Carnival in Rio de Janeiro, Brazil, accounts for an average of $1.6 billion USD compared to a paltry $465 million USD for the New Orleans, USA, Mardi Gras in 2014.[13] Finally, as an example of the countless pride parades throughout the world now, Toronto, Canada's contribution pulled in about $350 million USD in 2014.[14]

Participants and Spectators

What would garner this overwhelming interest in a parade? Not surprisingly, the needs of participants and spectators are different from those of the sponsor. Their mutual needs are concerned almost entirely with making connections with each other, with finding those emotional moments that I call moving encounters. If the connection is made, then the message has been delivered.

For participants, it's validation for what they are doing, be it marching in a band, riding on a float, or dressing up in historical costumes. Sustained applause over five kilometers of a parade is surely strong validation!

One participant in a Scottish procession summed this up. "There are certain points ... where everyone congregates ... where they are about ten deep ... and at the end of the day as you come to that final point ... all these people are there and the bands go wild ... you actually feel yourself lifting."[15] A second similarly commented, "I actually cried when I saw that amount of people that were there and it was a miserable day, and all these people had turned out and it really gave me a sense of pride to know these people were on the same side as you."[16]

Olympic athletes can have extremely emotional moments. Canadian speed skater and gold medalist Catriona Le May Doan had this to say about her participation in the Olympic Torch Relay—a sequential type of procession—preceding the 2010 Winter Olympics in Vancouver.

> Once downtown, I got my white torchbearer suit, met with the others, then we got into position. As they started the ceremony, it hit me.... We were the FIRST torchbearers!!!! Simon [Whitfield, gold medalist in triathlon] looked at me and we talked about how nervous we were. As athletes, we are individuals who are all about control, knowing and preparing for our situations. This was different—this was something we couldn't prepare for. Our names were announced. We walked on to the stage, waved, then walked to the cauldron, lowered the torch, and the first of thousands of torches began the route across this incredible country of ours. Simon and I proceeded down the path, but it was when we started to jog, that it really hit me. Thousands of kids and adults lined the way, waving Canadian flags. It was overwhelming. I was not prepared for how emotional that moment

was. It took me by surprise. I thought of my kids and how so many experiences in life will inspire them and how this was one of those moments for these kids here.[17]

For spectators, it's much the same. Numerous modern studies have confirmed repeatedly why spectators attend special events—also meaning parades.[18] They include the opportunity to socialize, to gain knowledge (e.g., history and culture), to experience high quality art, and to be emotionally rewarded or personally fulfilled (e.g., get excited, have one's ego enhanced, connect emotionally or spiritually).

One example should suffice here. The Russian Victory Day Parade celebrating the victory over Nazism, held on May 9, 2015, caused one member of the media to react strongly.

> To see the faces of thousands and thousands of ordinary Russians walking, optimism about their future beaming from their faces, young and the very old, including surviving veterans of the Great Patriotic War as it is known to Russians, moved this writer to quietly weep. What was conveyed in the smiles and eyes of the thousands of marchers was not a looking back in the sense of sorrow at the horrors of that war. Rather what came across so clearly was that the parade was a gesture of loving respect and gratitude to those who gave their lives that today's Russia might be born.[19]

What Are Moving Encounters?

I believe that participants and spectators choose to attend a parade because they seek moving encounters, those moments of emotional connection mentioned above. What are these encounters?

In the 18th century, philosopher Immanuel Kant proposed that all humans have aesthetic experiences—fleeting moments of "disinterested pleasure," as he called them—of beauty and the sublime (e.g., a feeling of awe at observing a sunset, a tingling up the spine, tears welling up in the eyes), but he did not attach any connection between the experiences and religion. Building on Kant's theories, philosophers Jakob Friedrich Fries and Rudolf Otto suggested that these were in fact transcendent, "holy" experiences of communication with a divine reality.[20] Finally, 20th-century anthropologist Victor Turner attached the term spontaneous *communitas* to such experiences, noting that they could occur either within or without a religious context, with the trigger often being ritual. As he put it, "Is there any one of us who has not known this moment when compatible people—friends, congeners—obtain a flash of lucid mutual understanding on the existential level, when they feel that all problems, not just their problems, could be resolved?"[21]

Whether or not they are religious *spiritual* connections has not been conclusively determined. Presumably they could occur in the middle of a football game or in the middle of a traditional religious service. Psychology has partially come to the rescue to explain them.

Recent studies have proven that something does happen to the brain when people participate in religious activities such as prayer or meditation. Neuroscientist Andrew Newberg and his team took brain scans of people participating in such activities and found that something happened to the parietal lobe, the part of the brain that processes sensory information. "When you begin to do some kind of practice like ritual, over time that area of the brain appears to shut down," he said. "As it starts to quiet down, since it normally helps to create sense of self, that sense of self starts to blur, and the boundaries between self and other—another person, another group, God, the universe, whatever it is you feel connected to—the boundary between those begins to dissipate and you feel one with it." Newberg also found that the frontal lobe, the other part of the brain heavily involved in religious experience and that normally helps us to focus our attention and concentrate on things, may shut down during these activities. "When that area shuts down, it could theoretically be experienced as a kind of loss of willful activity—that we're no longer making something happen but it's happening to us." Furthermore, these phenomena can also be experienced by non-religious people simply because of the way humans' brains have developed.[22]

Parades provide many opportunities for this to happen: an impeccably rehearsed dance routine; a spectacular float with an emotional theme and costumed performers; a silent squad of war veterans, as the observer in Russia documented; a nationalistic display of men and women in uniform marching to an upbeat song; a victorious sports team; and the list goes on. The connection can be felt by both spectators and participants alike. The fact that I have called such connections moving encounters is no coincidence—fancy word play, yes, but no coincidence. The encounters move with the parade, almost as if they become a series of encounters limited only by the viewing angle of a section of spectators and the length of time the participants of a parade element remain within that viewing angle. The encounter is physically moving—literally—and it is also emotionally moving. But it is not limited to spectators to participants; it can also be spectators to spectators and participants to participants.

Ritual is the single most likely way to trigger such encounters.

Creating Connections Through Ritual

Ritual is the "glue" that holds a parade together and provides the link between the message(s) to be delivered and the entities involved (i.e., sponsors, participants, spectators).

The word ritual often confuses people. It need not. One of the simplest definitions I have found is that it is "symbolic behavior that is socially standardized and repetitive."[23]

Catherine Bell, one of the world's foremost scholars on ritual, has found that such behavior has six characteristics: formalism, traditionalism, invariance, rule-governance, sacral symbolism, and performance.[24] In parades, one or more of these characteristics is operating at any given time. How they are used by parade participants is what creates moving encounters and successfully conveys the message desired by the sponsor. This book devotes at least one chapter to each of them.

Formalism contrasts formal activities and entities with informal ones. In a parade, this is seen in the attire of participants. It is covered in Chapter Three.

Traditionalism links activities in the parade with older cultural precedents. Processions such as those found in weddings, funerals, coronations, and inaugurations are strongly traditional. This is covered in chapters Seven and Eight.

Invariance refers to the precise repetition and control of actions in a parade. Religious processions are prime examples and are discussed in Chapter Six.

Rule-governance refers to rules that govern the behavior of spectators and participants. It is found in chapters Nine and Ten, which discuss protest marches and carnival parades.

Symbolism, at its heart, is the linking of something tangible to something intangible. In parades, floats are highly symbolic and are discussed in Chapter Four. Sacred space is also considered a form of symbolism and is covered in Chapter Two.

Performance relates parades to such events as theatrical plays and dramatic spectacles. It is covered in chapters One and Five and partly in chapters Eleven and Twelve.

The interesting thing about these characteristics is that they seriously affect what we do after witnessing or experiencing them. Emile Durkheim, sometimes regarded as the founder of sociology, first theorized that performing rituals created and sustained "social solidarity."[25] We have already mentioned Victor Turner who found that ritual could trigger the feeling of *communitas*. What these scholars theorized through direct observation of primitive peoples has now been reinforced through the research of biogenetic structuralists. This is a field that applies knowledge of human evolution to cultural behavior. In summary, here is the logic of their current thinking:

- Modern humans are "hardwired" for ritual behavior.[26]
- Ritual behavior overcomes social distance between individuals and helps to coordinate group action.[27]
- Emotions weight decisions and influence actions.[28]
- Emotions may be elicited by sensory stimuli.[29]
- Rituals with high levels of sensory stimuli (e.g., *rhythmic drivers* such as music and dance) will therefore be the most effective in bringing social groups and individuals together and in motivating action. One such rhythmic driver, electronic dance music, has recently been studied with near-conclusive results along this line.[30] This type of music is found in many types of parades, especially carnival. Another driver is marching and martial music, a topic covered in Chapter Five.

The key point to remember about the use of ritual and its characteristics in a parade is that they bring people together, creating Durkheim's social solidarity. Once social solidarity is gained, moving encounters are not far behind, and the message of the parade is more easily conveyed.

Dr. Neil Cameron, Director of the Centre for Creative Communities in Hobart, Australia, knows well the importance of ritual in events of all types. For more than 40 years he managed large-scale productions around the globe that created community involvement using giant imagery, fire, and music. In an interview I had with him a few years ago, he summarized the importance of ritual.

> Ritual is ingrained in us. It intensifies communication within groups of people.... We as a society and as communities have lost our prehistoric and historic traditions. People sang and danced in the past because they were drawn together by ritual. Nowadays, especially, many of our religious and church traditions are no longer bringing people together. However, they still crave ritual and so those religious rituals must be replaced by meaningful secular ones. People want to be involved. They want the structure and the formality that well-designed ritual brings.[31]

It is ritual that will guide us through this book, with occasional assistance from the periods of world history that will help to put many of the ancient parades in context. These periods break down as follows.

- **The Prehistoric Period**. Prior to 3500 BCE (Before Current or Christian Era). This covers the lengthy time between the emergence of anatomically modern humans around 200,000 years ago and the emergence of writing in civilizations around 5500 years ago in the Near East. It includes the beginnings of agriculture around 10,000 to 11,000 years ago, an important development in human culture. Major influences on parades during this period include animism, shamanism, and the acquisition of rational thought.
- **The Early Civilization Period**. 3500 BCE to 1000 BCE. This covers the emergence of river valley-based civilizations throughout the world. The most notable and well-documented is Egypt on the Nile. Others include the Mesopotamian city states along the Tigris-Euphrates rivers, Harappa along the Indus River, the Shang and Zhou dynasties along the Yellow River in China, and the Olmecs on several rivers in Central America. The difficulties with these civilizations, with the exception of Egypt, are that their writing systems were either minimal or poorly developed, with few meaningful descriptions of parades, and the archaeological record is not yet extensive enough to draw many conclusions. Influences on parades during the period include polytheism, writing, the understanding and use of sacred space, advanced symbolism, the introduction of state armies, and the invention of the chariot.
- **The Classical Period**. 1000 BCE to 500 CE (Current or Christian Era). During this period, the river valley civilizations generally expand into empires and other major civilizations emerge. In the Mediterranean, Greece and Rome flourish. In India, the Mauryan and Gupta empires take hold. In the area of Mesopotamia, Persia becomes strong. In China, the Qin and Han dynasties develop. Most of these provide good or superlative documentary evidence of parades. Many traditions that continued to influence parades are either invented or developed further during this period, such as complex polytheism, monotheism, advanced political experimentation, the notion of mythical heroes, advanced social systems, extended trade, and technological innovation such as parchment and paper.
- **The Postclassical Period**. 500 to 1450 CE. This is often considered a stagnant period in western civilization known as the Middle Ages or the medieval period between the fall of Rome and the Renaissance. In fact, the early part is sometimes erroneously called the Dark Ages. Nothing could be farther from the truth, particularly in the rest of the world. This era brings forth two major themes, the spread of monotheistic religions—especially Buddhism, Christianity, and Islam—and the expansion of trade connections. Because of these, civilization centers explode in the Middle East (Byzantine Empire), China (Tang and Mongol dynasties, among others), Japan, India (several empires), Southeast Asia (Khmer Empire), northwestern Europe, Russia, and sub-Saharan Africa. Unrelated but nevertheless amazing in their progress are the Central and South American classical civilizations of the Maya, Aztecs, Moche, and

Inca who all reached their zeniths during this same period. Technological innovation begins to seriously influence parades during this period. Important developments include the quill pen, gunpowder, the construction of castles and cathedrals, the rise of universities, and early printing.

- **The Early Modern Period**. 1450 to 1750 CE. This period is one of growing European strength with the discovery of the Americas and the Renaissance. Conventional emphasis in history has been on Europe and the Americas. However, Europe did not rule the world, and many other societies, called *gunpowder empires*, continued to develop and expand.[32] Additionally, what seems to be a common theme throughout all developed societies during this period, both European and others, is a vibrant royal court life, which influenced parades. The Reformation and the beginning of a gradual decrease of Christianity's popularity was a major influence on parades.

- **The Long 19th Century Period**. 1750 to 1914 CE. This is a clear period of western dominance and empire-building, particularly by Great Britain, but later by the United States. It is also a period highly influenced by the Industrial Revolution, especially for parades. The inventions of steam transportation, the internal combustion engine, the telephone, loudspeakers and microphones, and radio all have profound effects on parades. It is also during this period that the first rumblings of secular humanism begin to take hold. That movement will eventually strongly affect how parades are designed.

- **The Contemporary Period**. 1914 to the present. This period is one of overwhelming change: in cultural, religious, and political belief systems; in massive urbanization; in technological upheaval in the form of air transportation and information systems; and in expanding global influences on almost everything. These continue to change the face of parades every year.

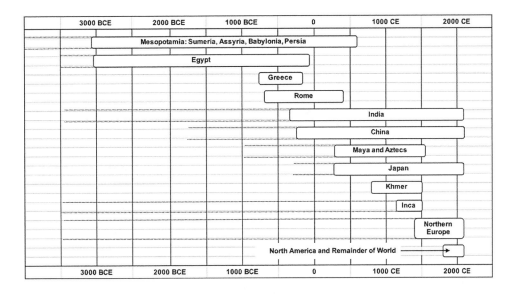

Figure I-2: World civilization timeline.

Figure I-2 illustrates in graphic form a timeline of these world history periods overlaid by major world civilizations. It is obvious that many civilizations are missing from this chart. It was not my original intention to ignore any of them; however, it was necessary to make choices of specific civilizations on which to concentrate. I made these choices primarily based on the availability of researchable information—including archaeological and written evidence—that adequately and accurately portrayed a variety of parades. Not only were parades from a variety of cultures important, but so were parades that represented the true nature of the time—political and cultural systems, the use of current technology, the influence of the parades on the civilizations involved and on the entire world or localized area of the world. Those chosen were benchmark spectacles of their eras.

The book is divided into two main parts and 12 chapters. The first part, "Crafting the Spectacle," is devoted to analyzing and explaining five of the primary "ingredients" of a parade in the context of ritual and how they have shaped societies. These are: human performance and its power to influence; the parade route and how it affects the psyche of spectators and participants; the part that formal attire, regalia, costumes, and uniforms play in adding meaning to a parade; the symbolic power of floats; and how marching and synchronous human movement can affect participants and spectators.

The second part, "Realizing the Spectacle," is devoted to an analysis and historical review of specific types of parades—religious processions, rites of passage, victory parades, protest marches, carnival parades, sailpasts and flypasts, and modern parades—once again in the context of ritual and how the parades have influenced societies.

Armed with this background, let's see what all the fuss is about.

Part I

Crafting the Spectacle

ONE

The Power of Performance

There is a clear theatricality to parades.

You may not be thinking about this as you stand on a steamy summer sidewalk waiting for the parade to begin, cranky children and jostling crowds impinging on your space from all sides, but you are about to witness the oldest and most sophisticated form of theatrical performance ever devised by humans.

Live theater began less than 5000 years ago; parades can be traced to prehistoric rock art. Some ingenious soul obviously thought about a mobile performance long before they thought about putting people in seats to watch a performance on a fixed stage. By the time live theater became popular, parades imbued with subtle messages were already being used in ancient societies to entertain, influence, and inform the populace. There was and still is a commonality between live theater and parades—or spectacles, as scholars call them.

Think about it.

The street and its surroundings form the theater building. The stage becomes that portion of the street that we can see in our field of view as spectators. The play is the parade itself and instead of occasional scene changes, it unfolds before us in a constantly changing kaleidoscope of colorful performances. In a play, the playwright/producer and the director seek to impart a message to the audience. Their raw materials to accomplish this are the script, the performers, and the stage sets. In a parade, the playwright/producer becomes the parade sponsor, the director the organizer, and the performers and stage sets the participants in the parade. The script is the layout and flow of the parade.

Ancient parade organizers quickly realized that to impart a meaningful message to their audiences and thus to influence their actions, a visual spectacle had to be created.[1] Many were breathtakingly inspired, and some of these will make appearances in later chapters. What these organizers understood was the power of human performance.

> If man is a sapient animal, a tool making animal, a self-making animal, a symbol-using animal, he is, no less, a performing animal, *Homo performans*, not in the sense, perhaps, that a circus animal may be a performing animal, but in the sense that a man is a self-performing animal—his performances are, in a way, reflexive, in performing he reveals himself to himself.
>
> This can be in two ways: the actor may come to know himself better through acting or enactment; or one set of human beings may come to know themselves better through observing and/or participating in performances generated and presented by another set of human beings.[2]

This statement by renowned anthropologist Victor Turner succinctly summarizes what a successful parade is about—communication. It is about live performers understanding their craft well enough to be able to communicate powerful messages, be they subtle or obvious, to spectators. As another anthropologist, William Beeman, has stated, "Through performance an audience is moved and transformed. They are made to laugh, to cry, to change their opinions, to take social action, to be surprised, to question their existence, to acquire a feeling of well-being and integration."[3]

As an aside, I have witnessed performers do this countless times in my career. Although not in a parade context, as examples I have seen audiences brought to tears by the simple, accomplished manipulation of a puppet on strings, and the heart-rending delivery of a single lyric-less song by a solo harmonica player.

Performers love to perform, even if they are only volunteers, as some in a parade might be. Their main goal is to connect with the audience and to receive validation for their abilities and recognition through applause. In so doing, they often enter a state of *flow*. Flow refers to "an interior state which can be described as the merging of action and awareness, the holistic sensation present when we act with total involvement, a state in which action follows action according to an internal logic, with no apparent need for conscious intervention on our part."[4] For performers, it is a feeling of wanting to remain in the moment. It happens particularly with group performances and only when members are completely in synch and performing together, each sensing what the others are doing as if they were a single, totally blended unit. It can be magical for them. It is their own moving encounter.

Anthropologist and event organizer Neil Cameron sums up these introductory paragraphs with the statement "Every project can be made richer by using a theme that taps into the real meaning behind the event. The 'spirit' held by the people involved is what really makes it [the parade] work."[5]

Defining Entertainment and Performance

A parade offers an enormous variety of human entertainment—singing, storytelling, dancing, music, athletic skills.[6] Often this entertainment is enhanced and augmented with what I call props. These props are non-human—animals, floats, machines (e.g., cars, bicycles, tanks, trucks), costumes and uniforms, balloons, computerized technology (e.g., lighting, video, recorded music). The point is that humans drive the entire parade, not props. For example, what would a float be like without a designer, a driver, or humans aboard? How would animals fit into a parade without human handlers? What would any parade be like without costumes or uniforms designed, made, and worn by humans? What would a marching band be like without human-invented instruments and musical structure?

Furthermore, it is not *who* but *what* makes a good—better yet, a *great*—performance? How are these human-prop combinations used to best effect? From my experience, it is by striving for perfection. After many years as an event producer, I finally realized that there are three key components to a masterful performance: flawless delivery of the act (i.e., as close to perfect as possible); incredible creativity; and audience interaction, preferably humorous and non-threatening, in other words, charisma. For a parade, all these apply, whether the humans are marching, dancing, inhabiting a float, prancing around in a costume, riding a bicycle, or sitting on an elephant.

Flawless delivery of an act, no matter how simple it may appear, can only be gained by way of hours and hours of rehearsal. Most audiences today have seen so much high-quality entertainment that they know when a performer has not put in the time. Indeed, they *expect* to be wowed, as if they were watching the winners of one of the Got Talent Shows. To not be wowed, even in a small community parade, leaves them wanting more and can leave them disinclined to view any repeat parades. They may even state that they "hate a parade" as the reporter did in the first sentence of this book's Introduction.

However, to be wowed is not always the result of strictly rehearsing and nothing else. It also requires creativity. Let's look at some examples. A parade can have a variety of performers. We'll take a juggler as the first example. Pretty well every juggler can keep three of four balls in the air. Add a wild, striped costume and the juggler attracts a little more attention. Now the juggler decides not to walk down the middle of the parade route while juggling but instead picks a section of the audience and asks them to give him any three items to juggle. They give him a ball cap, a portable beach chair, and a flag (a symbol like a pride flag). Besides that, he has started to talk to the audience and tells a couple of jokes while juggling. Things have gotten really interesting. Lo and behold, he keeps everything in the air for 10 seconds, earning a huge applause. It becomes a truly memorable moment for the audience in the immediate vicinity. Message well received.

The juggler has also shown that he understands the importance of audience interaction. As long as they can keep up with the parade and not create delays, most performers can have short performances like that along the route. This can include people on floats, marching bands, dancers, deejays, animals, and all the others mentioned.

Successful audience interaction is a combination of charisma and knowing what and what not to do with whom. For want of a better term, it's *rehearsed spontaneity*. I have seen many parades in which participants make little or no attempt to connect with the audience. They think that just putting on their once-a-year outlandish costume will gain the audience's approval. They need to do better, to approach the audience on all sides, or better yet, to rehearse a crazy dance routine with the audience that they can do every few hundred yards. Take a carnival parade for example. A scantily clad team of booty-wriggling revelers may be enough for some audience members but turn that into a well-rehearsed, high-energy dance routine with smiles and winks at the spectators and you have a winner. The spectators go home happy because they have had fun. The performers go home happy because they have connected with the audience. The parade sponsor goes home happy because their message has been delivered.

As I said earlier, it is up to the parade sponsor and their subordinate organizer to "write a good script" by first choosing the best and most proficient actors (i.e., performers and other participating entities) and then judiciously placing them in the parade for maximum effect. This means not only paying attention to their abilities but also being conscious of their placement among other parade entities such as floats or vehicles, as well as considering overall pacing and emotional high and low points. Throwing parade entries into the mix helter skelter does not make for success. The best way to illustrate this is by looking at some historical examples.

Performance in a Sample of Historical Parades

The classical civilizations of Egypt, Greece, and Rome were masters at parade design. We'll be seeing those parades in other chapters but here are some teasers that demonstrate how the organizers were aware of the importance of performance, especially in understanding what it took to win over spectators.

The Egyptian Opet Festival procession in the 2nd millennium BCE (see Chapter Six), when going by land, stopped at various waypoints where oracular proclamations were made. The oracle interpreted the movement of the god's palanquin-carried barque in the procession to answer if, for example, the king was the rightful ruler or if a particular person had committed a crime. Common people were also allowed to consult the oracle about anything they wanted, although simple yes and no answers were the only options.[7] Although we today would consider this akin to snake oil sales, the people of antiquity were a bit more naïve. What a sales pitch for the Pharaoh and the priests!

To add spice to the land procession, musicians, singers, and choreographed acrobat/dancers were also part of it (Figure 1-1).

King Ptolemy II of Egypt knew how to get parade participants to interact with spectators right from the start (see Chapter Four). He began his famous Grand Procession with two large floats built like a wine press and a wineskin, both overflowing with real wine, followed by 1600 costumed boys carrying wine goblets. The boys ran into the crowds with the goblets full of wine and continuously refilled them from the floats. Few politicians today are *that* good at campaigning.

Figure 1-1: Acrobat/dancers in the ancient Opet Festival procession carved in the Luxor Temple colonnade (photograph by the author).

General Lucius Aemilius Paulus's triumph (see Chapter Eight) was not the most lavish of the Roman Triumphs. Nobody was more vainglorious than the two rivals, Pompey the Great and Julius Caesar. Pompey had three triumphs over the course of 18 years—in 79, 71, and 61 BCE; Caesar had four over the course of a single month in 46 BCE. Both knew that Roman spectators loved outlandish spectacle. The last of Pompey's triumphs in 61 BCE was the gaudiest of his three. In it, his chariot was uniquely encrusted with precious gems and he arrogantly rode upon it dressed in Alexander the Great's cloak. As with other triumphs, he played with the lives of prisoners, executing some and saving others to show his toughness and clemency to the crowds. He also displayed a large, highly decorated globe representing the "world" that he had conquered—just Europe, Asia, and Africa—an indication that there must have been widespread knowledge at the time that the earth was round. In that same triumph, Pompey presented a massive head of himself made entirely out of pearls, what Pliny would later call "an offensive disgrace."[8] But, hey, if it excites the crowd, any publicity is good publicity.

Actually, Caesar and Pompey were friends and allies who ruled Rome together for a period in what was called the First Triumvirate, but after several years they drifted apart due to political differences. It seems that thereafter Caesar became driven to best everything that Pompey had done, especially in his triumphs, where the enduring admiration of the populace was at stake. Pompey, for example, in one of his triumphs, introduced spectators to the rhinoceros, the lynx, and an African ape. Caesar introduced them to the giraffe. Pompey, in his first triumph, used four elephants to pull his chariot. Embarrassingly, they could not fit through the opening of one of the triumphal arches, and had to be unhitched. Caesar had to do better and rode home after his last triumph accompanied by 20 elephants. Caesar also famously displayed the words "*Veni, Vidi, Vici*" [I came, I saw, I conquered] on a banner in one of his triumphs to prove how he had quickly dispatched the enemy, in contrast to the longer struggle that Pompey had with the same enemy.[9]

These western civilizations were not the only ones capable of performance-laden parades. In Meso-America, the fantastic painted murals at the ancient city of Bonampak in Chiapas, Mexico, prove that the Mayans were infatuated with processions during their civilization's classic period, 250 to 900 CE, and they used musical performance to enhance ceremonies. Bonampak's Temple of the Murals contains three rooms, each with what in ancient times would be vividly painted scenes. Room One has two registers, both depicting some sort of tributary procession intended to acknowledge the right of a certain king to rule. Included are singers, dancers, and musicians playing percussion instruments, including log drums, scrapers, gourd rattles and drum-like idiophones made from turtle shells. Also notable are wind instruments, such as ocarinas, flutes, and conch-shell trumpets.[10] All performers are elaborately attired in elegant formal ceremonial regalia with large, feathered back racks, in addition to various jaguar, quetzal and serpent elements. While the meaning is almost impossible to interpret due to the absence of any written description, it is obvious that the performers were integral to the proper conduct of the ceremonies and the processions.

In Southeast Asia between the ninth and 13th centuries CE, the magnificent city of Angkor arose as the capital of the Khmer Empire in what is today's Cambodia and part of Thailand. Khmer religion transitioned through Hinduism to Buddhism but always there were grand processions. The beautiful Elephant Terrace in Angkor is traditionally where processions and ceremonies took place. Much of what is known about the ancient Khmer comes from the writings of a Chinese chronicler, Chou Ta-Kuan, who accompanied a Chinese mission to Cambodia in 1296 to 1297 CE. His description of the king's rare appearance outside his palace leaves us with a vivid picture of a typical royal procession of the time.

> When the King leaves his palace, the procession is headed by the soldiery; then come the flags, the banners, the music. Girls of the palace, three or five hundred in number, gaily dressed, with flowers in their hair and tapers in their hands, were massed together in a separate column. The tapers are lighted even in broad daylight. Then came other girls carrying gold and silver vessels from the palace and a whole galaxy of ornaments, of very special design, the uses of which were strange to me. Then came still more girls, the bodyguard of the palace, holding shields and lances. These, too, were separately aligned. Following them came chariots drawn by goats and horses, all adorned with gold, ministers and princes, mounted on elephants, were preceded by bearers of scarlet parasols, without number. Close behind came the royal wives and concubines, in palanquins and chariots, or mounted on horses or elephants, to whom were assigned at least a hundred parasols mottled with gold. Finally the Sovereign appeared standing erect on an elephant and holding in his hand the sacred sword. This elephant, his tusks sheathed in gold, was accompanied by bearers of twenty white parasols with golden shafts. All around was a bodyguard of elephants, drawn close together, and still more soldiers for complete protection, marching in close order.[11]

This king—Indravarman III at the time Chou Ta-Kuan visited—knew his stuff. He began with the army, representing his reassuring protection of the people, and followed that with the joyousness of music and colored flags, representing his appreciation and support for tradition and the arts. The girls were probably Apsara dancers who performed in the king's court.[12] The remainder of the parade was an overtly ostentatious display of royal wealth and power, intended to impress—and no doubt humble—the populace. Bas reliefs of similar processions are carved into sections of another temple at Angkor, the Bayon. There are several scenes of entertainers such as wrestlers, jugglers, acrobats, dancers, and musicians, but a lack of written description and context makes it difficult to determine if they are part of a procession.[13]

During the eras of ancient Chinese history, emperors adopted a policy of strength in numbers, especially for their parades. They seldom went anywhere without enormous retinues. One documented example from the Northern Song Dynasty (960 to 1126 CE) reveals how performance in the form of symbolism, military marching, elephants, horses, gongs and drums, musicians, carriages, and floats all contributed to a substantial display of imperial power. Known as Grand Carriage processions, these spectacles were particularly large when the emperor ventured forth to visit temples—usually Buddhist or Daoist—on special occasions (see color insert Figure 1-2). Upwards of 20,000 or more participants was not unusual.[14] They were designed as political theater, intended by authorities "to dazzle an audience, gain its support, and impress upon it a vision of the social and political order."[15] They made use of strong visual parade elements to construct the message—"flags with written characters or pictures on them, carriages with images of dragons on them, ranks of guards in distinctive uniforms on color-coded horses [and] carrying weapons."[16]

Rehearsals for these processions began two months in advance with trainers teaching the elephants how to respond to the gongs and drums and how to trumpet on command. Even for the rehearsals the onlookers were densely packed on the streets where hawkers sold them miniature souvenir elephants.[17]

For the actual procession, attire differentiated participants by the color and design of their hats and robes and by emblems sewn onto them. Depending on their positions, participants might have also carried swords, shields, axes, large flags, and fans. The latter two formed much of the visual message and were painted with images of such things as dragons, tigers, mountains, rivers, lightning, and maps of heavenly bodies. Soldiers carried bows and crossbows. Six floats painted bright red were part of the procession, each with a symbolic design and one even carrying an automaton that struck a drum every 10 *li*.[18] The actual Grand Carriage and emperor's sedan chair were in the place of honor in the procession. Their coming was signaled—as was the approach of other units—by the placement of participants and the designs of their attire and flags.[19] The procession was thus a part of the visual culture of the Song. The audience understood what they were witnessing—an overt representation of the emperor's power—yet few words or interactive entertainment was needed.

Similarly, the later Ming (1368 to 1644 CE) and Qing (1644 to 1912 CE) Dynasty emperors regularly traveled extensively on Inspection Tours to the outer reaches of the Chinese provinces to consolidate their power. Even any shorter ventures outside the palace in public would require a protective procession. None of these were ordinary wanderings but involved a court retinue of thousands: standard bearers; soldiers, some carrying chains, whips, and cutlasses to keep the crowds under control if necessary; musicians; cavalry; and, finally, the emperor seated on a covered palanquin that was wheeled and pulled by an elephant.[20]

Today, the Chinese are still unparalleled in their ability to provide entertainment using the synchronous movement of massed groups of humans, one of the best examples being the Opening Ceremonies of the 2008 Olympics in Beijing.

No other rulers were more peripatetic than the Mughal emperors of India, descendants of Genghis Khan, famed leader of the nomadic Mongols. While early Mughal emperors roamed their territories more to expand them, by the time of Shah Jahangir (ruled 1605–1627 CE) the travels were seen more as a strategy for political control and centralization. Jahangir wandered more than most to the point that the Royal Court was almost never stationary. These processions were even larger than the Chinese retinues. The "emperor was protected by a personal bodyguard of 8000 horsemen on either side, followed by perhaps as many as 100,000 horsemen, 250,000 animals, and up to 500,000 persons in a procession stretching for a mile and a half.... A European merchant described the massive migration of the Mughal royal progress, 'All the face of the earth, so far as we could see, was covered with people.... All this moving in one, on so many huge elephants, seemed like a fleet of ships with flags and streamers ... so that all together it made a most majestical warlike and delightsome sight.'"[21]

These Chinese and Mughal processions, much like the Khmer king's appearances outside his palace, had a single goal—to demonstrate the power of the monarchy and to implant into the minds of the populace that they should submit to this power. They did this through performance, not the performance of strict, well-rehearsed music or dance, but by the sheer magnitude of raw military might that was under their control and hence could be brought to bear on any opposition, no matter where in the empire it might occur.

One of the best relatively recent historical examples of what I consider "performance extravagance" was the Delhi Durbar of 1903. "'Durbar' is a Persian term that was adopted in India to refer to a ruler's court. It could be used to refer to a feudal state council or to a ceremonial gathering. It was this latter sense that was taken up by the British Raj when, during the 'high noon' of Empire, three imperial Durbars were held in Delhi, each marking royal occasions. The first, held in 1877, marked the proclamation of Queen Victoria as Empress of India. The last, held in 1911, marked the coronation of King George V. The second, the 1903 Durbar, marked the coronation of King Edward VII."[22] It far outshone all the others (see color insert Figure 1-3).

"In a few short months at the end of 1902, a deserted plain was transformed into an elaborate tented city, complete with temporary light railway to bring crowds of spectators out from Delhi, a post office with its own stamp, telephone and telegraphic facilities, a variety of stores, a Police force with specially designed uniform, hospital, magistrate's court and complex sanitation, drainage and electric light installations. Souvenir guidebooks were sold and maps of the camping ground distributed. Marketing opportunities were craftily exploited. Special medals were struck, firework displays, exhibitions and glamorous dances held."[23] In short, it was what we call today a *mega event*, one that is international in scope.

It was organized by Lord George Curzon, the Viceroy of India, and has been termed a "Victorian invented tradition" that was ostensibly for gift exchange as a "sign of reciprocity and shared authority." It ended up, though, being a ritual of subordination to the British crown.[24] Nevertheless, it had its grandiose moments, thanks to the organizational skill of Curzon and his military assistant, Major (later Sir) James Robert Dunlop Smith. Although there was a glorious entrance procession that brought Curzon into the event on the first day, it was mostly an elephant procession and, according to a witness's account, it seemed to be no match for the second big review parade several days later, that of the Retainers, or state delegations from around the country. This was held in a large arena with the Viceroy in attendance and all passed in procession before him, in a manner much in keeping with the concept of ancient homage. Here are snippets of a first-hand account of the two-hour parade, thanks to an artist, Mortimer Menpes, who was present.

> A wail of weird native music was heard in the distance, and the first of the brilliant pageant, a huge elephant hung with emerald-green and surrounded by mahuts clothed in crimson, loomed into sight.... There were monstrous elephants hung with jewels; flaming banners; mail-clad horsemen; crimson velvet and cloth of gold; masses of precious metal; glittering fringes and tassels....
>
> No one in that arena had ever seen, or ever would see again, anything to approach it....
>
> Men on camels dressed in vermilion turbans carried salmon-and-gold banners surmounted by golden emblems.... Roars of laughter shook the audience as some men on rainbow-colored stilts, their heads on a level with the roof of the arena, passed by....
>
> Next came the gold and silver cannons of the Gaekwar of Baroda. As they advanced with the sun full on them, one could see nothing but golden rays shooting out from a clump of fire....
>
> Even the horns of the oxen were encased in gold, and precious golden tissue covered the sacred beasts....

A group of bards passed by, chanting as they went songs on the glories of their land....

Stiff with golden embroidery, the Gwalior elephants attracted all eyes. There were twelve of them the first three of blazing gold, and the rest grading off to silver and copper, becoming paler and paler until they reached a neutral gray....

Perhaps the most imposing spectacle of all as it swept past was Rewa.... First came a banner of vivid emerald-green, followed by a warrior on an elephant smothered with huge metal spikes. There were spikes on his breastplate, spikes on his back, spikes on his head, spikes everywhere—a most ferocious-looking creature! ....

The next group to attract attention was Orcha. This State was represented by a group of mounted bards playing on the quaintest instruments I have ever seen most of them two-stringed, others three-stringed....

How brilliant were the horses, and how proudly they marched past, tossing their gorgeous plumes, jingling their silver bells, and walking with a skittish movement, almost a skip.... The trappings were one blaze of color. Clumps of gold and silver succeeded old-rose and salmon tassels; green-and-gold and vermilion-and-gold saddle-cloths; massive silver anklets; plumes of every color—the sight was dazzling.... Many of these creations circled round the arena on their hind legs; others literally danced, springing forward in leaps and bounds with their legs gathered under them, and executing curious dancing steps in a way that could never be equalled by any circus horse....

In Rajputana we saw real workmen.... Here were horsemen in chain armour, stern and forbidding of demeanour, clothed in metal from head to foot.... More warriors followed from Rajputana—horsemen with bows and arrows; camel-riders with burnished swivel-guns that shone in the sun like great mirrors; spearmen and matchlock-men on foot; rough-riders and men carrying hand-grenades or rockets; and a crow-catcher in red and silver with green petticoats. Then, there were the Nagas or military ascetics, grotesque figures covered with ochre, performing wild dances....

There were brilliant carts of golden plush hung with violet tassels, the bullocks covered by jewels and silver scales, the drivers dressed in blue, silver, and gold; palanquins of gold and silver embroidery lined with green and old-gold, carried on carmine poles by attendants in red and yellow.[25]

    This parade had all the ritual characteristics to impress: colorful formal regalia and traditional costumes; rules and a controlled order of appearance; symbolism; and wonderfully unconventional performances of ethnic music, dancing horses, and dancing wild men, not to mention the magnificent variety of animals bedecked in rich fabrics and jewels. The placement and selection of participants were nothing short of brilliant, a credit to the labors of Curzon and Dunlop Smith. The politics of the time were complicated and as a result the reviews of the entire Durbar were mixed, but from the standpoint of a well-crafted spectacle that no doubt resulted in many moving encounters both for the Indians and the British, this particular parade was close to perfect.

A Well-Crafted Modern Parade

    What about modern parades? Is there one that demonstrates true thought for ritual and craftsmanship in its creation? I believe that the rapid emergence and acceptance of pride parades around the world within the last 30 years is one such remarkable example.

The movement to advocate for the rights of LGBTQ (lesbian, gay, bisexual, transgender, and queer or questioning) persons is universally believed to have begun in 1969 with the Stonewall riots.[26] These were spontaneous demonstrations by members of the gay community in response to a police raid that began in the early morning hours of June 28, 1969, at the Stonewall Inn in the Greenwich Village neighborhood of Manhattan, New York City. A few months later, homophile groups began to organize and recommend that demonstrations be held in cities across the USA annually to commemorate the riots. A year later, in June 1970, the first protest marches marked the anniversary in New York, Los Angeles, and San Francisco. By the 1980s, the activist nature of the marches had largely dissipated and they became celebrations of gay culture, using the more acceptable terms gay pride and parade. Since the early 1990s, the vast majority of actual parades have come into being around the world, some as part of larger festivals. They are immensely popular. The 50th anniversary parade in New York City in 2019 attracted roughly five million attendees.[27]

In my opinion, they are popular for several reasons and not entirely what one would think. Certainly, there is an element of solidarity in beliefs between spectators and participants, but ultimately it is superior organization and knowledge of ritual that lies behind the success. To begin with, their use of symbols is as well executed as almost any others, if not better, including the McDonald's logo and the logos of professional sports teams, even the Olympics. The six-color pride flag, originally designed with eight colors in 1978, has become so prominent that it is next to impossible to see a rainbow anywhere other than the sky—even though a real rainbow has seven colors—and not immediately think about gay pride.[28] After all, how can anybody not love a rainbow?

Their use of formalism is fascinating in that they have carried individual costuming to an extreme, in fact have encouraged such extremism to the extent that almost every parade participant has their own personalized, multi-hued attire. There is also a semblance of uniformity—body-hugging shorts, skimpy tops, and glitter-covered or painted exposed flesh. Invariance and tradition keep the parades on the same routes year to year and dates and times are consistent. There is consistent use of certain group placements, in particular the lesbian bikers known as Dykes on Bikes—a club founded in 1976 to promote pride, defiance, liberation, and empowerment—who usually lead many parades.[29] Rule-governance, while obviously present to keep the parades in order, takes a decidedly 180-degree turn in that the entire spectacle, much like carnival, has always been intended as a showcase for breaking laws (in the early days) but now for challenging moral codes (see Chapter Ten).

Everything comes together with performance in these parades and that is where they shine. Most participants are not professional performers, although the occasional name band might appear. However, a lot of supportive organizations go to much effort to rehearse dance routines. The lively music accompanying them keeps the mood uplifted. All the parades, no matter where, focus on positive messages of love, tolerance, and understanding. Combined with the overwhelming use of the rainbow colors, a plethora of outlandish costumes, and floats filled with exuberant partyers, these messages act as catalysts to generate moving encounters between participants and spectators (Figure 1-4).

Pride parades have been so successful that politicians now flock to march in

Figure 1-4: Vancouver Pride Parade (photograph by the author).

them. There has even been a backlash within the LGBTQ community that believes there is now too much *corporatization* as companies rush to take advantage of the pride phenomenon.[30] They are, in a sense, victims of their own success, but I would suggest that is a positive outcome, something of which to be "proud." Other contemporary parade organizers would do well to emulate them.

Two

Sacred Space
and Monumental Architecture

In the 2004 film *Alexander* there is a scene about five minutes in length in which Alexander the Great and his army march into the city of Babylon after defeating the Persian King Darius III at the Battle of Gaugamela. The army enters the imposing Ishtar Gate with its blue-glazed bricks (see color insert Figure 2-1), and then while advancing down the famous Processional Way, Alexander turns his head toward the sky with a look of sheer euphoria on his face. He drinks in the power of the moment, with the adulation of the crowd from every side and millions of flowers raining down on him.[1]

The year is 331 BCE and he is as close as anyone has ever come to being the "King of the World." His elation is not just from the adoring onlookers. He knows where he treads. The Processional Way bisects the entire city and is home to the king's palace, the beautiful Hanging Gardens, and a giant ziggurat and temple to the god Marduk. It is an awe-inspiring setting, made even more so by the impressive 20 meter width of the avenue and its bounding, 25 meter high walls on either side, all decorated with majestic tiled animalistic icons representing gods.[2] It is the very heart of the Persian Empire, and Alexander now owns it. But what do we make of this euphoria-inducing setting, this amazing place? It infers a certain sacredness, but is it truly sacred?

The Concept of Sacred Space

Religious scholar Mircea Eliade was the first to propose that, for what he called religious people, the world is divided into two kinds of space, the sacred and the profane. Profane—now more commonly called secular—space is the ordinary space in which we live and go about our daily activities free of all reference to a larger reality. Sacred space is experienced differently. When one enters a sacred space, he or she acts in accordance with the environment (e.g., in a church or temple one might bow, remove shoes and hats, or speak in whispers). Eliade claimed that before modern times, archaic people established towns, built sanctuaries, and organized space and time with reference to the sacred.[3] In those ancient times, the choice of location for a sacred space might have been simply due to a fortuitous sign (e.g., temples built on hilltops because they were closer to the gods) or it might have been planned as a result of some specific ritual. The one guiding principle was, however, that these sacred sites were entirely concerned with the worship of a higher power, in other words religion in its most strict sense.

Anthropologist Catherine Bell, whom we met in the Introduction, adds a new, more humanist perspective. She considers that geographic and historic—not necessarily religious—places can be in themselves sacred symbols where ritual-like activities occur. As examples she offers Niagara Falls and Pearl Harbor. The site of the Twin Towers memorial in New York City could be considered sacred in modern terms. Today, as Bell points out, thinking is along the lines that a specific space or location is made sacred by the ritual-like activities that take place within it. Thus, like other symbols, they are differentiated from profane spaces "by means of distinctive acts and responses and the way they evoke experiences of a greater, higher, or more universalized reality—the group, the nation, humankind, the power of God, or the balance of the cosmos."[4]

While Bell refrains from stating that *anywhere* can be considered sacred space depending on the ritual-like activities that take place within it, she nevertheless implies it. At least one academic, Robert Ellis, has taken Bell's implication one step further and suggested that sporting places can, through their design and the rituals performed within them, act as vehicles for divine encounters.[5] These encounters are, according to Ellis, much like the connections (i.e., moving encounters) to which I referred in the Introduction. Others have suggested that small, purpose-built public spaces could be used for personal reflection and therefore be considered sacred.[6] I have also previously stated in another book that I believe such places—and many others, including a parade route—can be considered sacred.[7] Theologians, on the other hand, may go as far as calling the route sacred only if there is a religious procession of some sort on it. I shall leave it up to theologians and anthropologists to debate if such spaces are indeed sacred or, more accurately, *quasi-sacred*.[8] For purposes of the remainder of this chapter, I will consider parade routes sacred, but only while the parade is in progress.

The Structure of a Parade Route as a Sacred Space

Architect Thomas Barrie identifies a basic three-part structure to sacred spaces: a marked origin, a path, and a sacred center (or destination) at the end of the path.[9]

While Barrie's structure is obvious for traditional sacred spaces such as churches and temples, it is not quite so obvious for the immense built environments that envelop modern parades. From a practical standpoint, though, there is more needed than just Barrie's basic three-part structure. In my personal experience of producing events—including parades—and in practical terms, I have determined that all these spaces have eight common physical components. Let's look at the components with reference to parades both historical and modern.

First of all, something has to enclose and define the space; it needs physical boundaries. These can be actual walls such as delineated the Processional Way through ancient Babylon. In modern terms, they can also be sidewalks, fencing, landscape and natural features such as trees or waterways, buildings on the sides of streets or plazas, or humans who have been purposely placed in guardian-type positions. Spectators must feel and clearly understand when they have crossed this threshold and entered the sacred space of the parade. More likely than not this happens when they enter the space from a side street.

There must be some sort of obvious way for the parade itself to actually enter and exit the space, to begin and end. Virtually all sacred spaces have at least one main entrance (i.e., the "origin" identified by Barrie) and often the same entrance is used as an exit. This is usually obvious through physical features (e.g., size, color, design) or strategic positioning along a boundary of the space. Ancient examples include city gates, a temple, or a palace. Modern parades might begin from plazas, stadia, parks, or side streets.

There must be allowance for a processional route. This is the "path" identified by Barrie. In a church, the obvious processional route is the aisle leading to the altar. However, in the case of a parade, logic would tell us that the processional route forms the *entire* sacred space, although in reality just a significant part of it. When one considers that the sacred space also encompasses the physical boundaries, then the real route itself would be the width and length of the avenue or boulevard.

There has to be a purposefully designed ceremonial space. Most sacred spaces contain smaller but more significant inner sancta in which the essential core ritual activities take place (i.e., the "destination" identified by Barrie). The most obvious of course is the altar in a church or the many sanctuaries of ancient temples. Not every parade will have a ceremonial space, but many do. Examples include the reviewing stand for a military parade, the stage in the Opening Ceremonies of the Olympic Games (used after the Parade of Athletes), even one or more of the elements inhabiting a processional route such as plazas or parks. For processions, by their definition, there is a designated ceremonial destination.

The orientation of the space could be a factor in making it more meaningful. This is usually obvious with ancient sites, especially religious ones. They were often oriented according to compass directions, the path of the sun, astronomical alignments or, as some have speculated, along lines of magnetic energy—sometimes called Ley lines—although this latter theory is mostly considered to be doubtful science. The Opet Festival processional route, for example, aligned with the direction of flow of the Nile River, the source of life. Similarly, water flow direction was responsible for the design of the Avenue of the Dead in Teotihuacan.[10] In ancient Mayan cities, processions moved towards and around commemorative stelae and temples, often along causeways and through central plazas, which tended to be developed in tandem with monumental building construction (e.g., temples).[11] Today's orientations are more concerned with accessibility and the presentation of a city's strongest architectural features, which may correlate more with the boundaries of the route. What is critical is that the boundaries and the overall setting are attractive enough to make spectators and participants feel proud and excited to be there.

There must be a performance space. This refers to the provision of space set aside for performances by dancers, musicians, theatrical shows with actors, comedians, and such. For example, in churches performance space is often designed into the architecture to accommodate an organ, choir, or musical group (i.e., a choir loft), and nowadays, often full theatrical productions on a stage that also serves as the altar. Parades require a unique perspective on performance space. On the one hand, it can be easily said that the performance space and the processional route coincide. This may not be entirely true. For the royal entries discussed in Chapter Four, it was common for the procession to stop along the route to watch *tableaux vivants* fixed in place. In modern parades, there may be certain locations along the route that lend themselves better to periodic performances than others, such as large intersections or city squares, or possibly anywhere if the parade must halt for a few moments.

Spectator space is a requirement. Otherwise, why have the rituals at all? For a church, the area set aside for the congregation usually comprises the largest area within the space, although to be correct, the congregation members are both spectators *and* participants. For a parade, spectator space is typically sidewalks or fenced-off areas of the actual processional route. This may extend further to specially constructed grandstands or bleachers. In some secular parades the "congregation" may also be both spectators and participants (see Chapters Nine and Ten).

Finally, somewhere is needed to prepare for the parade. Any special event as complex as a parade, or even as relatively simple as a church service, needs preparation. There is no reason to doubt why this area should not be considered part of the sacred space because it is essential to the completion of the necessary rituals. Prior to a Catholic mass, for example, the priest prepares and dons his vestments in an area known as the *sacristy*, while the remainder of the participants in the entrance procession prepare in the church foyer. Ancient parades had such areas; modern parades have them. One historical example is the Roman Triumph. Because most of them were so large, they assembled outside the city walls in an expanse of fields known as the Campus Martius. Likewise, modern parades generally assemble in side streets adjoining the major parade route. Because these areas—like the route itself—are often cordoned off, they are part of the sacred space.

Urban Space and Monumental Architecture

A parade is temporary, but much of the route itself is permanent. The structures and features that line and form the route contribute to the success of the parade and its emotional impact on spectators and participants. In other words, the structures and features are part of what influences people.

Throughout history, parade routes or processional ways have been designed to be grandiose. Along them one can find history and a sense of purpose. Their astute placement brings together religion, government, commerce, and the social life of the city. If one were to walk the length of such a "grand boulevard," it would be possible to understand the entire culture of a people. We have little knowledge of ancient designers, but we do know that, structurally, successful modern parade routes emanate from the creative minds of urban designers and architects.

From the point of view of urban design, the grand boulevards of today have several things in common with ancient processional ways. First of all, they are wide— not necessarily long—but wide. Twenty meters or about 66 ft in width was not at all unusual for ancient processional ways and seemed to be close to a norm (e.g., Babylon, Thebes in Egypt, Athens). The Boulevard Argeus in ancient Alexandria, along which Ptolemy's Grand Procession (see Chapter Four) weaved its way, was said to be 100 ft wide (30 m).[12] In Mesoamerica, the Avenue of the Dead in Teotihuacan, Mexico, was 40 m or more than 130 ft (Figure 2-2).

Modern boulevards are of similar and larger size, not including sidewalks. One of the smaller ones is the Rajpath in New Delhi at about 10 m (30 ft). The Mall in London is about 20 m wide (66 ft) and is purposely painted red to resemble a red

Figure 2-2: View of Teotihuacan looking south down the Avenue of the Dead from the Pyramid of the Moon (© nikonov/123RF.COM).

carpet. Unter den Linden in Berlin is around 22 m (74 ft) and then they just get bigger—Paseo de la Reforma in Mexico City (25 m or 82 ft), Pennsylvania Avenue in Washington, D.C. (30 m or 100 ft), the Avenue des Champs Elysees in Paris (30 m), and arguably the widest in the world, Chang'an Avenue in Beijing (a whopping 70 m or 230 ft). As a point of reference, the average four-lane city street is about 12 to 15 m wide (40–50 ft), not including sidewalks. These figures don't seem to mean much until you consider their psychological effects.

Wide avenues or boulevards inspire and elevate emotion. A sense of openness does this. In today's best-designed boulevards there is no overcrowded feeling since many have medians with trees and even smaller feeder routes separated by trees from the main thoroughfare.[13] When sidewalks—often overly wide and airy themselves—and feeder lanes are included, the width of many modern boulevards can approach more than 60 m or 200 ft (the width of Chang'an Avenue above does not include the sidewalks). Importantly, the inclusion of the trees and other green spaces has been proven to dampen feelings of oppression and improve health.[14]

Research has also shown that any boulevard design that leads to confusion and disorientation is a negative psychologically. If people cannot relate things spatially then they get stressed and upset, which is not what is wanted if parade spectators are to relate positively to each other.[15] For example, the rotational symmetry of Piccadilly Circus in London is disorienting; Champs-Élysées in Paris is not. Straight lines with symmetry just work.[16] After all, parade watchers don't want to get lost trying to get home.

For true inspiration, though, we must look to architecture. "'We shape our buildings and afterwards our buildings shape us,' mused Winston Churchill in 1943 while considering the repair of the bomb-ravaged House of Commons."[17] Indeed, the Parliament Buildings in London have become an iconic symbol for a nation, a culture, and a political system. They form part of a class of buildings known as monumental architecture, and these types of buildings are found in abundance surrounding, and on, ancient processional ways and modern grand boulevards. Pyramids, triumphal arches, obelisks, statues, temples, and cathedrals are typical of this type of structure. So are buildings such as parliaments, palaces, embassies, museums, and skyscrapers. As archaeologist Bernard Knapp has stated, "Unlike most other materials and objects that archaeologists study, monumental buildings are culturally constructed *places*, enduring features of the landscape that actively express ideology, elicit memory and help to constitute identity."[18]

Monumental structures are intended to induce awe, and awe does crazy things to your mind. Several years ago, I had the good fortune to take a helicopter ride over the Grand Canyon in Arizona, USA, with my wife and some friends. The chopper flew nap-of-the-earth from its base to the canyon edge so that passengers could not see the canyon. Suddenly it was there and the ground instantly fell away to reveal beneath our feet the mile-deep canyon with its rainbow of colors and billion-year-old geological striations. To say we were awe-struck would be an understatement. The experience literally took our breath away and one of our friends cried—not an unusual reaction. The sheer vastness and grandeur strongly affected us emotionally. Although this emotional reaction was not caused by a building, I have felt similarly upon first encountering the Egyptian pyramids, the jungle-covered complexes of Angkor in Cambodia, the Mayan temples of Tikal in Guatemala, and the Nabataean city of Petra in Jordan.

Current research has proven how experiencing awe affects us. Authors Yannick Joye and Siegfried Dewitte have summarized the psychological effects of awe-inducing monumental architecture. First, it can make us more spiritual and induce feelings of oneness with others. Even more interesting is the fact that awe-evoking stimuli can induce physical and mental immobility or *freezing*. This in turn, can literally slow people down and make them more susceptible to messages delivered to them.[19]

Joye and Dewitte's summary serves to suggest how these structures might affect parade spectators and participants who would be witnesses to an event on one of today's grand boulevards. As we know from the Introduction, it is desirable for people to have moving encounters at a parade. It is also desirable for the parade organizer or sponsor's message to be received clearly. Visible, awe-inducing monumental architecture along the parade route would thus assist in attaining these results.

What is the secret? It can't be the sheer size of a structure alone. Once again, the psychology of architecture comes to the rescue.

Boring buildings cause stress. Blocks and blocks of cookie-cutter tenements are asking for trouble. Ugly glass and concrete modernist apartments and office towers without personality do not necessarily make appealing places to live and work.[20] Therefore, choosing a parade route with buildings like these lining its sides would probably be a real downer for spectators and participants.

Strangely, though, some repetition in building facades is good, as long as it is interspersed with a different pattern or architectural feature. For example, building sections can be repeated but each section should be broken up with different window stylings, doors, and such. This type of patterning is best if it is symmetrical. Basically it still comes down to eliminating design boredom.

Finally, here's a secret that ancient architects must have learned early. If the patterns are aesthetically pleasing and rhythmic, our brains are conditioned by evolution to associate those patterns with safety, security, well-being, and survival, and this results in our body releasing pleasure drugs like oxytocin and endorphins.[21] Being in the presence of such buildings is therefore highly desirable. How did ancient architects do it?

The Influence of Classical Forms on Modern Monumental Architecture

To avoid writing an entire tome on the history of architecture, here in a nutshell is what happened. As for so many things, it all started in Egypt. Egypt influenced the Greeks, who refined and built upon the basic forms. The Greeks influenced the Romans, who rather crudely extended the Greek styles. Finally, in a spurt of inspiration, Renaissance architects, beginning with Leon Battista Alberti, thought it might be interesting to incorporate some of the classical styles into their buildings.[22] Not long after, the *Baroque* style arose which integrated multiple classical influences with an extravagant mélange of decoration. Then the *neo-classicists* of the 18th century went crazy incorporating more refined classical architectural forms into modern building design. This trend continued up to the present century.

One aspect of classical styles that carried through from the Egyptians to the Romans was the literal use of monuments for storytelling and political commentary. Temple walls, columns, and door lintels became their history books. Through colorful bas and haut relief carvings, they detailed military conquests, religious ceremonies, coronations, funerals and other public events. Although in most cases there was also some accompanying writing, universally illiterate populations could understand the gist of what was going on. Monuments *were* the mass media of the day. Parades and processions served to cement in memory what was or would be carved in stone.

There is a psychological component to this as well, according to behavioralists Melanie Green and Tom Baranowski, and architect Richard Buday. "Early architects embedded story in their buildings, combining narrative and multiple psychological theories into architectural behavioral interventions." They used "*Narrative Transportation Theory* (NTT), to produce buildings that changed what people thought and did.... Persuasive buildings aren't built today. The symbiotic relationship between psychology, narrative, and architecture disappeared at the beginning of the modern era, save for theme parks and an occasional world exposition. Today, in a time of declining architectural influence, that's a missed opportunity."[23]

What does this mean for parades? It means that for ancient parade sponsors, the battle was already half won. Spectators were in the presence of these stories and probably knew what the outcome and message of the parade were going to be before it started. For modern parade-goers, all they have is arcane architectural theory with which to begin their experience. Thus, the architecture must somehow speak for itself despite this. Using classical forms advances the experience at least partway to this goal.

Some examples are in order. The first is columns and their implementation in temples. If you rule out the rudimentary monoliths of Stonehenge in England and Göbekli Tepe in Turkey, the use of architectural columns began in Egypt around

2600 BCE. They had as many as 30 different forms of columns, most designed to resemble open or closed plants in the marshland vegetation that "sprang up around the primordial mound of creation."[24] This natural world was represented by the *hypostyle hall*, a cavernous hall just inside the entrance to temples in which the columns supported the hall's roof structure. The best example is the hypostyle hall in the sprawling Temple of Amun Re in Karnak (Luxor, Egypt), which dates from the second millennium BCE. Its size is mind-boggling.[25] It contains some 154 carved and painted columns representing papyrus plants. The largest are 21 m or 69 ft tall. It is said that 50 people can stand on the top of a single column. If this were not awe-inspiring for ancient Egyptians it would be surprising.

The Greeks adopted and modified these styles beginning around 650 BCE, as a result of expanding trade with Egypt, eventually resulting in the creation of three distinct column styles—Doric, Ionic, and Corinthian.[26] These styles became the basis of all Greek architecture, especially in temple construction. Most Greek temples were oblong, roughly twice as long as they were wide, and incorporated a colonnade of columns (*peristyle*) on all four sides. The roof was slightly sloping and had at each end an *entablature* that incorporated a horizontal *frieze* with painted sculptures and a *pediment* or gable also with sculptures.[27] Of course all the sculptures had their own stories to tell, be they historical, religious, or political. The Parthenon on the Acropolis in Athens, among dozens of others that still exist around the Aegean Sea, is perhaps the best and largest example of the classical Greek temple.

But here is the important part. This design was unbelievably popular with 18th- and 19th-century western architects, so much so, that we often take for granted the thousands of monumental buildings that line our avenues and plazas whose designs are based at least partly on Greek temples. It's impossible to list them all but here is a small sample of the better-known ones (Figure 2-3).

- Lincoln Memorial—Washington, D.C., USA
- White House—Washington, D.C., USA
- Supreme Court—Washington, D.C., USA
- Capitol Building—Washington, D.C., USA
- New York Stock Exchange—New York City, USA
- Buckingham Palace—London, England
- British Museum—London, England
- Pantheon—Rome, Italy
- The Vatican—Rome, Italy
- Bourse—St. Petersburg, Russia
- St. Isaac's Cathedral—St. Petersburg, Russia
- Palais Bourbon (French National Assembly)—Paris, France
- Brandenburg Gate—Berlin, Germany
- Reichstag—Berlin, Germany
- National Palace—El Salvador
- National Library of Greece—Athens, Greece
- Numerous national banks.

The fact that some of these are near or on important parade routes is significant. There must be something to the styles that influences people who approach or have need to be close to them, even without the benefit of explanatory sculptures

Figure 2-3: Comparison of Greek column architecture. Left: Ancient Greek temple in Agrigento, Sicily, Italy (photograph by the author). Right: United States Supreme Court building (photograph by Carol M. Highsmith, Library of Congress).

or paintings on the surfaces. I think it is because Greek design evokes timelessness and represents stability and order. Architectural expert Neil Collins sums it up well.

> Ultimately, Greek architecture presents us with a concrete illustration of moral and spiritual truth. The solid foundation platform; the down-pressing mass of architrave, frieze, and roof-structure, counteracting the otherwise too powerful sense of lift, from the columns; the serenity of the colonnade, modified by the exuberance of sculptured frieze and pediment—all this may be seen as a tangible expression of the Greek combination of freedom and restraint, of perfectly poised aspiration and reason, of invention and discipline.[28]

All this can only serve to amplify the positive feelings of parade spectators who are thrust into an environment—a sacred space—that includes such monumental architecture.

The second form of classical architecture that highly influenced western design was the Roman triumphal arch. Primarily during the Imperial era in Rome, arches were erected to honor triumphing emperors, those who won significant battles, like General Aemilius Paulus's victory detailed in Chapter Eight. It evolved as a distinct, freestanding category of architecture from monumental gateways that were major entrances to ancient cities (e.g., like the Ishtar Gate of Babylon). Most arches were of three distinct designs: a single opening, a triple opening (both usually spanning thoroughfares), and a four-opening quadrangular shape. The arches consisted of two or four main *piers* or upright supports and a flat entablature much like the Greek temple entablature. The piers and entablature were usually decorated with haut relief carvings of the emperor's exploits and accompanying written explanations. Columnar shapes were also part of the piers. Nearly 40 ancient Roman arches survive in one form or another scattered around the Mediterranean basin, home to the former empire. Most famous are the three triumphal arches remaining in the city of Rome: The Arch of Titus (81 CE), the Arch of Septimus Severus (203 CE), and the Arch of Constantine (312 CE). These three arches have inspired imitations throughout the world.[29] Often the modern imitations incorporate a *quadriga* or four-horse chariot sculpture crowning the entablature. Again, the actual arches are too numerous to list in their entirety, but some of the more famous freestanding examples are as follows (see Figure 2-4).

- Arc de Triomphe and Arc du Carrousel—Paris, France
- Monumento a la Revolución—Mexico City, Mexico
- Arch of Triumph—Pyongyang, North Korea
- Wellington Arch and Marble Arch—London, England
- Washington Square Arch—New York City, USA
- Siegestor—Munich, Germany
- India Gate—New Delhi, India
- Porta Macedonia—Skopje, North Macedonia
- Taq-e Zafar—Paghman, Afghanistan
- Triumphal Gate—Moscow, Russia
- Arco del Triunfo—Barcelona, Spain.

Many of these span parade routes in their respective cities, thus once again forming part of the uplifting, sacred space of parades. Although originally intended as symbols of state power, triumphal arches constructed in modern times have generally had their primary purpose as either the self-aggrandizement of a country's leader (e.g., the Pyongyang arch built by Korean dictator Kim Il Sung), or as war memorials.[30]

The triumphal arch shape has also been ubiquitous as part of the facades—frequently the main entrances—of important buildings in cities around the globe. Somehow architects have deduced that there is an inherent strength and noble character to the shape, one that can give the entire building a "dignity of appearance."[31] Train stations and especially national bank buildings have used this design extensively, but it is present in palaces, libraries, courthouses, schools and universities, cathedrals, museums, military buildings, private residences, and, unbelievably, suspension bridges. The Széchenyi Chain Bridge in Budapest, Hungary, is a good example. It is as if it were a prerequisite to acceptable design of virtually any building requiring a modicum of respect created between the mid–19th and mid–20th centuries (Figure 2-4).

For ease of explanation in the rest of this chapter and book, I will use the general term "neo-classical" to refer to an architectural design that incorporates Greek temple influence and/or Roman triumphal arch influence.

Figure 2-4: Roman triumphal arch architecture. Left: Arch of Septimus Severus in Rome, Italy (photograph by the author). Right: Kedleston Hall, Derbyshire, England (photograph by Glen Bowman, CC BY-SA 2.0).

Visualizing the Space

What were the imposing monuments that lined ancient parade routes? We've already seen Babylon, and in Chapter Six will see Thebes, the site of the ancient Egyptian Opet Festival. Here are two more examples.

General Paulus in his triumph (Chapter Eight) would not have encountered as many monumental structures as Roman Emperor Aurelian did in his later triumph of 274 CE.[32] Aurelian's nine-hour spectacle that included the captured Palmyrene warrior queen Zenobia, would have started at the Porta Triumphalis, the main city gate, then maneuvered slowly through the 150,000-plus seat Circus Maximus, and circled the Palatine Hill with its many mansions. After coming around the hill they would have proceeded through the first triumphal arch, commemorating Emperor Hadrian's victories, then immediately afterward, encountered the 30 m tall, bronze statue of Emperor Nero looming in front of the magnificent Colosseum. An abrupt turn left onto the Via Sacra would soon bring them to the Arch of Titus, and then they would move through the Forum with its many temples, columns, and *stoa*-lined shops,[33] and thence through the Arch of Septimus Severus. A final turn to the southwest would take them past the Temple of Saturn and up the Capitoline Hill to the Temple of Jupiter.

Meanwhile, 12,000 km to the west, in the pre–Columbian Central Valley of Mexico, around the same time, the feather and jade-bedecked lords and priests of Teotihuacan were gathering for a procession and sacrifices on the plaza at the base of the Pyramid of the Moon. After several initial prayers and offerings to the rain god, they proceeded south down the wide Avenue of the Dead, lined by small temples. Along the way, many of the 100,000 townspeople fell in behind the expanding procession. To the left soon loomed the Pyramid of the Sun, the largest building in the entire continent at the time, near which more offerings and sacrifices were made. Finally, the procession, now stretching over two kilometers, arrived at its destination, the Temple of the Feathered Serpent. Another plaza in front of it provided space for all the participants and there the official dedication sacrifices were made. They were all Teotihuacán warriors, for this was an honor.

How about modern parade routes?

Let's go back to 2011 in London, England for the first example, the wedding of HRH Prince William and Catherine Middleton. After the ceremony, the couple, riding in a 1902 state landau (horse-drawn carriage), left Westminster Abbey and turned up Whitehall where visible landmarks (i.e., monumental architecture) nearby or lining the road included a statue of Winston Churchill, the Houses of Parliament and Big Ben, Her Majesty's Revenue and Customs (neo-classical façade), the Cenotaph or National War Memorial, Foreign, Commonwealth and Development Office (neo-classical façade), Women of World War II statue, and the Cabinet Office (neo-classical façade). After about a kilometer, they turned west into Horse Guards Parade, a massive dirt parade square surrounded by neo-classical buildings and eight memorial statues and used for the Queen's Trooping of the Colour. They then proceeded up to The Mall and turned west. As they turned, they would have seen the magnificent Admiralty Arch (neo-classical) to their right (Figure 2-5). On The Mall heading towards Buckingham Palace in the distance, they had St. James Park on their left and Prince Philip House (neo-classical façade) on their right, followed by the

Figure 2-5: The Coldstream Guards Troop their Color along the Mall in London with the Admiralty Arch in the background (photograph by Cpl Stephen Harvey/MOD, https:// nationalarchives.gov.uk/doc/open-government-licence/version/1/).

King George VI and Queen Elizabeth Memorial on the right, then the Diana Princess of Wales Memorial Walk on the left. Within a few more minutes they arrived at the imposing Victoria Memorial with Buckingham Palace, their destination, immediately behind it.

For the last example, we look to the inauguration parades—more appropriately processions because there are ceremonies involved—of American presidents. They all follow a route along Pennsylvania Avenue from the Capitol to the White House.[34] Now Washington is one of the world's most beautiful capital cities and it has never disappointed or lacked for stately edifices. The parades pass: the George Gordon Meade Memorial and U.S. District Court; Andrew Mellon Memorial Fountain with the National Gallery of Art behind (neo-classical façade); Federal Trade Commission (neo-classical façade); National Archives Research Center (neo-classical façade); U.S. Navy Memorial and Naval Heritage Center (neo-classical façade); Old Post Office Museum; Ronald Reagan Building (neo-classical façade); the open and airy Freedom Plaza; the General William Tecumseh Sherman Monument; the U.S. Treasury Department (neo-classical façade); Internal Revenue Service (neo-classical façade); St. John's Episcopal Church (neo-classical façade); and Lafayette Square with the White House in the distance.

These spaces truly are the visual personalities of their respective nations. How could anyone not feel a sense of reverence and pride when standing in or marching through them?

But not every parade needs to—or should—use a city's most prominent and nationalistic thoroughfare. It's often a matter of formalism. Neo-classical buildings tend to reflect a formal atmosphere; narrow, shop-lined streets instill a more casual tone. Sometimes it just comes down to choosing the best neighborhood, the one that gels the easiest with a parade's goals and theme. Paris holds an annual parade to celebrate their national holiday, Bastille Day, along the Champs-Élysées, and comprising military units almost exclusively—perfect for the occasion. It also has an annual carnival parade in a less formal area of the city, a different district. Why? The informality of the carnival just would not fit on the Champs-Élysées, nor the formal Bastille Day parade on side streets.

My own home city of Vancouver on Canada's west coast hosts a large pride parade every summer. The parade follows a narrow street paralleling the city's most popular beaches on one side and apartment buildings on the other. Why this location? It exhibits the city's scenic beauty but it also traverses the heart of the city's most recognized gay neighborhood. It would not fit along an office building-lined, shaded, downtown thoroughfare, especially one that did not lend itself to the exposure of flesh.

New York's aptly named *Canyon of Heroes* is a route reserved for the homecoming of astronauts, military commanders, and sports heroes since 1886. It is in the financial district and is not a wide, nationalistic street but a dark, skyscraper-lined, narrow section of lower Broadway only about a kilometer in length. Why here and not somewhere else in this city with so many options? Because it lends itself to ticker tape parades, in themselves very nationalistic, but only successful when people can—or could—throw ticker tape from tall buildings in the financial district.

Meanwhile, in *upper* Manhattan, the annual Macy's Parade had been using the *Great White Way* (Broadway), New York's most famous street, for most of its route until 2008 when the route was changed to use wider streets (e.g., Sixth Avenue) to accommodate the giant balloons featured in it, and to avoid a pedestrian-only new section of Broadway.[35] Sometimes the route decision is quite innocuous.

By way of a tidy summary, a parade's route and the built environment that surrounds it can be considered a sacred space—during its performance—with all the attendant consequences of the rituals that take place within it. Some of these consequences are the positive feelings that can be attributed to the design of the space itself and of the buildings and monumental structures that inhabit it. Put simply, the space helps the parade influence people.

THREE

Looking the Part

He sat in a wheeled chair, waiting for dark,
And shivered in his ghastly suit of grey,
Legless, sewn short at elbow. Through the park
Voices of boys rang saddening like a hymn,
Voices of play and pleasure after day,
Till gathering sleep had mothered them from him.

About this time Town used to swing so gay
When glow-lamps budded in the light-blue trees,
And girls glanced lovelier as the air grew dim,—
In the old times, before he threw away his knees.
Now he will never feel again how slim
Girls' waists are, or how warm their subtle hands,
All of them touch him like some queer disease.

There was an artist silly for his face,
For it was younger than his youth, last year.
Now, he is old; his back will never brace;
He's lost his colour very far from here,
Poured it down shell-holes till the veins ran dry,
And half his lifetime lapsed in the hot race
And leap of purple spurted from his thigh.

One time he liked a blood-smear down his leg,
After the matches carried shoulder-high.
It was after football, when he'd drunk a peg,
He thought he'd better join. He wonders why.
Someone had said he'd look a god in kilts.
That's why; and maybe, too, to please his Meg,
Aye, that was it, to please the giddy jilts,
He asked to join. He didn't have to beg;
Smiling they wrote his lie: aged nineteen years.
Germans he scarcely thought of, all their guilt,
And Austria's, did not move him. And no fears
Of Fear came yet. He thought of jewelled hilts
For daggers in plaid socks; of smart salutes;
And care of arms; and leave; and pay arrears;
Esprit de corps; and hints for young recruits.
And soon, he was drafted out with drums and cheers.

Some cheered him home, but not as crowds cheer Goal.
Only a solemn man who brought him fruits
Thanked him; and then inquired about his soul.

Now, he will spend a few sick years in institutes,
And do what things the rules consider wise,
And take whatever pity they may dole.
Tonight he noticed how the women's eyes
Passed from him to the strong men that were whole.
How cold and late it is! Why don't they come
And put him into bed? Why don't they come?

This poem, *Disabled*, by First World War British poet Wilfred Owen, speaks volumes to the persuasive effect of the military parade and the military uniform on onlookers. How many countless women through the centuries have goaded young men into joining the military by innocently telling them how good they would look in a dress uniform? Or how great an adventure awaited them?

Marching and martial music will be covered in Chapter Five, but for now, I want to concentrate on one of the underlying meanings of Owen's poem—what parade participants wear and the effect of their dress on both spectators and participants. When we talk about what parade participants wear, we are getting into the ritual characteristic of formalism. As anthropologist Catherine Bell said, one of the obvious ways that formalism can be demonstrated is through attire.

For most parade participants, whether they are members of the military, cowboys on horses, clowns, majorettes, dancers on floats, bagpipers, or even fully vested priests in the entrance procession of a mass, they will undoubtedly be attired in the best, most impressive clothing that their calling allows, in other words their equivalent of formal attire. This attire will have some sort of effect on both the spectators and on themselves as participants.

I consider that there are four types of attire that might be exhibited in a parade— formal dress, regalia, costumes, and uniforms.

Formal Dress

Formal dress is the best of what most people keep in their closet, or occasionally rent; it's what we put on for occasions of varying importance. It might be as lowly as a business suit for our job or as lofty as a tuxedo for a wedding.

But wait a minute. Haven't sociologists and social commentators been telling us for several years that there has been a mass casualization of dress and that people have abandoned their public persona in favor of their private one?[1] They have let go of the tailored business suits and dresses, ties, polished oxfords, high heels, stockings, and hats and moved to a more fluid, creative interpretation of themselves. Their personal values are no longer wrapped up in their ability to adapt to a universally accepted standard of dress but more in how many likes they can garner from photos of their outlandish outfits posted on social media. Does this mean that any appreciation of formal social occasions and indeed, formal attire itself, has been lost? The answer is a resounding "No." In fact, quite the contrary appears to be happening.

At least one observer, Bruce Boyer, has opined that there is a longing for nostalgia, for a time when there was a sense of occasion to dress up for a special event like a wedding, a party, or the theater. As he states, "Frustrated by the demands of individual expression, some have begun to yearn again for a shared and public happiness.

Behind their desire lies a realization that was once universal: A society hospitable to the down and out will not be afraid to dress up."[2]

In 1975, author John T. Molloy published a book titled *Dress for Success* about the effect of clothing on a man's success in business and personal life. It was followed two years later by *The Women's Dress for Success Book*. Both became bestsellers and popularized the concept of *power dressing*. The advice provided in these books, although considered by some to be outdated, is still relevant today mainly because as humans, we still judge a book by its cover. We form opinions about someone's status, income, job, personality, and yes, even political leanings solely from the clothes they are wearing.

Much more has been done in recent years.

In 2000, an important study showed that people make rapid judgments, often very accurate judgments, within a very short period of time of observing another person. These short perceptive interactions are known as *thin slices*.[3] A thin slice is defined as "a brief excerpt of expressive behavior sampled from the behavioral stream." These excerpts can be as short as five seconds. The traits judged include trust, competence, dominance, nervousness, warmth, likability, expressiveness, sympathy, and politeness. Of course, one of the attention-grabbers in this short time span is attire.

In recognition of this, in 2010, Swiss bank UBS issued a 44-page dress code manual that, among other things, stated:

- A flawless appearance can bring inner peace and a sense of security.
- Adopting impeccable behavior extends to impeccable presentation.
- The garment is a critical form of non-verbal communication.[4]

In 2013, researchers using a customer/salesperson interaction in a store, proved Molloy's contentions experimentally.[5] They found that salespersons perceived customers (strangers) who dressed more conservatively to be higher-class members of society.[6]

Five more studies done by Columbia University social psychologists in 2015 on 60 students reached the following conclusion.

> Dressing up makes people feel and seem more powerful and impacts their thinking and speech. Subjects in formal clothing spoke more abstractly and less concretely, and this was unrelated to socioeconomic backgrounds. For example, instead of describing mechanical actions, like saying "I'll lock the door," they'd use intentional speech by saying "I'll secure the house."
>
> When subjects dressed informally they felt, acted, spoke, and thought differently, and others responded according to those signals, regardless of their upbringings. The findings were consistent with other studies on formal speech, which have found that formality influences social distance—how approachable someone is—which is associated with feelings of personal power, competence, and abstract thinking. When dressed up more formally, subjects were less approachable but felt and appeared more powerful, but the opposite is true when dressed casually.[7]

This idea is not new. Hundreds of years ago the importance of formal clothing in a social setting was more than apparent. The famous meeting between Henry VIII of England and François I of France at the Field of the Cloth of Gold in June 1520 is a great case in point. One of the most ostentatious displays of wealth, culture, and courtly sports that Europe had ever seen, some 12,000 noblemen and women from both countries took part. Having the right attire was a ticket into the event and social competition was very much a part it. One French memoirist described the nobles as literally "carrying their castles, woods, and farms upon their backs" because they had mortgaged their lands to buy the best clothes they could.[8] These were on full display for the great procession that brought the two delegations together and that is represented by numerous paintings and drawings (see color insert Figure 3-1).

Two other published studies in 2013 and 2015 showed some of the very subtle ways in which clothing influences all kinds of impressions about us. Our clothes make a huge difference to what people think about us—and without us knowing or in ways we couldn't even imagine. As with previous work, they found that people make their assessments in the first few seconds of seeing another; assessments that go way beyond how well you are dressed and how neat and tidy you might look. For example, in one study, after just a three-second exposure, people judged a man more favorably in a tailor-made suit than in an off-the-rack suit. And the judgments were not about how well dressed he was. They rated him as more confident, successful, flexible and a higher earner in a tailor-made suit than when he wore a high street equivalent.[9] In a second study on subtle differences in women's workplace attire, people rated a senior manager less favorably when her dress style was more provocative, and more favorably when dressed more conservatively (e.g., longer skirt, buttoned up blouse). The clothing in the provocative condition was still very conservative in style and look; it was not a short skirt and a revealing blouse, but a skirt slightly above the knee and one button on the blouse undone.[10]

Even shoes, hairstyle, and one's choice of clothing colors influence what viewers think.

A 2012 study found how first impressions were formed based on the shoes one was wearing. Of the many findings, some of the positive ones included: colorful and bright shoes indicated extroversion; conscientiousness was indicated by attractive shoes in good repair; and shoe attractiveness correlated with income level. Overall, the study found that age, gender, income, attachment anxiety, and agreeableness were most accurately predicted.[11] As an aside, in my career as an entertainment agent and producer, one of the first things I insisted on was that all performers onstage ensure their shoes were in good order and polished. It made the audience respect them as dedicated practitioners of their craft. On the other side of the coin, it also showed the audience that the performers respected *them* enough to take care of all the minutiae of dress.

Not many studies have been done on hairstyles for either men or women. However, of the little that is known from experience, the consensus seems to lean toward shorter, well-maintained hairstyles for both sexes. In general, these indicate confidence, dependability, and intelligence.[12]

The psychology of color has been widely studied. In terms of clothing color and its effect on the perceptions of spectators or viewers, there have been some interesting findings. For example, some tests found that red clothing on sports teams favorably influenced referees' decisions because of the color's association with dominance and aggression.[13] In another study, red attire on women meant sexual attractiveness and the same on men; however, the red on men signaled higher status.[14] Generally speaking, the effects of colors on viewers has not changed much over the years. Keeping in mind the context of their use, particularly in a parade, here are some accepted guidelines.

- Trust and credibility—blue
- Friendliness and approachability—light tones of colors
- Assertiveness—red
- Confidence (women)—blue-green
- Dependability—green
- Neutral—grey or beige
- Authoritative and professional—dark blue or dark grey
- Accents of color can help to convey certain messages.[15]

Here is a simple example from two different countries of how color affects us. In the USA, a politician wearing a red tie is assumed to be a Republican while a politician wearing a blue tie is assumed to be a Democrat, almost to the point that now *anything* colored red—especially clothing like hats—has become a symbol of Republicanism. In Canada—although not to quite the same extremes—the opposite is true: red for Liberal or left-leaning, blue for Conservative or right-leaning.

What does all this mean, then, for parades?

First and foremost, it means that participants must be very conscious of dress style before they choose what to wear in a parade. For the most part they would want to command respect. Second, the choice has to be congruent with the context. Too dressy or not dressy enough could be disastrous for their image.

Let's take another simple example, a politician in a gay pride parade. He might have two choices for attire. One might be an over-the-top *coat of many colors*—in other words a costume, which we will be discussing shortly—and the other might be a conservative suit accessorized with a rainbow tie. The message he would be sending with the first choice would be that he is fully into the cause and is willing to go to almost embarrassing ends to prove it. It also might be sending the message that he is unstable. The second, more conservative choice, would indicate that he is supportive of the cause yet still commands respect. It also leaves room for observers who do not share his political views to respect him. In other words, he will probably garner more support and respect by using the more conservative, formal choice.

Of course, the *most* formal type of regular dress is formal wear. This can be a tuxedo for men and usually a long gown for women. In a parade one might encounter this on beauty queens and princesses, often sitting atop a float and occupying a place of honor in the parade (Figure 3-2). The psychological effects of the formal gown or tuxedo on both the wearer and viewer would necessarily follow and be similar to those for regular dress, with one exception. Formal wear such as a gown or tuxedo could label the wearer as being unique, and thus worthy of increased attention. On the other hand, the intended effect of most non-casual business attire (e.g., suits for men, dresses for women) is to make the wearer "*indistinguishable* ... to erase peculiarities of personal style."[16]

I once participated on the organizing committee of a festival in Nova Scotia, Canada, called the Apple Blossom Festival held annually in the spring. It was a celebration for all the small communities along the length of the Annapolis Valley. One of the defining events was a large parade that consisted primarily of decorated floats upon which sat in all her formal splendor, each community's queen, her attire being a formal gown and tiara. Certainly, her gown, but more importantly her relative beauty

Figure 3-2: Beauty queens and princesses on a parade float (©robertogalan1983/123RF. COM).

plus the attractiveness of her float, were sources of pride for her community and became key points of connection between her and the parade spectators.

Regalia

While formal attire like a gown or tuxedo is mainly intended to elevate the value or relative importance of an individual amongst their socio-economic peers, regalia do much more. Regalia are neither formal dress nor costumes, a term that is often mistakenly used to label them. "Regalia refers to the symbols, emblems, and physical artifacts traditionally associated with a person of significance or with official titles and powers. While culturally specific, regalia generally reflects the authority, legitimacy or insider status of the person who wears or owns it."[17] Four examples of regalia that are often found in parades and especially in ritual-filled processions are royal regalia, religious regalia, academic regalia, and Indigenous regalia. Of all types of parade attire, they command the most respect because they combine long-standing—sometimes mythical—tradition with respect for the status of the wearer. Likewise, of all attire, regalia are the most instantly recognizable by onlookers, particularly royal regalia.

Royal regalia consist of such items as crowns, mantles, gloves, and jewels, accessorized with hand-held items such as scepters, swords, orbs, crooks, and flails. All have deep symbolic meaning, often linking a sovereign to a god in keeping with the divine right of kings to rule. Such regalia go back to the very beginnings of recorded history in Egypt and Mesopotamia. Typically, these regalia are seen in processions leading up to some sort of ceremony like a coronation, wedding, or funeral. Depending upon the respect earned by the ruler, such processions can be intensely emotional. In the case of British royalty, one clear example was the state funeral for Queen Elizabeth I on April 28, 1603, in London. A much-beloved queen, it was said of the funeral procession by chronicler John Stow, "Westminster was surcharged with multitudes of all sorts of people in their streets, houses, windows, leads and gutters, that came out to see the obsequy, and when they beheld her statue lying upon the coffin, there was such a general sighing, groaning and weeping as the like hath not been seen or known in the memory of man."[18]

The statue on the coffin was a wax effigy of the queen, a "'lively picture of Her Highness's whole body, crowned in her Parliament robes, with her sceptre in her hand, lying on the corpse, embalmed and leaded, covered in purple velvet.' The effigy was borne in a chariot drawn by four horses trapped in black velvet; the chariot was covered by a canopy and surrounded by twelve noblemen (six on each side) carrying banners representing Elizabeth's lineage."[19] We thus have all the royal trappings on view for the public, all the better to identify with the dead queen and all the easier to mourn her.

Religious regalia have a history at least as old as royal regalia, going back to the shaman of hunter-gather societies. Although occasionally the subject of scorn and persecution in history, those wearing this clothing command much respect among the followers of a particular faith. To these followers, the regalia are instantly recognizable.

Taking Christianity and Roman Catholicism as an example, the regalia are called *vestments*, and vestment design goes back to Greco-Roman times where it began as the ordinary dress of the day. However, by the late Middle Ages it had ceased to undergo any major changes and is to this day virtually the same as at that time. The multiple ranks of the clergy are indicated by a variety of differences, the number and meaning of which are far too esoteric to go into here. Suffice it to say, such vestments are in use in every single mass or service that is held today, all of which generally begin with a procession. Lastly, it should be mentioned that for Catholics, the priest or bishop is considered to be Christ's direct representative on earth and is endowed with the power to change bread (the *eucharist*) into the real body of Christ and to forgive sins. The mere presence of such a person in such vestments in a procession, is ultimately important—for this religion at least—to the lives of roughly a billion practitioners in the world, or more importantly, to saving their souls.

As a comparison, Buddhist regalia do not have quite the complex history, although there are differences among the regions where Buddhism is practiced. In Theravada Buddhism, for example, practiced in Southeast Asia, it is claimed that the regalia have not changed in 25 centuries. These are comprised of three parts, an undergarment called an *antaravasaka,* a main robe called a *uttarasanga* or *kashaya,* and an extra robe called a *sanghati,* often used for warmth.[20] All these are saffron or orange-yellow-colored, and form the regalia with which most western observers are familiar. Monks wear these in processions such as the daily alms-giving ceremony in Laos, in which "several hundred monks and novices from the various monasteries in Luang Prabang walk barefoot through town. They collect donations of food and rice in their alms bowls from locals—and tourists alike—lining the streets."[21]

Academic regalia, sometimes called—mistakenly in my opinion—dress, cloth-ing, or costume, began their history as the ordinary daily wear of medieval scholars and derived from the outdoor dress of the clergy, since early European universities were run by religious orders. Hazy history seems to lean towards explaining part of their design as being functional, so students could keep warm in the poorly heated church buildings that served as early university classrooms. By the 15th century, the design of the academic gown had been all but standardized with an open front rather than the originally closed version or *cappa clausa*. The *mortarboard*—square-topped hats of undergraduates—may *look* like the mortarboards of a bricklayer, but it is thought to have developed from the *biretta*, a similar-looking hat worn by Roman Catholic clergy starting somewhere in the inexact fog of time. Modern aca-demic regalia are, for the most part, not much changed since medieval days, except for customization of colors and some outer accoutrements based on the university and faculty.

These many colors that represent faculties at universities are seen in their most vibrant form and use during convocation ceremonies. Academic Kathleen Man-ning succinctly sums up the inherent importance of the event's rituals and regalia as follows.

> Although most colleges in the United States are secular, the religious nature of institu-tional life remains firmly embedded in higher education rituals.... The most significant vestige of the sacred nature of campus ritual life is academic regalia.... During graduate student hooding ceremonies, regalia is bestowed by an academic on graduating masters and doctoral students.... The already established academic bestows the honor and obli-gations of status as an educated person upon the graduating student. The solemnness of the ceremony [including the procession] as well as the use of these almost holy vestments engenders meaning and significance upon the ritual action.[22]

Interestingly, although academic regalia are intended more to help celebrate a col-lective tradition, recent attempts to partially customize them to make them more personally meaningful have met with some success, particularly for groups such as Indigenous graduates.[23]

In fact, Indigenous regalia themselves nicely bridge the gap between this type of attire and costume, which we will discuss next. Besides being worn by persons in authority such as chiefs and spiritual leaders, some Indigenous regalia can be worn by ordinary Indigenous citizens as a sign of honor. As such, "pieces of regalia are sig-nificant to both personal and collective identity. They tell a story, transmit heritage and serve as badges of honor. Regalia can reflect an individual's connection to their ancestors, family members and clan."[24] It is this unique personal aspect that differen-tiates them from other regalia.

Indigenous regalia are often seen in processions within Indigenous communi-ties, a prime example being grand entrances to powwows. Within the greater com-munity, Indigenous people and their regalia may often be seen in major parades and processions in which their heritage may be honored and appreciated. One example is the appearance of Indigenous peoples of the Canadian prairies who ride on horse-back in the annual Calgary Stampede parade in Alberta, Canada (Figure 3-3).

In my career as an event producer, I frequently worked with Indigenous per-forming dance troupes. Some of the most popular events we had were opening cer-emonies for large conferences hosted by our city that began with what we called a

Figure 3-3: First Nations in Calgary Stampede Parade (courtesy Petra König).

Talking Stick Ceremony and involved Indigenous dancers. A loud clap of thunder initiated proceedings as the room went dark. The dancers then processed into the conference hall in full regalia accompanied by drums and singing, and the sound of the rainforest in the background. This was followed by a dance performance and prayers onstage, and then the gift of a "talking stick" to the conference chairman. The stick was about five feet tall and carved with totem symbols. Its purpose was to signal that all listening to the speaker who held it were to remain silent, an Indigenous tradition. This procession and performance often emotionally affected the audiences and helped to create a connection between cultures.

Costumes

As opposed to regular formal dress and regalia, costume is much more individualistic. As Pravina Shukla points out in her excellent book on the subject, costume is "special dress that enables the expression of extraordinary identity in exceptional circumstances" and is "deliberately used to project an elected identity, specific to the time, place, and audience."[25] In simple terms, it is a person trying to be somebody else.

While at first glance this would imply a lack of formality, especially in a folkloric sense or when one imagines Halloween, if the context for its use is a specific performance such as a parade, then it becomes a formal and necessary component of the performance. The persona of the wearer also changes when they inhabit the costume so that the result is a new person with a new personality. Generally, this is obvious in stage performances or movies, but when ordinary, non-actors choose to wear a costume and "take on a role" things get interesting (Figure 3-4).

Again, in the many special events I produced, one of the more popular activities involved making one's own hat, no more, no less. We provided the materials and watched as accountants, salespeople, doctors, nurses, and scientists—often from different cultures—instantly transformed from mild-mannered introverts into wild and crazy party animals.

This is the gist of what costumes are all about; the more elaborate and authentic the costume, the more extreme the personality transformation. One of the more unconventional phenomena of modern times, yet one that proves this theory, is that of *cosplay* or costume play. Individual fans transform into the fully costumed and accessorized characters from movies, books, comics, video games, and the Japanese genres of *manga* and *anime*. Superheroes such as Superman, Thor, Spiderman, Wonder Woman, Iron Man, and others are always popular. The phenomenon now boasts several annual conventions, the most notable of which is called Comic-Con, held in San Diego, California. As of 2018, annual attendance had surpassed 130,000 over three days. Many conventions include parades of costumed attendees.

Figure 3-4: The Rosenmontagszug (carnival parade) moves through the streets of Mainz, Germany. In the foreground is a so called Schwellkopp, which is a traditional carnival figure. In the background are costumed spectators. Rosenmontagszug in Mainz is one of the largest and most famous carnival parades in Germany with approximately 500,000 spectators (©olio, www.istockphoto.com).

The lure of costume, whether for ordinary people dressing up as superheroes or ordinary people dressing up in elaborate ethnic and historical carnival costumes for Mardi Gras parades, is the social connection. Comic-Con was initially considered to be a gathering of nerds, ironically and typically less social than most. Mardi Gras in its many incarnations around the world, is successful because of the enthusiasm of the groups that build floats, displays, and costumes. Groups like samba schools in Rio de Janeiro, *krewes* in New Orleans, and historical societies in Venice provide the impetus for these events and members are emotionally fulfilled by the social connections within their groups, and between the groups and their enthusiastic audiences.

Quotes from participants prove the point. "Cosplay makes me happy"; "It's worth it just to put some smiles on people's faces"; or "Costuming is more fun if you do it with other people.... You create your own look, but you also feel like part of a universe when you surround yourself with people who enjoy it as much as you do."[26]

Uniforms

The last type of parade attire is uniforms. Although other participating groups in parades may wear uniforms, this discussion is about military uniforms, since the uniforms of civilian marching groups are typically only derivations of them.

Most military units in all countries have different uniforms, or accessories they add to regular uniforms to make them ceremonial, what they would wear when on parade. Until recently, military battle dress was the same as ceremonial parade dress, and ceremonial parade dress was, once it became standardized for armies in the mid–17th century, very colorful. As the thinking went, conspicuous colors were necessary to distinguish one side from the other on "musket-produced, smoke-filled battlefields."[27] Also, once standardization was achieved, common uniforms instilled a sense of individual pride in the wearers and increased unit esprit de corps.

It was from this time until well into the 19th century that male dress uniforms reached the zenith of exhibitionism. It has been argued that three competing principles have governed fashion design, including military uniforms, throughout history. These include the *hierarchical principle*, the *seduction principle*, and the *utility principle*.[28] By far the most influential of these in military uniform design appears to have been the seduction principle. At least one scholar has observed that "a smart uniform enhances a man's masculinity.... It gives him a headdress which exaggerates his height; it puts a stripe on his trousers to exaggerate his apparent length of leg; it gives him epaulettes to exaggerate the width of his shoulders."[29] Vamp/comedienne extraordinaire Mae West famously said, "You know, I always liked a man in uniform.... That one fits you perfect. Say, why don't you come up some time. I'm home every evening." She recognized the appeal.

Furthermore, the seductiveness and erotic aspects of this type of design cross societal and national boundaries and have been found equally effective with both sexes.[30] In the 1970s, the popular vocal group the Village People understood this and satirized the appeal of uniforms to a homoerotic audience.[31] In simple terms, it is the uniformed soldier—or seaman or airman—who wins the girl—or guy. As Wilfred Owen implied in his poem, this can have profound effects on both an individual and a nation.

As far as the hierarchical principle goes, this refers to the fact that officers in the military have traditionally had more attractive uniforms, often of better-tailored quality. They are the ones with the more exaggerated epaulettes, the gaudy sashes, the swords, and the "scrambled egg" gold on their hats. Their attraction meter registers higher. But that does not mean that enlisted ranks miss out on the effects of the hierarchical principle altogether. For them, rank insignia, achievement badges, and medals all contribute to differentiate them from their comrades. It has been proven, for example, that genuine war heroes, those military men sporting combat medals, are seen to be even more alluring to the opposite sex, although the same cannot be said for female war heroines.[32]

Military uniform design took a major direction change toward the end of the 19th century with the advent of smokeless gunpowder and the introduction of longer-range automatic weapons. Standing or marching forward in full view of the enemy on a battlefield was to become a technique of the past. Armies could now hide closer to the ground in foxholes.[33] This resulted in a new focus on camouflaged attire (i.e., the utility principle) for battle and to the familiar image of the modern soldier. Most national militaries did, however, continue to recognize the benefits to be gained by their members from the appeal of a well-designed, colorful ceremonial parade dress uniform. This is the situation today, so that anytime military personnel parade in public, they usually do so in all their peacock resplendence.

This has placed some forces in almost embarrassing situations because they have chosen to retain the male uniforms representative of their nations' past glories going back hundreds of years. Examples abound, including the Vatican Guard with their armored breastplates and helmets, the strange head plumage of Indian army units, skirted Greek guards (Evzones), bearded and aproned French Foreign Legionnaires, British Beefeaters, and even excessively be-medalled American and Russian generals.

Is the seduction principle still applicable after all this time, especially with anachronistic apparel like this? Journal and newspaper articles suggest it is alive and very well. In 1995, Midge Wilson, a psychology professor at DePaul University in Chicago, stated, "The erotic value has to do with *masculinity*. A man in uniform taps into ... father figures, heroism, protection and power. He also suggests a chance for excitement and adventure."[34] As more recent articles confirm, smitten females continue to literally throw themselves and their phone numbers at military personnel in uniform.[35] Indeed, the attraction has now spread to even those in non-descript camouflage since these types of uniforms reinforce the belief that the wearer is heroic and strong.[36] This notion would have been unheard of in the Vietnam War era when the civilian adoption of camouflage tended to be more of a fashion statement in protest against the war.[37] However, in the early 21st century, the more publicly popular anti-terrorism fight has come home to western shores and requires extensive use of camouflage by fighting forces; hence the continuing attraction for women.

But what of the appeal of women's military uniforms? Famous women warriors have been adding spice to history books for centuries—Joan of Arc of France, Celtic Queen Boudicca, Artemia I of Caria, Japanese archer and swordswoman Tomoe Gozen, Queen Zenobia of Palmyra. There are dozens of others. They are exceptions, though. Apart from the semi-mythical Amazons of ancient Greek lore, women did not have any real combat—or other—military roles en masse until the early 20th century, although many did fight disguised as men over the centuries. Russia formed 15 women's units in 1917 but only two battalions saw action in the First World War, and all were disbanded by the end of 1918. In the Second World War, countries on both sides of the conflict began bringing women into the military fold in both combat and non-combat roles. It is from this time that serious attention began to be paid to the design of women's uniforms.

The design process in all countries has been—and continues to be—fraught with conflicting opinions. Should the uniform conform to male standards and appearance or should it be obviously female? What about female comfort compared to men? Sorting out the intricacies of a design has not been easy—hat size and shape, jacket length, breast pockets or not, shoe heel height, pants or not, skirt shape, hem length. As Cynthia Enloe points out, "women in the military must not be mistaken in public for soldiering men. Neither, however, should women in military uniform be mistaken for bar waitresses or flight attendants. Women soldiers must look like representatives of the state's military. Women soldiers must be attired in a manner that enables them to do their job effectively for that military." She goes on to opine that getting it wrong can lead to a woman appearing "mannish," which is a "threat to the proper order of things."[38]

It's not surprising that disagreement has existed. There has been almost no evidence or research other than anecdotal to indicate there exists the same attraction of a woman's uniform to men that a man's uniform has to women. Were there evidence, it could make a case that the uniform would attract male spectators to females on parade. In a logical world, this type of appeal would also suggest that men could influence decisions of their mates to join the military. Since one of the main reasons for designing the right attire for military women is to help in recruiting other women, this has no doubt complicated the design problem.

If it is possible to summarize the design problem at all, it would be this. A military woman's dress uniform design must appeal to the woman and only the woman, not to both sexes as in the case of a man's uniform. Therefore, what it looks like on parade is only important to female spectators.

Occasionally, designers have gotten it right. Cultural researcher Kathleen Ryan has interviewed female war veterans and talks about what she found.[39] During World War II, the U.S. Navy and Coast Guard brought in famous fashion designer Mainbocher and he created four optional uniforms for the women, all universally praised by these women for their quality and looks. Tailor-made, lady-like, gorgeous, sophisticated, high-class, refined, comfortable, and magnificent—these were some of the descriptions of the uniforms by those wearing them. One of the key things that the design did was to elevate the social status of the women no matter where they came from. One Navy member had this to say.

> I looked at myself in the long mirror. By heavens, I did look impressive. The suit was beautifully cut, trim and efficient-looking without being stiff and masculine. It was the kind of tailored outfit I might have bought in civilian life—but in navy blue, with the folded-anchor embroidery on the collar and black regulation buttons, it gave me the bearing of a woman in whom great responsibilities were vested. Unconsciously, I straightened and got a look of fire in my eyes.[40]

In 1943, according to Ryan, the WAVES (U.S. Navy enlisted women), along with other women in uniform, were named as *Vogue's* "Best Dressed Women in the World Today." It was assured that recruiting would be no problem (see color insert Figure 3-5).

Even today, many nations' militaries still get women's uniform design horribly wrong. The result is often that the uniforms simply look ridiculous on parade, no matter how enticing the marching cadence, synchronization, and music might be (see Chapter Five). I would go so far as to say that the uniform design actually detracts from the effectiveness of the overall parade and its purpose. Examples center on the use of very short skirts—and occasionally hair that is too long—by military units of Russia, China, and North Korea, among others. There's just something about goose-stepping, automatic rifle-toting women in mini-skirts that seems a little incongruous.

If there is one single statement to be made about attire it is that making the right connections with parade spectators is highly influenced in numerous ways by what participants wear.

Four

The Symbolism of Floats

The story of parade floats goes back to the origins of civilizations. It is a story about symbolism, which is another of the characteristics of ritual laid out in the Introduction. A symbol is a mark, sign, or word that indicates, signifies, or is understood as representing an idea, object, or relationship. The golden arches of the McDonald's restaurant chain, for example, even without the company name emblazoned under them, still conjure up in our minds thoughts of tasty hamburgers, a pleasant and bright dining environment, and happy children. In the same way, the term "parade float" and what it may represent is in itself a symbol, and frequently a very powerful one.

The Semiotics of Parade Floats

Semiotics is the study of signs and symbols and how they are used to communicate meaning. They can help us understand what floats are all about.

Let's be honest. Some of the things we love the most about parades are the floats. We wait with anticipation to see what the next fantasy creation will look like. We want to be wowed. We want to connect with the people on the float. We want to understand what the entire mobile work of art means and how it connects to us. As mentioned in the Introduction, when they attend an event like a parade, spectators want to gain knowledge about history and culture, and they want to be personally fulfilled. This is what floats do, and semiotics can help us figure out just how they do it.

Floats themselves are inherently symbolic. They are literally and metaphorically vehicles for the interpretation of symbols. In general terms, they represent three concepts: achievement, power, and validation.

The building of a float and its acceptance into a parade is no small achievement. It involves countless hours from dedicated volunteers and/or a contracted company to design and build, not to mention the contribution of money from the sponsor. What is it about achievement that impresses us? Probably the fact that it is deep-rooted in our society, a core value of capitalism. In the USA, it's the American Dream. Striving for perfection is what keeps us motivated. We constantly want to see—and be—bigger and better, and like the Olympic motto, *Faster, Higher, and Stronger*. Think about it. Ultra-wealthy people are celebrated and ranked. Countries compete to build the world's highest building. We are entranced by giants, Amazons, and superheroes in the arts. Companies endeavor to outdo each other by building large "things" (e.g., at the time of writing Royal Caribbean had the largest cruise ship in the world at 230,000 tons, five times larger than the *Titanic*). Individuals and even entire countries attempt to gain unique records that will live on in the *Guinness Book of Records*. In fact, the *Guinness Book of Records* has become so popular that it now holds its own world record as the best-selling copyrighted book of all time. It has sold more than 100 million copies in 100 different countries and is printed in 37 different languages.[1] Intriguingly, the book contains numerous records about parades and their sizes, and the sizes of such elements as floats.

While a float is an achievement, it is also a large mobile prop, as mentioned in Chapter One, upon which actors, automata, or static design elements play their parts in telling a story or relaying a message. However, the audience, albeit perhaps subconsciously, still treats the very short performance as if it were a true story unfolding before them in a real theater. In fact, they expect to be entertained and challenged; they expect to have the same emotions elicited from the performance as if it were a Shakespeare play. "Theatre is an art form that brings people together to celebrate, challenge and provoke through the telling of stories. Theatre is unique, you see transformation right in front of you—created in the moment.... What you witness in any given moment is unique and only you and the audience will ever experience that."[2] That is what is expected to happen—and does happen—with floats.

This prop, the float, is elevated above the eye level of the audience. By this simple consequence of the float's construction, the audience's perception of the people and actions on the float changes. Over the centuries, we as human beings have come to subconsciously equate positions of power with a physical difference in height. Most political and religious leaders have always spoken publicly from raised positions or platforms, and hence we consider anyone who speaks or performs from such a position as special in our eyes. We attribute more importance to their utterances, whether those utterances are serious or humorous, true or false.[3]

Power is also enhanced by spectators' perception of the performing space, which is in most cases a street. We saw this in Chapter Two, in that we treat this kind of space with more reverence than we do other spaces. The float, being in this space, instantly gains a measure of power in the sense that it owns the space. As an example, "carnival floats have power and use power, as spectacle and as a physical occupation of the street."[4] This is more a result of the upside-down nature of carnival in which lower classes can be seen as those in power. Nevertheless, it does demonstrate how such floats can be perceived when occupying a unique space.

The last concept that floats represent is validation. The Merriam-Webster dictionary defines "to validate" as "to recognize, establish, or illustrate the worthiness or legitimacy of."[5] For floats there are two logical premises that concern validation, both interconnected and not unlike the concept of celebrity endorsement of products. The first premise is that the parade, being sanctioned by a municipal governing body of some sort, is therefore legitimate and worthy of being a public event. Logically then, any participant such as a float and the float's sponsor must also be legitimate and worthy as an entity or organization. This premise gives the float and the float's sponsor legitimacy in the eyes of the spectators. The second premise is just the reverse and starts with the assumption, proven or not, that the float's sponsor is already worthy and legitimate. It follows that by the sponsor's participation in the parade then the organizer of the parade and its cause or theme must also be legitimate and worthy of the attention of the spectators.

It is this validation in the eyes of the spectators that makes parade participation by different organizations so popular as a form of marketing, as mentioned in the Introduction.

One Victoria, British Columbia, mobile entertainment franchisee says this about an annual parade in that city, "It's fantastic exposure … an inexpensive way for small businesses to showcase themselves to a large amount of people.… Our target market is lined along the side of the road."[6] Similar sentiments are echoed about participants in the famous annual Rose Parade in Pasadena, California. According to Tim Estes, CEO of Fiesta Parade Floats, "I would say the overall average [cost of a parade float] is around about $250 to $260,000," and also according to Estes, a number of corporate sponsors have told him they've received anywhere from four to six dollars in return for every dollar invested in a float. "It's a great ROI for anyone … trying to give a message about who you are and what you do," he says.[7]

While floats have extrinsic symbolism, they also have *intrinsic* symbolism. They are constructed *as* symbols in order to convey specific messages. The symbols can be obvious or abstruse. For example, the Dole Pineapple float in the 2020 Rose Parade was in large part comprised of three-dimensional, graphic sun's rays, which normally form part of the company logo. This worked well because the theme of the parade was the "Power of Hope." It was a little esoteric but not so much so that the connection could not be made. At the other end, some European carnival parades have, as of late, taken to mocking political leaders using floats depicting giant effigies of political leaders in various coital positions, the symbolism of which is hard to miss. But these are only two recent and simple examples. We can get a much better overall picture of the efficacy of floats in conveying messages by analyzing how they fit into some of the great parades of history.

A Brief History of Parade Floats

The story begins around 3400 BCE in the Early Civilization historical period, the approximate time when wheeled vehicles made their first appearance in the archaeological record. Early evidence has been found in present-day Iraq, Poland, Germany, Russia, Turkey, and Hungary. Most of the evidence is in the form of written signs, rudimentary drawings, preserved wagon parts, and clay models. The first invented wagon (i.e., a four-wheeled vehicle) came from Mesopotamia, and the technology spread north and east from there.[8] Cart (i.e., a two-wheeled vehicle) technology reached India by the beginning of the Harappan Civilization around 2600 BCE.[9] Based on a recent find of wagon tracks in Henan Province, the technology reached China by about 2200 BCE.[10]

Wheeled vehicles were a big deal, one of the great human inventions. Items previously hauled cross-country on sledges (e.g., crops, fertilizer, lumber, clay) could now be hauled much more efficiently on wagons. It is not a stretch to speculate that soon after wagons were invented, they would have been used to carry people in processions, especially powerful rich people and kings, or objects such as statues of gods.[11] This would have been in ritually significant cities with early roads of stone like Babylon's Processional Way.

The first real proof comes about a thousand years after the wagon came into service. A beautiful artifact in the British Museum called the Standard of Ur, is a small trapezoidal box whose two sides and end panels are covered with mosaics made of shell, lapis lazuli, and red limestone set into bitumen. It dates to about 2500 BCE, and is from Mesopotamia. One side shows "war" and has three registers. On the top, a king, standing taller than any other figure and with his bodyguard and four-wheeled wagon behind him, faces a row of prisoners, all of whom are portrayed as naked, bound and injured with large, bleeding gashes on their chests and thighs. In the middle register, eight identical soldiers give way to a battle scene, followed by a depiction of enemies being captured and led away (see color insert Figure 4-1). The lower register shows more wagons. The king's wagon looks like it was configured slightly differently. It was conceivably used for a purpose other than strictly fighting, and if for a victory procession, then it is an indication of its use as a *proto-float*. Because it also resembles a chariot (two wheels) it might even be considered a *proto-chariot*.[12]

Kings were carried in chariots in both Mesopotamia and Egypt from at least the second millennium BCE onwards. Today, monarchs and VIPs are transported in parades and processions in unique vehicles—everything from classic cars to Renaissance carriages and our modern version of floats. From a symbolic point of view, the mere sight of an ancient royal chariot or wagon coming into view in a procession could have induced a whole range of emotions in onlookers, from fear to elation, depending on whether the onlookers were, for example, conquered or conquerors.

The first real mention of what might be considered floats in today's terms comes from Greece and the two processions described in Chapter Six (Panathenaic Procession) and Chapter Ten (Dionysian Procession).

Every four years in the Great Panathenaic Procession beginning around the middle of the 6th century BCE, an enormous *peplos* (dress) was taken to the Acropolis in Athens to enrobe the statue of Athena in the Parthenon. Since it would have been virtually impossible to put this peplos on a 39 ft high statue, the dress may have been merely hung in the Parthenon. This peplos was so large that it was carried in the procession on the mast of a ship on wheels, like a float in a modern parade. The connection between the ship and Athena is unknown, but the use of a ship to carry the peplos must have seemed appropriate since Athens dominated a large part of the Aegean world with its sea power.[13]

For the Great Dionysian Procession beginning about the same time, there are paintings on pottery of four-wheeled wagons with structures made to resemble ships that carry Dionysus and two *satyr* musicians, undoubtedly costumed performers. Like modern floats, the decorative structure appears to cover most of the wheels so that the vehicle would look like it was floating (Figure 4-2). Both these wagons/floats (Panathenaic and Dionysian), with their religious symbols, served to emphasize their importance to the procession audiences.[14]

Nowhere in antiquity is there a more obvious example of early float structures and their use as symbols than in the Grand Procession of Ptolemy Philadelphus held in Alexandria, Egypt, around 278 BCE, as part of a larger festival called the Ptolemaieia.[15]

Ptolemy II (Philadelphus) was the son of Ptolemy I who was an army general and

Figure 4-2: Ancient Greek wagon or "float" in a Dionysian Procession depicted on a Greek postage stamp. Note that it is shaped like a small ship (photograph by the author)

member of the Royal Bodyguards of Alexander the Great. Ptolemy I established the famous Ptolemaic Dynasty in Egypt when he broke the power of the Egyptian priests and named himself pharaoh. In order to prove he was legitimate, he linked himself to Alexander (considered a god by the Egyptians for liberating them from Persian rule), just as pharaohs throughout Egyptian history had taken steps to prove their relationship to gods. With Ptolemy II, the link was not there, or at least weak. At the time of the procession, it had been more than 54 years since Alexander had liberated Egypt and the memories of his importance were probably fading. Ptolemy II now had to re-legitimize himself.[16] He used the procession to do it. The extensive use of symbolism in the parade elements—mainly floats as described below—and their arrangement in the procession was brilliant. It was crafted to perfection, the goal we discussed in Chapter One. The Grand Procession had its end purpose in mind from the very beginning. Like a staged performance, it began slowly and built to its impressive conclusion with the appearance of statues of Dionysus, Alexander, and Ptolemy I that linked them to Ptolemy II.

The procession was enormous and probably lasted from sunrise to sundown. Rather than describe its entirety I will concentrate on *some* of the main float-like components. The descriptions below are part of a much longer account written by Kallixeinos of Rhodes, presumably a witness to the procession.[17]

- A four-wheeled wagon, eight cubits wide, was drawn by 60 men. In it was a statue of Nysa, eight cubits high, in a sitting posture, clothed in a gold-embroidered tunic and a cloak. The statue rose up by a mechanism of some sort, without any one applying his hand to it, and then it poured libations of milk out of a golden bottle, and sat down again. In its left hand it bore a thyrsus wrapped round with turbans, and it was crowned with a garland of gold ivy-leaves, and with gorgeous bunches of grapes inlaid with precious stones. It also had a parasol over it and on the corners of the wagon were fastened four golden lamps.[18]

- A large wagon with 180 slaves pulling it by ropes. It held a tall statue of Dionysus wearing a purple garment.[19] The statue was posed as if pouring wine out of a golden goblet. A canopy shaded the entire statue.

- More than 300 slaves pulling a huge cart on which sat a gigantic wine press full of grapes.[20] Sixty satyrs trampled the grapes, singing a song in praise of the wine press to flute music. The bald and fat, drunken tutor of Dionysus, Silenus, presided over them. The newly pressed wine ran out from the bottom of the cart, leaving a purple trail in the dirt.

- Six hundred men drawing a cart with a sack on it of sewn leopards' skins that held 3000 measures of wine.

- Sixteen hundred boys crowned with ivy and vine leaves and clad in knee-length white chitons. They carried a variety of gold and silver wine coolers. After them, hundreds more boys carried drinking cups. They ran into the audience and offered the entire a draught of sweet Mareotic wine, refilling the cups from the coolers (the large wine-skin float presumably) as necessary.

- A wagon decorated as the bedchamber of Semelê, the mother of Dionysus and another decorated as a large cave, the cave where Dionysus was raised. Live doves and pigeons flew out of the cave for the audience to catch by long threads attached to their legs.

- A wagon containing a beautifully painted statue of the god riding on an elephant. Sitting in front of him on the elephant's neck was a satyr crowned with a golden chaplet.[21]

- A cart containing a colorfully painted statue of Dionysus flying to the altar of Rhea, the earth mother, being pursued by his real mother Hera. Priapus, his son, stood by him crowned with gold ivy leaves.

- A cart containing exquisitely designed statues of Alexander and Ptolemy I, both crowned with gold. A statue of Arête with a gold crown stood beside Ptolemy. Again, another statue of Priapus was with them, wearing a gold crown of ivy leaves. A fourth statue wearing a golden diadem and representing the city of Corinth also stood beside Ptolemy. The two carts were followed by women in sumptuous dresses, jewelry, and gold crowns. They all held signs announcing cities in Ionia, Greece, Asia, and islands, all of which were under Persian control before Alexander conquered them.

- Two chariots with oversize symbols of the cult of Dionysus. The first had a golden thyrsus 90 cubits long and a silver spear 60 cubits long; the second contained a gigantic golden phallus 120 cubits long wreathed with golden garlands and having on the end a golden star six cubits in circumference.[22]

- A magnificently decorated golden statue of Alexander borne on a chariot drawn by lumbering elephants, their trunks constantly swinging. Beside him stood statues of Nike, the companion of Zeus and the winged goddess of victory, and Athena, the goddess of war.[23]

In addition to the wagons/floats, there were thousands of other costumed participants, animals, and gold and silver objects of art. The procession ended with a march past of more than 80,000 soldiers and cavalry. From its beginning, it had the clear intent of shaping Egyptian society. In my opinion, it was the first well-described ancient procession that solidly established floats as highly persuasive ingredients in parades.

In the Postclassical Period of history (500 to 1450 CE) floats started to become more obvious as specific parade entities and began to look a little more like those of today.

The Tang Dynasty, considered to be a high point in Chinese culture, ruled from 618 to 907 CE. Public celebration was a significant part of it. By the middle of the eighth century, there were 28 official holidays and numerous festivals. For their version of carnival, a parade of floats drawn by horses or cows was the highlight.

> The floats at Tang carnivals were called mountain carts or drought boats. The former were wagons that had superstructures hung with colored silks formed to resemble mountains. The latter, also draped with colored cloth, were ships made of bamboo and wood. Men inside the boat floats carried them along the avenues. Since they did not float on water, they were called drought boats. Musicians rode on the tops of both vehicles and performed as they moved along. Other carts carrying musicians, dressed in rich fabrics and summoned from counties as far as 100 miles from the capital, were drawn by bullocks covered with tiger skins or outfitted to look like rhinoceroses and elephants.[24]

During the Tang Dynasty, the technology of these floats must have made its way to Japan across the East China Sea. In 869 CE, the Shinto Festival, Gion Matsuri, in Kyoto, Japan, was inaugurated to appease the gods and prevent plague from ravaging the city. It was thereafter held annually starting in 970 CE, and with spectacular floats since 999 CE.[25] It is still held today. In fact, "many Shinto festivals [*matsuris*] involve parades in which the *kami* (Shinto gods) are carried through the streets on floats (*kasahoko omikoshi*) by people wearing traditional costumes."[26] Other large float festivals are held in Takayama and Chichibu.

The floats in all these festivals closely resemble the Tang floats, but the symbolism is entirely religious. The main float parade incorporates two types of floats. The first is called a *hoko* or halberd. These are made to roughly resemble the medieval, two-handed pole weapon of the same name, and symbolically represent the structures built around the city to ward off the original plague (Figure 4-3). There are nine such floats and they each weigh 12,000 kg and reach 25 m in height.[27] Riding on these floats, much like the Tang floats, are musicians and performers. The superstructures housing the performers are incredibly decorative. Rich textiles cover the sides, a traditional Japanese roof covers the top, and bright lanterns festoon the entire structure for night processions. No nails are used. The wooden wheels can be as large as two meters in diameter. These spectacular floats take 30 to 40 men to haul them using ropes only. They are more like "wheeled palanquins" than our image of a modern float. Going around corners is especially difficult since the wheels do not change direction. Smaller floats, the *yama* or mountain floats, can be up to 1600 kg in weight and six meters tall.[28] In symbolic terms, this festival re-enacts the rites of separation, transition, and re-incorporation of the kami,[29] not dissimilar to the hero's journey that will be encountered in Chapter Eight.

Similar are floats from India that form part of the almost 500-year-old Hindu

Figure 4-3: Gion Matsuri float, Kyoto, Japan (Corpse Reviver, CC BY 3.0, https://creative-commons.org/licenses/by/3.0/deed.en).

festival known as Jagannath Rath Yatra, which takes place annually in Puri, India. In this procession the god Jagannath and his brother and sister are transported via large floats—also called, confusingly, chariots—from their temples to another temple to reside for nine days. These floats are enormous, with the largest towering to 45 ft and carefully crafted anew each year with wood, cloth and resin (see color insert Figure 4-4).[30] They are pulled by humans as with the Japanese floats. It is amazing how much this relatively modern religious procession resembles the Opet and Akitu Festivals of ancient Egypt and Mesopotamia (see Chapter Six). It begs an answer as to whether there was a link at some point over the course of 1500 years.

From East and South Asia, we return to Europe to investigate what some believe to be the main forerunner of today's floats, pageant wagons. But a little backstory first. In the Middle Ages, the Catholic Church was the only game in town as far as processions and entertainment for the common folk went. Unfortunately, the church mass was boring. It was delivered completely in Latin (save for the homily) by a celebrant (priest) and his assistants, all with their backs to the congregation. The mass left the mainly illiterate audience, who were standing throughout, with minimal understanding of what they were witnessing.[31] Then someone had a brilliant idea. Why not make actual stage plays out of the stories from the Bible to make them more palatable?

The concept developed slowly. As early as the fifth century CE, living pictures were introduced into sacred services, especially on festival days. By the 10th century, small additions to the liturgical text called *tropes* had been added, the most popular being the *Quem quaeritis*, a dramatized dialogue between the angel at the tomb of Christ and the women who were seeking his body.[32] Other biblical stories—mysteries or miracles—were soon added and the short plays took place on church altars.

By the next century, especially in larger cities, musicians and secular variety entertainers were banding together to perform public shows on portable wooden stages. Performances expanded and soon the liturgical plays were taking place on those same fixed public stages. By the Late Middle Ages, likely as a result of waning church attendance due to humanism, the church sought to renew itself, and *mystery cycle plays* were initiated. In these, "costume, scenery, and language, contemporary with medieval life, gave vividness and urgency to the church's stories."[33] From this initiative, pageant wagons were born.

Designed and operated by various secular guilds, the wagons would process around towns on special days in the liturgical calendar, pulled either by men or horses, and stop periodically to perform their religious plays. These were significant efforts. In York, England, for example, beginning in the mid–15th century, there were 48 different plays staged at waypoints as part of the performance (Figure 4-5).

The wagon decks were about five or six feet high, with horizontal dimensions averaging about 20 × 10 ft, although some were purported to be much larger. Some wagons had more than a single tier and with the stage sets, may have reached heights of well over 20 ft.[34] They also incorporated working mechanisms such as pulleys and winches for special effects, plus props, scenery, and stage skirting to cover the wheels. From illustrations of the day it is known that many had beautiful architectural canopies framing the biblical tableaux.[35] On one wagon in a 1594 procession in Leuven,

Figure 4-5: A stage mock-up of Noah's ark mounted on a wagon (i.e., a pageant wagon) is drawn in procession during a dress rehearsal of "Noah's Flood," a pageant play acted in the streets of York in the medieval manner as part of the York Festival (PA Images / Alamy Stock Photo).

Belgium, a multi-storey tower housed dozens of singers and required two men at the wagon's sides holding guide ropes to prevent it from falling.[36] Also leading the Leuven procession was a wagon decorated as the Garden of Eden complete with allegedly naked Adam and Eve who acted out the original fall from grace.[37] Most wagons were set up to play to one side only, but some were open on all sides.[38] Pageants were popular in Northern Europe through to the mid–16th century when the Reformation began to de-popularize them.

That was not the end of the pageant wagon, though. As the popularity of religious pageants was waning, the popularity of royal entries was ascending. Pageant wagons ended up playing a role in this new form of political display.

Royal entries, intended to recall the Roman triumph, paralleled the proliferation of ostentatious court life across Europe during the Early Modern historical period, from approximately 1450 to 1750 CE. The royal entry, also known as triumphal entry or joyous entry, consisted of festivities accompanying a formal entry by a ruler or his representative into a city.[39] The entry centered on a procession carrying the entering prince/king/queen into the city, where he was greeted and paid appropriate homage by the civic authorities. A feast and other celebrations would follow.

Early entries began as a gesture of loyalty and fealty by a city to the ruler, but later morphed into lavish propaganda exercises for the ruler and conversely, appeals from the city for the ruler's help in various political matters. Most entries, particularly the later ones, incorporated pageantic displays of both religious and secular themes. Examples included three dimensional, decorative triumphal arches sometimes with performers on them, temporary statues, either real or constructed, large painted images, and many tableaux vivants or allegorical/thematic set scenes. These last were stages upon which costumed actors performed a short symbolic story. They would be positioned at strategic locations along the procession's route. The stages could be either fixed or portable as on a pageant wagon; history does not make the distinction very well and we are frequently left to guess which ones were used.[40] If they were pageant wagons, they could also be positioned along the route or be part of the procession. In either case, the procession would have to stop to observe the plays.

In the lexicon of royal entries, another confusing term, *triumphal cars*—or sometimes carts, even chariots—came to replace pageant wagons, or work alongside them linguistically. Obviously referring to the Roman triumph, the triumphal cars of royal entries were just floats that carried performers or symbols as opposed to being used to stage a short play. Figure 4-6 is an example of such a car designed as part of a theoretical royal entry by Maximilian the Great, Holy Roman Emperor from 1508 to 1519.

It is known that some of the entries in Spain used triumphal cars to carry singers and musicians, particularly the entry of Ferdinand of Aragon into Valladolid in 1513.[41] Likewise, Alfonso the Great's victorious entry into Naples in 1443 had at least three cars with allegorical scenes. One "bore seven ladies who turned a large globe over which a standing male figure carrying a sceptre and wearing a laurel wreath presided. The standing figure, representing Caesar, saluted the new King and then presented him with his throne and crown." The second "represented a scene from Arthurian history. The float depicted the legendary throne whose seat would ignite in flames if an unworthy ruler sat upon it. The seat was surrounded by five figures representing the virtues of Justice, Fortitude, Prudence, Charity, and Faith. The figure of Justice addressed the

Figure 4-6: The Triumphal Chariot of Maximilian I (The Great Triumphal Car) by Albrecht Dürer, 1523 (Rosenwald Collection, National Gallery of Art, Washington).

newly crowned King while Charity distributed gold coins to the spectators." The last was the throne of Alfonso himself. "He rode on a four-wheeled cart drawn by four white horses covered in red and white silk whose harnesses were decorated with the arms of Aragon. The cart was decorated like a fortress and had a crenellated top and turrets at the corners.... Alfonso, dressed in purple robes, carried an orb and a sceptre and wore around his neck the collar of the Order of the Lily decorated with a gold griffin. The throne on which he sat had the crowns of his kingdoms laid out in front of it and had the mantle of the defeated Renè of Anjou draped across the back."[42]

In the same period as royal entries, another form of entertainment arose as a result of the expanding court culture across Europe. This was the almost mythical tournament, or joust. Knightly tournaments were popular from the 13th to the 16th century. However, what started as no more than spirited medieval games or *hastilude*, slowly transformed into "a form of artistic expression. The element of real combat had been increasingly sacrificed to the elements of display and disguising—that is the dressing up of combatants in fanciful and exotic costumes—and, in its most highly developed form, the tournament became an incipient drama in which the participants represented particular characters and even uttered speeches, so that the actual fighting would arise from a dramatic dispute or allegorical story."[43] Much of this pomp was intended to reflect the knightly code of chivalry. Pageant wagons or cars/pavilions again helped to do this.

During the week of a Tudor wedding tournament in 1501 (Katherine of Aragon and Prince Arthur), the king (Henry VII) entertained his guests with four banquets. The shows, using pageant cars as the focal points, were spectacular and would have been considered compelling dramatic entertainment even today. The symbolism of chivalry was obvious. Here is a description of one evening's procession and accompanying theatrics (transcribed as originally written).

The first [pageant car], bearing eight disguised ladies, was a castle drawn into the hall by four great beasts—a golden lion, a silver lion, a hart with gilt horns, and an ibex.... The castle had four towers, each containing a child singing sweetly. The second pageant was a fully rigged ship whose master and men in their "countenauns, spechis, and demeanour usid and behavyd them self after the maner and guyse of marynours." This ship, without any "leders in sight," proceeded through the hall "as though it hade been saylyng in the see," till it cast anchor near the castle. In the ship was a fair young lady, "in her apparell like unto the Princes of Hispayne"—though her relevance in the ensuing débat is obscure. Hope and Desire, ambassadors from certain Knights of the Mount of Love, now descended from the ship "by a ledder," passed to the castle, and endeavoured to gain the favour of the ladies therein, only to find their blandishments utterly refused. The ambassadors, in anger, warned the ladies that the knights would make such an assault on the castle that it would be "grevous to abyde there power and malesse." The eight knights themselves now entered on a third pageant, like a mountain, decorated with their banners. The ambassadors reported the ladies' refusal, whereupon the knights, "with moch malés and curvagyous myend," sallied forth, "hastely spede them to the rehersed castell," and soon compelled the ladies to surrender, descend from their stronghold, and join them in "dyvers and many goodly daunces."[44]

In April 1612, King Louis XIII of France staged a three-day tournament called the Romance of the Knights of Glory, focused entirely on the chivalric code. The first day was entirely occupied by a procession of all the knights into the lists. It included animated chariots (wagons), an elephant carrying a tower full of spears, an elephant carrying a tower of the universe with seven floors, and to conclude, Pegasus, the mythical winged horse, which spat water and fire and pulled a large rock. On the second day there were more decorated wagons, including ones with exotic animals and one with a sacred wood adorned with caves and fountains—and this was only a small part (see color insert Figure 4-7).[45] Note that the elephants seem to be on a par with floats in terms of their purpose in the parade.

The pageant wagon's transition from wagon—or car/cart/chariot—to float was completed during the golden age of processions, from the mid–16th to mid–18th centuries, particularly in the Flemish Low Countries (e.g., Belgium). The first description of a wagon as a float or *"gheestelijcke puncten ende vercierde waghen"* (sacred floats and decorated wagons in Flemish) comes from there.[46] The *ommegang* was a medieval pageant of the Flemish region that, from its early beginnings as a religious procession in the 14th century, morphed into a civic event with royal entry overtones by the 17th century. It was resurrected in 1930 CE and today is an annual major event in Brussels. A magnificent painting by the Dutch artist Denys van Alsloot, used on the cover of this book, depicts in minute detail an ommegang from 1615 in Brussels titled "The Triumph of Archduchess Isabella." Its description follows.

The procession begins in the lower left-hand corner with four camels, followed by the huntress Queen Semiramis of Babylon with the huntress Diana and Phoebus Apollo. Next come two Amazons carrying banners with the monograms of the Virgin and St. Anne.

The first car, which bears the Jesuit emblem, is that of King Psapho of Lybia, who taught his parrot to say "Psapho is God." The king is seated on the car; inside the cage a boy in feathers is teaching the birds to say "Isabel is Queen."

The second car represents the Court of the Archduchess Isabella. Fame, blowing two trumpets, is seated on a column, and under a portico bearing an escutcheon with the Lions of Brabant sits a woman representing Isabella. The motto at the side of the car reads "Aeternelle memoire te chante une grande Victoire."

The next car contains Diana and her nymphs, who have come to honor the Archduchess. It is inscribed "Vaincu de plus faute lour(de) Je vien(s) faire mon (?) homage."

The fourth car (second row, on the right) represents Apollo and the Nine Muses. The motto on the front reads, "Cedoes voster arc," and that on the side, "Nous chantons une belle victoire," a reference to Isabella's victory in an archery contest that preceded the festival.

The next car contains the tree of Jesse, with the Evangelists at the corner. This is followed by a car containing the Annunciation and another with the Nativity.

In the top row, on the left, are four artificial animals—two camels, a unicorn and a fantastic bird—followed by a car showing Christ disputing with the Doctors in the Temple. The ninth car, containing figures of Justice, Charity, etc., glorifies the virtues of the archduchess. In the front is a panel inscribed "Heroina Isabella."

The last car, in the form of a ship drawn by marine monsters, was made more than half a century earlier for the funeral procession of Charles V [the Holy Roman Emperor] in Brussels in December 1558. A print of it is reproduced in "La magnifique et somptueuse pompe funèbre faite aux obsèques et funérailles du très grand et très victorieux Empereur Charles Cinquieme.... Antwerp, Plantin, 1559." This "ship of Charles V" contains the Virgin and Child with a court of ladies, while at the end are the pillars of Hercules inscribed "Plus oultre," the insignia and motto of Charles V, drawn by two sea elephants.[47]

While this description may seem rather baffling, the procession's symbolism becomes much easier to understand when one realizes that the entire triumph was intended as an exaggerated event—perhaps even a tongue-in-cheek send-up—to honor Isabella's victory in a minor archery contest.

Before leaving the Early Modern period, I should mention a little about *automata*. The incredible automated float of Ptolemy's procession in Hellenistic Alexandria was probably the first recorded example. Not many more were known until the 16th century.

Tableaux vivants were often animated with moving limbs and heads of statues, and animals occasionally moved on their own, thanks to the genius of contemporary inventors such as Leonardo da Vinci who had quite a career designing such objects. "Accounts of the joyous entries of Louis XII into Milan in July of 1509 and the entry of François I into Lyons in 1515 both describe a captivating performance by a Leonardo device. In both these accounts, a mechanical lion is said to marvellously move of its own accord before stopping, bowing before the monarch, and then opening its chest to present a bouquet of lilies to the monarch."[48]

One of the most spectacular automata was a float known as Hellmouth, a popular theme for tableaux in this period. A description comes to us of its use in a parade in Bourges, France in 1536. It was "'fourteen feet long and eight wide, in the form of a rock on which was constructed a tower, continually blazing and shooting out flames in which Lucifer appeared, head and body only.' There were four small towers at the corners of the rock inside which souls were visible 'undergoing various torments.' The Hell-mouth proper was at the front of the rock in the form of 'a great serpent whistling and spitting fire from throat, nostrils and eyes.'"[49]

Automata were not overly complicated by modern standards, but were ingenious. The movable statue in Ptolemy's procession was undoubtedly controlled by a mechanism of pulleys and hooks—with the help of a human inside—since these were widely used in Greek theater as early as the fifth century BCE.[50] Renaissance devices showed more sophistication. They often came from the brilliant minds of not only da Vinci but also engineers such as Giovanni Fontana and Brunelleschi, and artists ranging from Mantegna to Raphael. Some of da Vinci's drawings reveal experiments with novel gear arrangements and special tie-rod and pulley arrangements for the theater that could have been transformed into innovative designs for floats or tableaux vivants.[51]

At this point we leave the history of floats with this tantalizing foretaste of the future. The amazing advancements in float technology and parade design that take place through, and because of, the Long 19th Century and Contemporary historical periods, will be the fitting conclusion to this book in Chapter Twelve.

FIVE

Mesmerizing Marching

The ritual characteristic of performance was introduced in Chapter One with our examination of it as the key to crafting a parade that turns mere viewing into a moving encounter. Chapter Three referenced Wilfred Owen's heartrending poem *Disabled*, about the persuasive power of the military parade—"And soon, he was drafted out with drums and cheers." In that chapter, the subject was uniforms on display; in this chapter, it's the actual marching, a specific type of performance. It boils down to pomp and circumstance.

At the age of 21, even I fell victim to it, much like Owen's soldier.

I'm standing at attention on the massive lawn in front of Canada's parliament buildings, my gaze fixed on the peace tower and the blue sky beyond. It's a hot May afternoon and I can feel tiny trickles of sweat slithering down my back underneath my scarlet broadcloth tunic. The stiff sides of my small oval pillbox hat dig into my head. It's particularly tight today to avoid the embarrassment of having it fall off in the middle of the parade. And a most important parade it is. We, the 500 officer cadets of the Royal Military College of Canada, the Canadian cousin of West Point in the USA and Sandhurst in England, are about to perform a unique ceremonial drill celebrating the 100th birthday of Canada. Thousands of onlookers line the periphery of the lawn. I hear the command that launches us into action and from then on for about an hour, every step, every turn, every movement is rote, guided only by the commands of our Cadet Wing Commander and the mellifluous steady rhythm of our massed brass and pipe bands. We end with a spectacular feu de joie, rifles crackling up and down the perfectly dressed rows of cadets. Only after we leave the lawn and march along the nearby streets to the cheering, clapping crowds, do I feel a tingling up my spine, a faint lightness in my heart, and a swelling pride of what I have just accomplished with my fellow cadets. We are not just comrades in arms, we are loyal Canadians, and we are appreciated. I wonder if I will ever feel this way again.

I was lucky. I only fought in the Cold War during my ensuing military career of 19 years. No bullets were exchanged. Owen and his comrades fought in the deadliest, most gruesome, most futile war in history. Owen died in that same war at the age of 25, less than a year after he wrote the poem.

These two extremes—cold war and hot war—illustrate how military parades can affect us. In both cases, similar motivations brought men into the military, even though the outcomes of their enlistment were profoundly different. Indeed, why *have* young men—and more so nowadays young women—so readily embraced the call to arms? Why do onlookers love marching troops? Why are marching military units and other organizations so ubiquitous in parades?

Mesmerizing Marching

It begins with a military ethos.

Every country that has an army—or navy or air force—has a military ethos. It is invariably wrapped up in a code of conduct defined by such noble ideals as honor, truth, duty, valor, bravery, patriotism, loyalty, and discipline. Some ideals such as honor "summon a deep-seated ethic to moderate an inherently violent profession."[1] It has guided warriors throughout history, including the extreme bravery of the Spartans, the chivalry of medieval knights, the ritual suicide of Japanese samurai when reputation was compromised, and the early-modern concept of duels between "gentlemen officers." That has always been the purpose of the military ethos—to act as a moral and ethical guide for soldiers.[2]

Of the ideals noted, discipline is the grounding, common feature of the military ethos.[3] Unquestioning obedience is at the very heart of military service, no matter the country, the leader, the religion, or the political system. The public manifestation of discipline and the military ethos in general is the ceremonial military parade in its many forms.

Fashioning a public military parade cannot be done without investing considerable time in the indoctrination process known as drill. The concept of utilizing mass coordinated movement (i.e., drill) to control armies goes back to before the Romans. While there are no written records of actual drill from the oldest civilizations, there are existing artifacts that would suggest the armies of both ancient Egypt and Sumer moved in synchronization.

The 15th-century-BCE mortuary temple of Queen Hatshepsut near Luxor, Egypt has wonderful, painted carvings of Egyptian soldiers marching in step (Figure 5-1). The Opet Festival temple carvings mentioned in Chapter Six also have them. There are many more.

Figure 5-1: Marching soldiers with axes and lances carved in Hatshepsut temple (photograph by the author).

A similar artifact, the Stele of the Vultures, is a monument from the Early Dynastic III period (2600–2350 BCE) in Mesopotamia celebrating a victory of the city-state of Lagash over its neighbor Umma (Figure 5-2). It shows what appears to be an army, not only marching in step but also wearing identical uniforms and using a *phalanx* battle formation (heavy infantry with armor, shields, and spears). Use of the phalanx with its protective shield movements requires training and discipline and this stele portrays what is considered "the first evidence in human history of a standing professional army."[4]

The ancient Greeks and Romans were masters at warfare and both engaged professionally trained armies. Marching, the major part of drill that involves synchronized lateral movements rather than stationary movements, is mentioned numerous times in the famous *Anabasis* by the Greek professional soldier and writer Xenophon in the fifth century BCE. One particular passage is a very clear reference to the strict coordination of troop movements. "Simultaneously he [Xenophon] began leading on the troops in battle line; and, placing the peltasts [shields] on either flank of the main body, they moved against the enemy. Along the line the order had sped 'to keep their spears at rest on the right shoulder until the bugle signal; then lower them for the charge, slow march, and even pace, no one to quicken into a run.'"[5]

Philip II of Macedonia advanced even further the *hoplite* phalanx style of coordinated troop movement in battle mentioned by Xenophon.[6] First, he initiated a full-time professional army rather than the part-time army of farmer-soldiers that the hoplites were. This meant that the soldiers were "fired by nationalism and personal loyalty to the monarch ... and could operate and train all year round."[7]

Figure 5-2: Stele of the Vultures (Ernest de Sarzec, *Découvertes en Chaldée* [Paris: E. Leroux, 1886]).

In other words, their minds were on the task at hand, that of defeating the enemy as a coordinated unit. To this end, they trained extensively with "thirty-five-mile forced marches and extensive drilling."[8] Second, Philip and his son, Alexander the Great, further modified the phalanx to replace the heavy armor and shield of the hoplites with a smaller shield and lighter armor, while at the same time increasing the size of the spear—now called a *sarissa*—to a formidable 16 ft in length. Thanks to these innovations, both leaders were able to move their armies great distances at speed, thus giving them the upper hand and the element of surprise in numerous instances. Alexander and his army once reportedly covered 278 km in just over three days.[9] This could never have been done without extensive drill training and marching in step, more than likely to a steady tempo either called out or played musically.

The Romans further improved the phalanx with the more tactically flexible legion incorporating several differently-equipped types of soldiers whose service was obligatory. At the same time, they established an oath of allegiance and a system of rewards and punishments. During the empire, this system was "increasingly used to enforce an understanding of discipline that included training, especially training in collective forms of fighting."[10] Famous writers of the period, Josephus and Vegetius both described how much this training resulted in the army being able to move as a single body and in military step.[11] Obviously, by this time (i.e., late fourth or early fifth centuries CE), drill and coordinated movements were an integral part of basic military training.

At around the same time in China, similar advances were being made, although references are scarce. One archaeological discovery that would imply rehearsed, synchronized army movement is the famous Terracotta Warriors found near Xian, China in 1974. They date to the first emperor Qin Shi-huang, founder of the Qin Dynasty, 221–206 BCE. The thousands of infantrymen, archers, and cavalry, as well as chariots, are all lined up in perfectly dressed battle array. The standardized uniforms and complex battle positioning would have reflected real life. Indeed, it has been suggested that the individually painted and cast soldiers resembled actual men in the emperor's army of the time.[12]

During the medieval period, the emphasis on drill as the basis of military training waned. However, "during what historians have reluctantly come to call 'The Military Revolution,' European armies between 1550 and 1720 [CE] became generally state-controlled, financed, and permanent. 'There was a resultant loss of individuality, with the need for better organization, good training—especially in drill—and strict discipline.' Training became an institution."[13] This period produced an emphasis on drill to enable the effective use of gunpowder and the synchronized firing, reloading, and advancing of army units in battle. From then until the start of mechanized warfare in the early 20th century, this form of war was the norm.

By the turn of the 20th century, the industrial revolution had begun to affect the way in which war was conducted. Tanks, sophisticated artillery, and aircraft soon added to the mix and essentially put an end to the practice of two armies lining up against each other on an open field, all the while using their individual firearms in well-rehearsed patterns. Parade square drill turned into exercises designed to train and instill discipline in military recruits and to rehearse for ceremonial parades, rather than for actual battle. That is still the state of drill today.

What exactly, then, is drill? A statement by an American Marine paints a realistic picture (see Figure 5-3).

I was a Marine, and like other branches and militaries, the Marine Corps takes drill very seriously. For the majority of our three months there [basic training], me and my boot camp platoon spent virtually every free minute in drill, rehearsing a drill movement or command, and being reminded of the importance of drill.

I can think of literally dozens of reasons why it is important for any military unit, especially a professional one, to use drill to sharpen and mold civilian recruits into disciplined and well-trained troops. When we first arrived at Parris Island what would become Platoon 3078 of follow series, India Company, Third Battalion, could hardly even walk in coordination.

You would be surprised how difficult it is to get seventy or more young men to go in the same direction, to stop when they need to; it is almost a cliché, but many people when under pressure move *right* when you say *left* and vice versa!

At the end of three months of intense drill, sometimes on the hot black pavement of a parade deck in summer in the humid weather of a swampland island, over seventy men marched with a singularity, each of the hundred and forty some odd footsteps sounded like one, there was one voice, one mind, and one commander calling the cadence.

Under the instruction of our drill instructors, we each stepped on the same step, halted with a word, turned on a dime, acted without questioning or doubt or second-guessing. Our allegiance was to unit, Corps, god, and country, but there was also the immediate pride and love of the platoon that made us each respect one another like brothers—even though we all came from different cities and towns and started out as strangers. We didn't necessarily love each other; sometimes we downright hated each other. We could and did fight, used the foulest of language, and schemed behind each other's backs. The drill instructors weren't there to break up each fight, and it wasn't a miracle that held the platoon together, it was purely discipline that kept us in check. Like sled dogs all yoked to the same sled, we had a common goal and direction and were determined to get there together. Failure was not, nor was ever, an option.[14]

From my own experience, I can attest to the truth of this marine's comments. When my comrades and I first entered the military, it took weeks before we were confident and capable enough to perform what resembled a full parade without someone messing up. Achieving this successful goal required competing yet simultaneous thought processes; on the one hand a buying in to the necessity of rote physical movement while on the other an acute, continuous awareness of exactly where one was spatially in relation to one's comrades. And it was definitely not easy. In fact, it was at times painful. We were trained in the traditional British style of stationary drill, one in which most movements included some form of raising one's leg so that the thigh was parallel to the ground, then driving the leg down into its new position with considerable force. This produced a loud stomp of the hard-soled boot which, when done in unison, gave the impression of authority. When multiple such movements of a unit of some 500 or more men—and/or women—were made, the impression on any onlookers was quite intimidating. Unfortunately, it also produced injuries. Within about a month of beginning this rigorous training, I was laid up with a case of shin splints, serious lower leg pain caused by physical stress. The fact that part of our training also involved running on pavement in our hard-soled boots without any cushioning or arch support no doubt contributed to my and my comrades' injuries. Part of the military mindset, however—and it is not without its benefits as a

Figure 5-3: U.S. Marine Corps recruits marching for final drill evaluation at Parris Island, SC, USA (photograph by Lance Cpl. David Bessey, USMC).

life lesson—was that one should, as much as possible, drive through the pain for the sake of one's unit and future tenacity as a leader of men. As a result, I was back on the parade square in relatively short order.

It is thus here, on the parade square, under the strictest of conditions, where a ceremonial, public military parade is born.

"Left, left, left right left." This shouted or chanted guiding command is imprinted on the brain of every person who ever set foot on a parade square—the word "left" sounded on every second step. It firmly starts and keeps the soldier's brain in marching cadence (also called pace or tempo). Once perfected, it generates synchronous movement and the synchronous movement of large groups of humans has always held a fascination for observers. How could we forget the amazing synchronized displays of the opening and closing ceremonies of the 2008 Beijing—and other—Olympics? Why is color guard culture so popular around the world? What would we do without the "wave" at football games?

Recent studies have proven that such movement does indeed foster cooperation and that "synchronous action functionally directs the experience of compassion in response to the plight of those around us, interests us in their well-being, and motivates us to help on their behalf."[15] This holds true for both observers and participants. In other words, watching a precision military unit will influence us emotionally just as much as watching a winning dance team. Furthermore, observers will consider the group that exhibits synchronous drill as a more cohesive unit than one that is not synchronized.[16] Likewise, that very same movement will have both a cooperative and altruistic effect on the participants, the soldiers who are required to have these attitudes in a battle situation. Put simply, it is now proven that well-executed drill does accomplish its mission

A natural walking or marching cadence comes from somewhere deep inside the human brain. Most of the military forces in the world use a marching cadence of 120 steps per minute—with some variations to the lower end—for standard quick marches. This is about the same pace as normal walking. This is the pace that they would, for example, use in a ceremonial parade along city streets. Research has recently proven that this pace corresponds to an innate "highly tuned resonant frequency of human locomotion at 2 Hz."[17] At this pace, dynamic visual acuity or the ability to focus on a target is also optimum, which helps marchers maintain good alignment.[18] The frequency is irrespective of gender, age, height, weight, or body mass index, which means every human being has a tendency to walk close to this pace whether or not the pace is set by an external driver such as music or the "left-right" commands.

This resonant frequency is also thought to be the reason the Broughton Suspension Bridge near Salton, England, collapsed on April 12, 1831. Seventy-four soldiers were marching in step across the bridge when it began to vibrate and then quickly collapsed, throwing some of the soldiers into the river. Since then, troops are given the command to "Break Step" (march/walk out of step) when they cross a bridge.[19]

Martial Music

When music is brought onto the parade square, the range of brain activity and subsequent effects caused by simply basic marching tempo is enriched through complex instrumental rhythms (i.e., drums and other percussion), volume, melody, pitch, harmony, timbre, and dynamics. Of all musical genres, march or martial music is one of the most emotionally compelling (see color insert Figure 5-4). Who does not feel uplifted by a marching band, want to cheer and wave flags when a patriotic march is played by a brass band, or be moved to tears by a bagpipe band? This happens because the above musical elements all combine in just the right proportions in this type of music. As a result, we unconsciously become emotionally attached to it.

The field of study of the psychological effects of music on participants and passive listeners (i.e., in this context, military musicians and marchers, and parade spectators respectively) has grown immensely over the past few years. It is now widely known that music affects the neurochemical systems of the body, and martial music abounds with examples. Most of it is written in 2/4, 4/4, and 6/8 time, with heavy accents on the main beats, especially using bass drums and lower frequency instruments like trombones, tubas, and bassoons.

Such highly rhythmic music has a tempo that puts us into a state of wanting to connect with others. It also stimulates the decision to take action, a highly desirable outcome for a parade sponsor who wants spectators to buy their products or avow loyalty. This tempo corresponds to—guess what—approximately 120 bpm (beats per minute), the same optimum tempo for marching, even *without* music. Is it any wonder that most martial music is therefore written around this tempo?

It causes a phenomenon known as *sonic entrainment*. Entrainment is "an aspect of sound that is closely related to rhythms and the way rhythms affect us. It is a phenomenon of sound in which the powerful rhythmic vibrations of one object [e.g., a military band or simply marching soldiers] will cause the less powerful vibrations of another object [e.g., other marchers or audience members] to lock in step and oscillate at the first object's rate." Furthermore, within our own bodies, "our heart rate, respiration and brain waves all entrain to each other."[20]

The rhythmic marching pace of 2 Hz (120 bpm) falls within the range of brain waves known as delta waves (0 to 4 Hz), the lowest frequencies of all the brain waves, and the ones that we also find in our most relaxing state of deep sleep. They are responsible for helping to produce anti-aging hormones, tranquility, harmony, mind and body rejuvenation, the release of growth hormones, a stronger immune system, and most importantly in this context, a deeper empathy for others. As a result, if the regular boot plants of marching soldiers—especially augmented by music—can be heard by the soldiers and observers, then this entrainment should occur in both groups of people. The parade spectators should more easily enjoy the parade, and the soldiers should be in a positive, relaxed, and happy state. As an aside, other human physical actions also seem to naturally converge on this frequency such as hand clapping and heart rate at orgasm. Other types of music have similar effects. "Trance," a genre of electronic dance music played at a slightly higher tempo than military marching (i.e., above 125 bpm), is said to induce "euphoria, chills, and an uplifting rush."[21] To make a long story short, it is possible, although not yet proven conclusively through rigorous scientific research, that playing music at certain tempos may induce entrainment of an audience's brain waves.

But martial music is not all rhythmic; melodic content is equally important. Part of the secret to its effectiveness is its purposeful creation of musical tension and release through the use of major keys, chordal structure, and unique sections of music.[22] Although martial music has been doing this for centuries, it has not been until recently that researchers have found that this type of music corresponds to the body's need for reward and pleasure. Such reward and pleasure comes about when the brain senses a build-up of tension and an anticipation that the tension will be released. Once it is released, the body's neurochemical systems in turn release pleasure-causing dopamine and opioids.[23] As an example, think about the feeling you have when a rock group hangs on a chord for an extended period just before the end of a song. Your brain goes crazy waiting for the release back to the tonic chord.[24]

Ironically, part of the reason for the popularity of martial music and no doubt its ability to influence the thought processes of young men and women is—in my opinion—its *anti*-antagonistic nature. The buoyant, major key melodies of the strains (one section of the march) interspersed with the flirtatious innocence of the trio section (a different section of the march), all emphasized with an authoritative rhythm, tend to impart a piece with pleasant excitement and a feeling of camaraderie that only the military life can offer. The music belies the exciting adventure—and potentially agonizing death—that might await those same young men and women.

Missing from this theory is bagpipe music. The bagpipe is a unique instrument at the heart of the second main type of military band, pipes and drums. With drums performing the same rhythmic role as with a brass band, the pipes are the only instruments responsible for the melody. Therefore, the structure of bagpipe music is different. The pipes usually play in unison and because of their construction, they possess a rich timbre. The melody is played over top of a continuous *drone* which imparts a sense of longing.[25]

One final point about pipe band music is that it is traditionally played slightly slower than brass band music, at a tempo of around 90 bpm, and its songs form a unique sub-genre of martial music. This tempo also translates to 1.5 Hz, still within the delta brain wave spectrum, an attractive frequency for brainwave entrainment.[26] Again, from my own personal military experience when marching to the lilt of the pipes, I was so calm and relaxed that I felt as if I could march forever. It was quite mesmerizing.

Marching as a Political Statement

Military marching has been used to reinforce political agendas since ancient times. Large army components climaxed processions in Thebes, Egypt (the Opet Festival—Chapter Six), Alexandria (Ptolemy II's Grand Procession—Chapter Four), and Rome (Paulus's triumph—Chapter Eight). Emperors, kings, dictators and presidents have relied on marching armies to support their legitimacy. Put simply, they have trusted that these marching armies will be so loved—or feared—by spectators that these emotions will be transferred to them, the leaders.[27] Why does this work?

David Kertzer, in his excellent book on ritual and politics, answers this question well.[28] Essentially it begins with cognitive structures called *schemas.* Our brains tend to take everything that is absorbed through our senses and organize it into patterns of thought that are then used to form our belief systems. We interpret what we encounter in daily life in terms of these pre-established schemas that tell us what to expect. However, we tend to ignore information that conflicts with our schemas, unless it is emotionally interesting and presented in concrete, vivid detail. An example from the 1960s is appropriate here.

The USA has always had a strong appreciation for, and positive view of, their military, even during the early years of the unpopular Vietnam War. American soldiers marched proudly in victory parades following the two World Wars and the Korean War—although this one was not until 1991.[29] That schema began to change on March 16, 1968, in the small Vietnamese village of My Lai. On that day, 504 innocent Vietnamese civilian men, women, and children were raped, tortured, and killed by American servicemen under the command of Lieutenant William Calley. The military immediately tried to cover up the massacre and the truth did not come out until 1969. By then the damage was done. The American public's perception of fighting men and women had changed—as had their schemas—and those returning from Vietnam received scorn rather than praise. No parades were held in their honor.[30]

History also provides us with an extreme example of schemas being influenced by all the psychological aspects of marching and parades that have so far been introduced in this book. That example is the annual rallies that took place in Nuremberg, Germany after the Nazi Party and Adolf Hitler rose to power in 1933. The rallies lasted until 1938. Their primary purpose was to act as propaganda events for the Nazi Party.

That purpose, meant to influence the schema of the German people, can be seen in passages from Hitler's 1925 book, *Mein Kampf.* In it he says the following about his audience.

> All propaganda must be presented in a popular form and must fix its intellectual level so as not to be above the heads of the least intellectual of those to whom it is directed.... The art of propaganda consists precisely in being able to awaken the imagination of the public

through an appeal to their feelings, in finding the appropriate psychological form that will arrest the attention and appeal to the hearts of the national masses.

And about the methods to be employed:

> [Propaganda] must present only that aspect of the truth which is favorable to its own side.... The receptive powers of the masses are very restricted, and their understanding is feeble. On the other hand, they quickly forget. Such being the case, all effective propaganda must be confined to a few bare essentials and those must be expressed as far as possible in stereotyped formulas. These slogans should be persistently repeated until the very last individual has come to grasp the idea that has been put forward.[31]

These statements are the gist of how schemas operate and can be influenced to change. To accomplish this, Hitler and his team (primarily architect Albert Speer and propaganda chief Joseph Goebbels) pulled out all the stops to create events that were meticulously orchestrated. They brought together every imaginable element of ritual and theatricality to achieve their ends.

It began with the design and construction of the Nazi Party Rally Grounds covering 11 sq km of real estate to the southeast of Nuremberg.[32] Architecturally, the grounds reflected the conflicted Nazi personality—partly a worshipful homage to ancient Rome and Greece and partly the cheerlessness of modernistic grey concrete blocks. Several structures became regular venues for the rallies and had all the attributes of sacred spaces as described in Chapter Two. There were three main structures used for marching and displays.

The first was the Städtisches Stadion (municipal stadium), a relatively small stadium with a seating capacity of 50,000, used for Hitler Youth activities such as marching, athletics, games, and artistic displays.

The second was the Luitpoldarena, an open-air field with spectator stands and other commemorative structures. This arena had a seating capacity of 50,000 and space on the arena floor for 150,000 persons. The arena was used for massed parades of Nationalist Socialist organizations like the SA (Sturm Abeilung), and SS (Schutzstaffel).

The last main structure was the Zeppelinfeld (Zeppelin Field, after Count Ferdinand Graf von Zeppelin who landed one of his famous airships on the location in 1909). This field was immense, the size of 12 football fields, with space for more than 200,000 participants.[33] It was used extensively for marching displays (at the prescribed 120 bpm, of course), dance performances, athletic demonstrations, parades of tanks and military hardware and highly charged, emotional speeches by Hitler. It is famously remembered for the Cathedral of Light (*Lichtdom*) conceived by Albert Speer, which used 152 anti-aircraft searchlights, spaced at intervals of 12 m around the periphery of the arena. When turned on during a night-time rally event—at the most emotionally dramatic moment possible—they shot skyward 4000 to 5000 m to create a series of vertical bars surrounding the audience, interspersed with vivid red and black Nazi flags.[34] Speer described the effect. "The feeling was of a vast room, with the beams serving as mighty pillars of infinitely lit outer walls." The British Ambassador to Germany, Sir Nevile Henderson, described it as "both solemn and beautiful ... like being in a cathedral of ice." Art historian Kathleen James-Chakraborty went so far as to assess its effect in the following words.... "The single most dramatic moment of the Nazi Party rallies ... was not a military parade or a political speech but the Lichtdom, or Cathedral of Light."[35] See Figure 5-5.

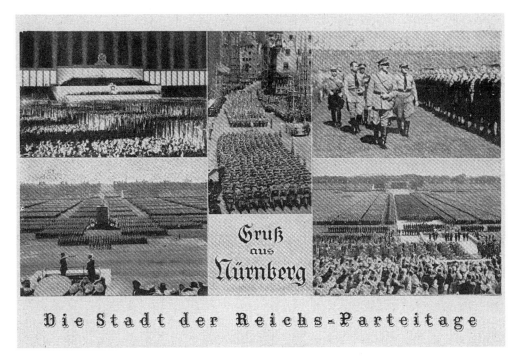

Figure 5-5: Vintage postcard that reads, "Greetings from Nuremberg, the city of the imperial party congresses." Scenes clockwise from top left: Cathedral of Light; troops marching in downtown Nuremberg; Hitler reviewing troops; and two scenes of massed troops in stadia, probably Luitpoldarena and/or Zeppelinfeld (Documentation Center Nazi Party Rally Grounds / Schlothauer).

With the marching at the rally events in the stadia, plus marching through Nuremberg's old streets with banners and flags waving from all the buildings, and with the nationalistic music of Wagner blaring everywhere, it would have been impossible not to get swept up in the emotion of the day. Cap it off with *Zeig heils* every few minutes during these parades and the schemas of all red-blooded Aryans could hardly resist being converted to Nazi thought.

A ground-breaking film, *Triumph des Willens* (*Triumph of the Will*), was produced by German actress/producer Leni Riefenstahl in 1934. It chronicled the entire rally of that year and was rife with marching scenes. It was thereafter used throughout Germany as a propaganda film to convert German citizens to the Nazi way (i.e., to help change their schemas). Riefenstahl's innovative techniques—which included moving cameras, aerial photography, the use of long-focus lenses to create a distorted perspective, and the revolutionary approach to the use of music and cinematography—have since earned *Triumph of the Will* recognition as one of the greatest propaganda films in history.[36]

A few years ago, I had a conversation with a surviving participant from the 1937 rally, Herr Reinhold Schwiddessen. Herr Schwiddessen, who was 17 at the time, participated as part of a unit representing laborers who carried special symbolic spades. His remarks bear witness to the excitement of the event and how much he was personally affected by it. Here is a condensed and edited version of his comments.

First of all, we had to march in front of our commanding officers and were selected for the rallies [in June 1937]. Maybe six or eight persons out of 80 or 85 people were chosen to take part in Nuremberg.

I felt as a special selected man who is very good at marching and in doing the "Spatengriff" (how the men hold the spades). But I really just felt ... a certain pride because of my marching.... It was an honour to be a participant of the rallies in Nuremberg.

Around four weeks before the rallies the participants were brought together for the first time ... in Kattenvenne.... The last six days before we went to Nuremberg, we stayed ... near Paderborn.

We arrived in Nuremberg on Sunday, 5th September 1937.

On Monday, 6th September, we practised on the Zeppelin Field Grounds, but only those who would march in front of the fuehrer on Wednesday.... This made us who were allowed to march even prouder.

On Tuesday, 7th September, all participants practised the marching one more time.

On Wednesday, 8th September, the actual rally took place.... We wore our uniform which was brown-green. On the back we carried our bag and a blanket. We also had a canteen/water bottle and of course our spades.... It was "fuehrer-weather." ... The sun was shining and it was neither too warm nor too cold.

Between 8 and 9 am we went from the camp Langwasser to the Zeppelin Field Grounds.... I can remember we had to go a long way straight.... From time to time we had short breaks and then we had to put our spades together. The whole time bands played music.

On the way, marks gave us orders.... As an example, red might have been the order "Attention! Start marching!" Other colours showed us where the fuehrer was or when we could finish marching.

Every group had special music and their own brass band. The band entered the grounds first, then the group followed. On the right side of Hitler the band turned right and formed up next to him. They were playing the whole time.... The music was called the "Petersburgermarsch." ... We marched past them and the band followed us out of the stadium.

It was an atmosphere in very high spirits. I especially remember the end. After we left Hitler behind us, we could have stopped marching, but on the left hand side of the stadium, a group of Austrians clapped their hands and cried. They were absolutely enthusiastic. So we continued marching until we had left the stadium.

Then we entered [re-entered] the Zeppelin Field Grounds from the back.... After all the groups ... had formed up on the field.... Hitler talked to us. Later on, planes flew above us, dive bombers and biplanes. We thought, "Great!"

In the afternoon we marched through Nuremberg. On the Zeppelin Field Grounds we marched in rows of 18, I think. In the town, we marched in rows of eight or ten. I remember the people standing at the street. They were waving and waving. Sometimes they even threw some chocolate. The march through town was an experience as well.

I was proud that everything went so well and that I was allowed to take part in the rallies. I am not sure if it is was the march in front of the fuehrer. I do not think so. I often thought about it. But I was proud of being selected as a man who is good at marching. It did not matter whether I would have marched in front of the fuehrer or the pope.... During this time in the 20th century, "marching" itself was different from today. "Marchmusic" was often played on the radio and belonged to our daily life. My father was a soldier under ... the emperor Wilhelm II. He loved marchmusic and my brother as well. At least in my family this music was often heard and liked. I enjoy this music until today. Therefore, to be selected as one who is good in marching was very, very special to me.... It was an important experience in my life.[37]

Herr Schwiddessen's experience would lead one to believe that his schema might not have been changed, that he was only impressed by the importance of nothing more than his participation. While I never intentionally asked him if he had become sympathetic to Hitler's cause, I got the distinct impression that he was very aware of the importance of the rallies in which he participated and was also proud of his country. His conversion journey perhaps took a different route but ended up at the same destination.

Marching and Rhythm as Pure Entertainment

Most countries that maintain military forces display them occasionally in public, typically on Independence or National Days, days commemorating war victories, and special days like coronations or state funerals. Some attach more importance to these displays such as China, North Korea, and Russia, whereas others, especially western democracies like the United States and Canada, tend to downplay excessive displays of force, preferring instead to "walk softly and carry a big stick."[38] The United States, especially, has downplayed military braggadocio in recent years due to the difficulty in gaining public support for wars in Vietnam and Iraq, as mentioned earlier. Instead, they, like Canada and the UK, have resorted to a softer, cuddlier form of persuasion to gain support.[39] This is the use of marching and drill as pure entertainment.

Some of the most impressive displays of drill as entertainment come from silent military drill teams that use real rifles as if they were simply lightweight batons, tossing them around in synchronized, timed routines. This takes a tremendous amount of skill and self-control, first because the movements have to be absolutely perfect and second because there is no audible beat for pacing and each soldier must use his internal clock to maintain order with his fellow performers. The pace is slower than regular marching, around 70 to 80 bpm, but this is no doubt to permit the intricate movements.

All branches of the U.S. military have such teams whose purpose is to make frequent appearances at private and public events and subtly market patriotism. Russia has several similar ceremonial teams as do a few other countries (India, Canada, Malta, Norway, Singapore). For impressive synchronous, mass marching on a public parade, though, one need look no farther than China or North Korea whose military units settle for nothing less than absolute perfection.

Another more rhythmic form of related entertainment is the drumline or batterie/battery. Drumlines are teams of percussionists often taken from a musical marching ensemble such as a marching band or drum and bugle corps. The battery usually consists of snare drums, bass drums, tenor drums, and cymbals. Like silent drill teams, drumlines require tremendous precision and rehearsal to perfect their act. They are used in both marching and stationary formats. Tempos usually vary between 120 and 160 bpm. Drumlines come in both military and civilian versions (see color insert Figure 5-6).

Marching bands and drum corps, which begat drumlines, have also held the attention of the public for many years, especially in large venues such as football fields. These are massed bands with varied instrumentation that perform intricate marching routines more the product of choreography than strictly military-type drill. This marching is more impressive when seen from above, especially with the addition of color guards, where their elaborate, rehearsed patterns can be clearly seen. Color guards are essentially dance teams that use flags and fake rifles as props. More are civilian community or school organizations, although there are some military versions. The tempo for these bands can be as high as 160 to 170 bpm for drum corps and 110 to 120 bpm for marching show bands. Whatever the pace, these bands are universally loved by audiences. Several quotations tell the tale of these organizations.

First, a motivational speech by staff:

> It started in November as an audition process. You went through all the steps, and you became a member of the Phantom Regiment. And that process, throughout all of the summer; all the camps, all the flights, all the rain all summer—it's all part of the process. And now you're here. You've practiced, and practiced, and practiced. You've performed a lot, too. And tonight will be the performance of your life—and it has to do with that process. And it'll be done, just like that. And, while it's a little unfortunate that you don't get to enjoy it.... You'll remember it forever.[40]

Emotional thoughts by members:

> To me, Bucs is teamwork. It's about working together to accomplish something indescribably powerful. It's a feeling that I can't clearly explain, but can sense and will always remember years beyond the field. It's learning how to communicate and collaborate; essential skills which I bring into my own classroom as a middle school teacher.[41]
>
> It has changed me, challenged me, it has given me wonderful friendships and a stronger bond in my family with me and my sister ... and strengthened my love of performing.[42]

Emotional thoughts by audience members:

> Unreal. Goosebumps all over the place.[43]
>
> Finally hearing the sounds that bring tears of pride, followed by that comes the most beautiful sight!! The flags ... just as they reach the top of my vision.... I'm in awe each and every time, it never gets old, nor does it ever have less pride or emotion.[44]

These quotations demonstrate how certain particular ingredients—uniforms, martial music, mind-blowing performance creativity, an emotion-inducing environment or sacred space—all combine to produce feelings of *communitas* and connection in the audience

One final type of marching entertainment that also incorporates all the necessary ingredients is the military tattoo (unrelated to the Tahitian origins of an ink tattoo). The tattoo is a peacetime variety show of everything military. Simple versions began appearing in the early 19th century but today's elaborate live productions did not get started until the latter half of the 20th century. Although there are others around the world, the king of them all is the Royal Edinburgh Military Tattoo held annually in Scotland (see color insert Figure 5-7).

It's no wonder. As a sacred space, the esplanade or parade ground of the castle is unmatched. Sitting in the grandstands here, with the imposing grey towers of the 12th-century castle in the background—on a rocky outcropping that commands a spectacular view of the city—one has no doubt about being in the presence of something unique and timeless. The space soon comes alive with intricately choreographed and emotionally moving displays of pipe bands, brass bands, drill teams, dancers, ethnic performers from abroad, and lighting. By the time a floodlit lone piper plays from the castle ramparts to end the show, there is not a dry eye anywhere. Very few would not love *this* parade.

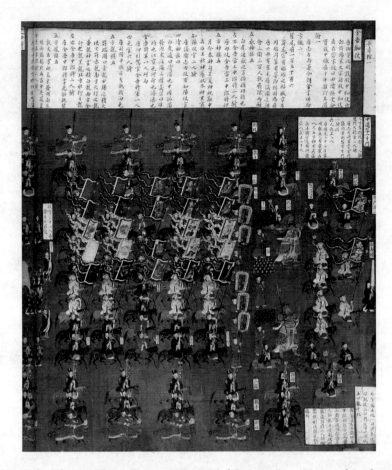

Figure 1-2: Part of a Chinese Song Dynasty Imperial Procession. Note colored attire and flags with emblems (Photo: akg-images / Pictures From History).

Figure 1-3: "The State Entry" by Roderick MacKenzie. Entrance procession of British officials and Indian princes at the Delhi Durbar of 1903 to hear Edward VII proclaimed as Emperor of India. Lord Curzon and the Duke of Connaught, as representatives of the British monarchy, head the procession (Photo: akg-images).

C2

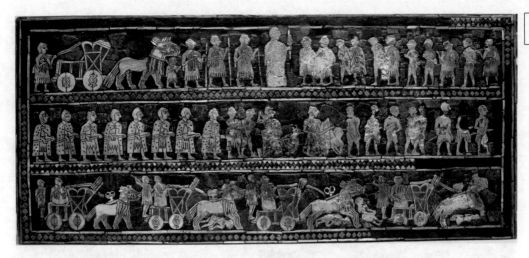

Figure 4-1: Standard of Ur (War Side) (photograph by the author).

Figure 4-4: Jagannath Rath Yatra floats preparing to be moved (Dinodia Photos / Alamy Stock Photo).

Opposite, top: Figure 2-1: Artist rendering of the ancient Ishtar Gate and Processional Way in Babylon (Madain Project, https://madainproject.com).

Opposite, middle: Figure 3-1: "The Field of the Cloth of Gold." Entry procession at the Field of the Cloth of Gold, 1520 CE. Note the elaborate dress of the attendees in the procession and around the field (Photo: akg-images / WHA / World History Archive).

Opposite, bottom: Figure 3-5: Women's uniforms used in recruiting posters for World War II. Left: Royal Canadian Air Force (courtesy Canadian War Poster Collection, Rare Books and Special Collections, McGill University Library). Right: Women's Army Auxiliary Corps, United States Army (courtesy Kittleson World War II Collection, Hennepin County Library).

Figure 4-7: Romance of the Knights of Glory Entry Procession, *Le "Roman des chevaliers de al gloire,"* oil, 150 × 240 cm, 1612 (CC0 Paris Musées / Musée Carnavalet—Histoire de Paris).

Figure 5-4: Marching Band at New Year's Day Rose Parade, Pasadena, California, USA (©Visions of America LLC/123RF.COM).

Figure 5-6: The University of Pittsburgh Varsity Marching Band Drumline ("The Crew") performs their pregame routine prior to the Pitt Panthers football game against the Virginia Cavaliers in Pittsburgh, PA, USA (Jeffrey Gamza).

Figure 5-7: Royal Edinburgh Tattoo (Andrew Wightman / shutterstock.com).

Figure 6-2: The Opet Festival procession in ancient Thebes, Egypt, is depicted as it exits Karnak Temple heading to the Nile River to transport the gods Amun-Re, Mut, and Khonsu to the Luxor Temple (Xiuyuan Zhang, http://xiuyuan.deviantart.com/gallery/).

Figure 6-4: King David bringing the Ark of the Covenant to Jerusalem (© sedmak, 123RF.com).

Figure 6-5: A group of tuskers parades past the Temple of the Sacred Tooth Relic in Kandy, Sri Lanka, during the Esala Perahera (Photo 73421856 © Thomas Wyness | Dreamstime.com).

Figure 6-6: Feast of Fools parade. A false pope plus several fools and costumed individuals can be seen in the crowd. (Heritage Image Partnership Ltd / Alamy Stock Photo).

Figure 7-2: Young Maasai warriors (morani) on parade as part of their Eunoto ceremony, or coming of age (John Warburton-Lee Photography / Alamy Stock Photo).

Figure 7-4: The marriage procession of Napoleon I and Marie-Louise crossing the Jardin des Tuileries on April 2, 1810, by Étienne-Barthélèmy Garnier (Heritage Images / Fine Art Images / akg-images).

Opposite, top: Figure 6-7: Inca King being carried by palanquin into the Inti Raymi celebrations at the fortress of Sacsayhuamán, near Cusco, Peru (©torukojin, www.istockphoto.com).

Opposite, bottom: Figure 7-1: Ottoman circumcision procession of 1582 showing the coffee-sellers guild. Note the sultan looking on from his palace in the upper left of the image (Photo: akg-images).

Figure 7-6: Entry of Emperor Charles V and Pope Clement VII as part of the coronation ceremonies in Bologna, February 24, 1530 (Photo: akg-images / Erich Lessing).

Figure 8-3: Part of the Triumph of General Lucius Aemilius Paulus (Carle Vernet, oil on canvas, 129.9 × 438.2 cm, 1789 (Gift of Darius O. Mills, 1906, Metropolitan Museum of Art).

Opposite, top: Figure 9-1: Peasants meeting King Richard II in London, 1381, during the Peasant's Revolt (GL Archive / Alamy Stock Photo).

Opposite, bottom: Figure 9-3: More than 7000 students from local colleges and universities march to Tiananmen Square, Beijing, May 4, 1989, to demonstrate for government reform (AP Photo/Mikami).

Figure 10-1: Participants in the Greater Dionysia. This vase depicts a large phallus being carried and ridden (by permission of the National Archaeological Museum of Florence [Regional Directorate of Museums of Tuscany]).

Figure 10-3: Feast of Fools parade. A false pope plus several fools and costumed individuals can be seen in the crowd. (Heritage Image Partnership Ltd / Alamy Stock Photo)

Figure 10-4: Throwing beads at Mardi Gras in New Orleans (GTS Productions / Shutterstock.com).

Figure 10-5: Bikini and Beads revelers at Pretty Mas' during Carnival in Port of Spain, Trinidad (John de la Bastide / Shutterstock.com).

C14

Figure 11-3: The funeral procession of Lord Nelson, seen from Bankside on the River Thames. Colored etching by John Thomas Smith, 1806 (Wellcome Collection).

Figure 11-4: The Return to Amsterdam of the Second Expedition to the East Indies, 1599 (Photo: akg-images).

Figure 12-1: St. Patrick's Day Parade along Fifth Avenue in New York City (Steve Edreff / Shutterstock.com).

Figure 12-3: A float in the annual Zundert Flower Parade, Netherlands (Photo 188097272 © Elena Podolnaya | Dreamstime.com).

Figure 12-4: Rio Carnival parade float in the Sambadrome, Rio de Janeiro, Brazil (lembi / Shutterstock.com).

Part II

Realizing the Spectacle

Six

It Started with Gods

How could we function as humans without our daily habits and rituals? We rise and rest at the same times every day. We eat the same meals. We drive to work on the same route. We watch the same TV programs at the same time. We are invariant in both our thinking and our actions. This chapter is about the behavior of humans toward the ritual characteristic of invariance as it relates to parades. If a parade is a regular occurrence (e.g., weekly, monthly, annually), we would have a lot of trouble accepting its credibility if it were to change dates, times, and even its structure each time it is held. The mere fact that there is a built-in stability to its reliable repetition is comforting to us. This is another reason for our infatuation with parades.

But what this is really about is not so much our attraction to consistency as our fear of change. We fear change because we fear uncertainty and we fear uncertainty because it reminds us of life's impermanence.[1]

There was a lot of uncertainty in prehistoric times. In the oldest hunter-gatherer societies, there was belief in a spirit world separate from the daily world, and a belief that there were forces at work beyond human understanding. It was also believed that a bridge between the two worlds could be established by a shaman, or religious leader. These beliefs were the beginning of a fascinating trajectory that religion has taken over the centuries, because it has been the invariance of religion that has allowed humans to live with the uncertainty of life. This invariance has frequently been manifested in parades, more specifically processions and pilgrimages. Even today, with many western countries moving towards secular humanism, religion and its invariant processions and rituals still act as a stabilizing force for 84 percent of the world's population—and this figure is growing.[2] Do people love their religious processions? You bet they do! Life's uncertainty has not disappeared, no matter how many times we try to convince ourselves that we rule our own destinies.

Although many secular parades are invariant, this chapter concentrates on a historical review of religious processions because they are the ones that exhibit invariance the best; they have been around the longest. I am hoping that my cherry-picked choices are acceptable for the reader to discover the importance and pageantry of these ancient events, because the sheer surfeit of them is impossible to cover completely.

Religious Processions in Prehistory

Evidence of prehistoric processions is frequently found in rock art. There are hundreds of sites all over the world, but art resembling a religious procession, like a row of stick figures, could be interpreted as anything from a dance to a procession to a hunting or war party. Furthermore, dating is imprecise unless a piece of identifiable art falls off and becomes part of surrounding datable material (i.e., that is carbon-based). If there is a shaman-like figure present in the art, then there is more likelihood it was part of a religious ritual.

Around 10 to 12,000 years ago humans began to construct independent, freestanding structures of stone. Indications are that most were religious centers. Current research indicates that they were associated with a transitional phase between humans being nomadic hunter-gatherers and being fully committed, city-dwelling agriculturists.

The oldest of these yet discovered is Göbekli Tepe in southeast Turkey, which dates from about 10,000 BCE. Thought to be a spiritual center, it contains circular structures made of stone within which are larger anthropomorphic monoliths, shaped much like the stones of Stonehenge but not as high.[3] Some have obvious arms carved on the sides. Some of the circular structures appear to have had entranceways that might have been used as processional routes although that is my own interpretation as there is no other evidence unearthed to prove they were. Likewise, other younger stone circles thought to be ancient religious centers, in particular the cromlech in Almendres, Portugal, which dates from about 6000 BCE, is laid out in such a way that processions could have easily moved amongst the stones.[4] Again, there is no evidence yet discovered to prove this but the implication is there.

What makes this implication more credible is the fairly recent discovery that Stonehenge, the 5000-year-old stone structure in southwest England, had a long cursus or pathway nearby as well as an avenue of approach to the monument itself, both indications that processions could have been a part of ceremonies at what was almost certainly a major religious center.[5] Unfortunately, because there is no supporting evidence in the form of writing or carvings of processions at any of these monolithic sites, the concept of processions being associated with them remains purely speculative.

Religious Processions in the Early Civilization Period (3500–1000 BCE)

By the dawn of writing, about 5000 years ago, religious processions were well established. Tangible objects were emerging with what appeared to be scenes of religious processions, although full interpretations are still not available for some of these.

One artifact, dating from 3200 to 3000 BCE, resides in the Iraq Museum in Baghdad. Known as the Uruk or Warka vase, it is a carved alabaster stone vessel found in the temple complex of the Sumerian goddess Inanna in the ruins of the ancient city of Uruk in southern Iraq. The vase is decorated in relief in four registers, showing rows of plants, sheep, nude males carrying baskets or jars, and a cultic scene, in which the ruler of the city of Uruk delivers provisions to the temple of the goddess Inanna (Figure 6-1). It appears to represent a religious procession and a "ritual enactment that may be associated with the idea of a marriage between a god or a goddess and a mortal."[6]

Figure 6-1: Warka Vase (Osama Shukir Muhammed Amin FRCP [Glasg], CC BY-SA 4.0, https://creativecommons.org/licenses/by-sa/4.0/deed.en).

Another artifact, a carved steatite seal, comes from the early civilization centered in the Indus valley, the Harappans, dating to 2200–2000 BCE. It depicts some sort of revered person or horned deity standing amid a sacred tree, with a second horned image kneeling in front of the tree, presenting an offering of a human head on a short stool.[7] The lower portion of the seal depicts a possible procession of humans wearing headdresses, the purpose of which is unknown.

The fact that these two artifacts are among the oldest of any containing actual language or interpretable images is noteworthy. That they contain some semblance of a religious procession means this form of human activity was important to these civilizations. The activities represented were the ancient equivalent of headline news.

As we move forward in time, beginning around the middle of this period, civilizations are more clearly using religious processions as expressions of their societal values and belief systems. What is being depicted becomes more obvious and interpretation less of a chore. More than anything, it is from this time that representations of processions start to appear on the actual monumental architecture of ancient civilizations.

One of these was the enigmatic Minoans. The Minoans inhabited Crete and other Aegean islands between about 2600 and 1000 BCE, with the civilization reaching its zenith between 1700 and 1350 BCE.[8] Most of the details of their society have yet to be interpreted from numerous records written in an as yet indecipherable language.

The name of the civilization refers to the mythical King Minos from the city of Knossos on Crete. His palace at Knossos covered 22,000 sq. m and had more than 1500 rooms. From this the Greek imagination conjured up the legend of the labyrinth. Its function was to contain the Minotaur, a monster with the head of a bull and the body of a man. In the legend, the hero Theseus eventually killed the Minotaur. It's no surprise then, that the Minoans did, in fact, worship bulls, and much of their art depicts this.

While there are several artifacts from Knossos showing processions, the most interesting depictions are within King Minos's palace itself.[9] The exquisite frescoes painted on its walls portray processions of girls and boys in colorful attire against vivid backgrounds that resemble modern graphic art in style. The purpose of the processions is unknown but likely related either to worship of their main deity, a Mother Goddess, or an accompanying god of fertility, the famous bull. The importance of processions in their culture is further reinforced by a Corridor of the Processions, identified as a main path into the palace.

Eventually, the Minoan civilization suffered from two fatal blows. The first occurred around 1450 BCE when the volcano on the island of Santorini erupted and destroyed all the main centers on Crete. The palace at Knossos survived; however, within 100 years, the Myceneans from the Greek mainland overran it and the rest of the island of Crete.[10]

Unfortunately, from the middle of the second millennium BCE until 1799 CE, attempts by scholars to understand more than the most basic meanings and details of ancient processions in any country were universally thwarted by the lack of any translation guides. In that year, Pierre-François Bouchard, an officer in Napoleon's army in Egypt, discovered the Rosetta Stone. It contained writing in three languages—Egyptian hieroglyphic script, Egyptian Demotic script, and ancient Greek. It proved to be the key to deciphering Egyptian hieroglyphs, once the stone was fully translated by Jean-François Champollion in 1822. Thanks to the work of the French, it finally became possible to translate the hieroglyphs on Egyptian temples and their accompanying carvings of processions. A similar breakthrough, called the Behistun Inscription, was discovered in 1764 CE and has since been used to decipher ancient Sumerian cuneiform script (i.e., writing from early Mesopotamia), and thus provide an interpretation of their parades, but not to the same extent as for Egypt.[11]

For anyone who has visited the temples of ancient Egypt, it quickly becomes obvious how prolific were their religious observations and processions. Most temples are completely covered with combinations of hieroglyphs and bas/haut relief carvings of the events. Thus, once the French had the key to deciphering them, it became easy to understand what had been going on. One of the most famous examples of a well-documented ancient Egyptian event of this period was the Opet Festival in Thebes (present day Luxor), located in Upper Egypt, the primary component of which was a magnificent procession. As with the Grand Procession of Ptolemy Philadelphus, this one influenced western religion and parades in general for centuries afterward.

The festival began with offerings made by the Pharaoh to the god Amun-Re (by then the most important god in Egyptian religion) in the god's temple in Thebes, today's Karnak Temple.[12] These offerings supposedly rejuvenated the Pharaoh's divine power, although the exact nature of the rituals is unknown, and this rejuvenation may also have taken place in the Luxor Temple. From the Karnak Temple complex, the Pharaoh and his queen led a procession of the god in his statue form plus the other gods of Thebes, Mut the Mother Goddess and Khonsu, their offspring (see color insert). All the statues were borne aloft on small barques carried on palanquins on the shoulders of temple priests who made their way to the temple dock and small harbor just off the Nile.[13] The statues were loaded onto larger, highly decorated river barges which were hauled by laborers or specially chosen people out of the waterway to the Nile where they were towed upriver to the Luxor Temple. A boisterous land procession moving south along the eastern bank of the Nile accompanied the water procession. Nubile, bare-breasted female dancers and contortionists took up a position in the lead. Sistra-playing temple musicians were joined by scores of singers, tambourine and lute players, trumpeters, flautists, and drummers behind them. Making up most of the formal contingent was the army garrison from Thebes, hundreds or perhaps thousands of marching soldiers in full battle dress armed with lion-skin shields, lances, and killing axes. A squadron of richly caparisoned chariots followed them, plumed horses prancing in time to the shouts and music of the joyous crowd.[14]

Once at the Luxor Temple, the statues were offloaded and a short procession took them into the temple where the second part of the ceremony took place, the symbolic divine marriage of Amun-Re to Mut, which was in essence a fertility rite related to the rising waters of the Nile that re-fertilized the valley every year in the spring.

About three weeks later the entire process was reversed and the gods' statues returned to the Karnak Temple, this time via a processional land route lined with sphinxes.[15] Throughout the long history of the festival the routes changed occasionally, depending no doubt on the Nile floodwaters and/or the whims of the powerful temple priests and Pharaoh, but the basics remained.

The Opet Festival and procession were held annually in the springtime when the Nile flooded and provided water for the valley's extensive crops. It was the Pharaoh's principal responsibility, acting as the earthly manifestation of several gods, including Amun-Re, to maintain *ma'at*, or harmonious earthly order, and especially to ensure the gift of the Nile's life-giving water. He did this by symbolically remarrying each year via the rituals of the festival.

The Opet had important legacies for religion and for parades in general. The first legacy was related to the god Amun-Re and the beginnings of western religious thought. A papyrus written during the reign of Ramesses II attests to Amun being "the image of every god" and "too great to investigate, too powerful to know." It goes on, "All the gods are three: Amun, the sun, and Ptah." As one scholar notes, "Although the text speaks of three gods, the three are merely aspects of a single god. Here Egyptian theology has reached a kind of monotheism ... one more akin to that of the Christian trinity."[16] By the time of Ramesses II, Amun had combined with the sun-god Re to become Amun-Re, a clear indication of the beginning of a unified concept. It's also worth noting that this was around the same period when Moses led the Israelites out of Egypt, so the Opet's rituals would have been fresh in all their minds. It would be surprising if they did not affect the establishment of later Jewish and Christian rituals.

A second legacy concerns the ritual characteristic of performance. There was a plethora of instruments used in the Opet procession, including sistra (metal rattles usually made of bronze), lyres, flutes, castanets, tambourines, ivory clappers, barrel drums, and trumpets. There was also singing and dance. All the music and dance scenes, taken together, could be interpreted as an early documentation of music and dance used to bring greater understanding of the festival's arcane rituals to spectators, in this case the illiterate general populace who awaited the appearance of their gods and pharaoh outside the temple enclosures. This would make it one of the clearest early examples of how such performance was used to accompany religious observances.

Contemporaneous festivals in Mesopotamia (the Akitu Festival) and in Hatti (the Ah.Tah.Sum Festival) had similar purposes and included processions.[17]

The Akitu Festival became one of the major annual springtime events in Babylon and involved the ritual enactment of the abdication and re-investiture of the king as a comparison to spring's revival of vegetation and commencement of the annual rains. As in Egypt, a large procession escorted the gods between the main temple and the Akitu festival house where more rituals—most importantly the sacred nuptials of the king and queen representing the gods—were performed to ensure spring's creation. Exact sequences and details still await discovery.

The Ah.Tah.Sum was a Hittite springtime festival also like the Opet, intended to regenerate the powers of nature and reconfirm the gods' endorsement of the king's authority. The major procession of this festival took place in several cities, the main ones being the capital Hattusa, and Nerik (both in modern Turkey). As with the Opet, the procession included the king and queen, statues of the gods held aloft, musicians (drums, castanets, cymbals, tambourines), singers, acrobats, jugglers, jesters, and dancers. The cities' processional ways were, of course, lined with spectators waiting expectantly to view their gods and the king and queen.[18]

These three festivals were indicative of how and why festivals began in the first place. Their purpose was to mirror, by way of human celebration, what was occurring in nature, thereby hoping to ensure that nature (their gods) would respond with bountiful crops. They were clearly religious and helped to regulate and time the agricultural cycles of their respective societies.

Religious Processions in the Classical Period (1000 BCE–500 CE)

Around the mid- to late 12th century BCE, something strange happened. Virtually all written and carved recordings of contemporaneous civilizations ceased. They did not re-appear until 300 years later. This included any records of parades or processions. Historians have referred to the period as the Late Bronze Age Collapse. To date, no single cause for this calamity throughout the civilized world of the time has been found, although there are theories that range from a climate catastrophe to marauding/migrating peoples from Asia and the Mediterranean.[19]

After the ninth century BCE, early civilizations generally expanded into empires and new civilizations emerged.

Greek civilization flourished and with it came depictions of processions. One was the annual mid-summer Panathenaic Procession (see Chapter Four) that took place in Athens and was carved in glorious detail on the lintel surrounding the

Figure 6-3: Two sections of the Parthenon Marbles taken from the frieze on the Parthenon. These two depict on the left, several people readying the peplos, and on the right, mounted soldiers, all in the Panathenaic Procession in Athens (photograph by the author).

famous Parthenon atop the Acropolis (part of which were the famous Parthenon Marbles—see Figure 6-3).[20] The procession was held to honor Athena (goddess of war and the protectress of Athens) and was Athens' most important festival. It was one of the grandest regular processions in the entire Greek world. It included priestesses of Athena and Athenian women carrying gifts, sacrificial animals (cows and sheep), visiting dignitaries, musicians playing the *aulos* (flute-like instrument) and the *kithara* (seven-stringed lyre), a colossal peplos (for Athena's statue in the Parthenon) hung on the mast of a ship on wheels, four-horse chariots with a charioteer and fully armed man in each, craftswomen (weavers of the peplos), infantry and cavalry, and victors in the games associated with the main festival, the Panathenaia.[21]

The procession made its way up the Panathenaic Way from the Agora (main town square) towards the Acropolis, making sacrifices along the way. It ended up at the great altar of Athena in front of the Erechtheum (temple dedicated to Athena and Poseidon) where there was an animal sacrifice at Athena's altar, and representatives from each *deme* (subdivision of Athens), chosen by lot, enjoyed a meat banquet along with bread and cakes.[22] Like so many other celebrations and processions of this historical period, it tied together political success and power—in this case of Athens—with a god/goddess, a concept to which the western world of today could never return.

There were two more noteworthy religious processions from Greece, among many. One was the final event of the ancient Olympic Games, which saw spectators, judges, and victors make their way in a religious procession to the Temple of Olympian Zeus, where the victors were crowned, followed by the sacrifice of animals, feasting, and celebrations.[23] This religious event and procession was also one of the most enduring of the ancient world, lasting from 776 BCE to 67 CE, almost 1200 years. As we all know, the games were resurrected in 1896 CE as a secular event, and continue to this day, complete with pseudo-religious opening and closing ceremonies and accompanying processions.

The second was the annual Dionysian Procession through Athens to the theater on the south slope of the Acropolis. It was a highlight of the seasonal festival, the Great Dionysia. According to legend, the festival was established after Eleutherae, a town on the border between Attica and Boeotia (not far from Athens), had chosen to become part of Attica. The Eleuthereans brought a statue of Dionysus, their fertility god, to Athens, which was initially rejected by the Athenians. Dionysus then punished the Athenians with a plague affecting the male genitalia that caused them to remain erect, which was cured when the Athenians accepted the cult of Dionysus. This was recalled each year by a procession of citizens carrying *phalloi* (erect penises).[24] I will be discussing the Dionysian Procession in more detail in Chapter Ten.

The next great classical empire, Rome, produced the famous Roman Triumph, which we will cover in Chapter Eight. Besides being a victory parade, it was also a religious procession dedicated to the god Jupiter. Its impact on Christian processions cannot be overstated.

The apostle Paul wrote his letters to the people of Corinth around 56–57 CE, just near the beginning of the Empire in Rome. He was well aware of the triumph. In 2 Corinthians 2:14 he famously referred to "God, who made us his captives and leads us along in Christ's triumphal procession." He further compared the Christian way of life to the smell of temple incense at a triumphal procession wherein "to those who are perishing [i.e., sinners] it is a fearful smell of death and doom, but to those who are being saved [i.e., followers of the Christian way] it is a life-giving perfume." Of course, the inevitable comparison of Christ as a triumphator has been made ever since that period, with Christ's passion along the Via Dolorosa and even with his triumphal entry into Jerusalem, represented by the church's entry procession on Palm Sunday.[25]

These comparisons were not lost on the early popes in Rome who might have made the obvious connections by pure observation alone. Whatever happened in the years between Constantine, the first Christian emperor in the fourth century CE, and the fall of the Empire, it appears that the papacy adapted many of the rituals and symbols of the triumph. For example, the title *Pontifex Maximus* originally referred to the chief priest of Roman religion and was conferred on a person other than a ruler. From Augustus onwards the title was part of those given only to the emperor. At some indeterminate date after 376 CE, the title went to the Christian pope, thus relating him to the same person who would be considered a conqueror. Furthermore, the vestments worn by priests and higher-ranking church officials today are all descended from the formal regalia worn by the Roman triumphator. Part of Papal coronations mirrored triumphal processions.[26] Even today, the eminently practical and secure "popemobile" could be compared to an absurd offshoot of the triumphal chariot, and a priest's entry procession into a church to a mini-triumph.[27]

Rome also had numerous lesser religious processions. The second most famous was known as the *pompa circensis*, or circus parade, that led off regular games held in the Circus Maximus, the chariot racing arena in the heart of the city. It was said that at least 150,000—perhaps even up to a quarter million—spectators could be accommodated in the Circus, making it the largest arena anywhere—ever.[28] Details of the pompa come to us from the ancient historian Dionysius of Halicarnassus in a lengthy description, a shortened version of which is below.

> Before beginning the games, the principal magistrates conducted a procession in honour of the gods from the Capitol through the Forum to the Circus Maximus. Those who led the procession were, first, the Romans' sons who ... rode on horseback if their fathers were entitled by their fortunes to be knights, while the others, who were destined to serve in

the infantry, went on foot.... These were followed by charioteers, some of whom drove four horses abreast, some two, and others rode unyoked horses. After them came the contestants in both the light and the heavy games, their whole bodies naked except their loins.

The contestants were followed by numerous bands of dancers.... These were accompanied by flute-players ... and by lyre-players.... The dancers were dressed in scarlet tunics girded with bronze cinctures, wore swords suspended at their sides, and carried spears of shorter than average length; the men also had bronze helmets adorned with conspicuous crests and plumes.... After the armed dancers others marched in procession impersonating satyrs and portraying the Greek dance called *sicinnis*. Those who represented Sileni were dressed in shaggy tunics ... and in mantles of flowers of every sort; and those who represented satyrs wore girdles and goatskins, and on their heads manes that stood upright, with other things of like nature. These mocked and mimicked the serious movements of the others, turning them into laughter-provoking performances.... After these bands of dancers came a throng of lyre-players and many flute-players, and after them the persons who carried the censers in which perfumes and frankincense were burned along the whole route of the procession, also the men who bore the show-vessels made of silver and gold, both those that were sacred owing to the gods and those that belonged to the state. Last of all in the procession came the images of the gods, borne on men's shoulders.... After the procession was ended the consuls and the priests whose function it was presently sacrificed oxen.[29]

The Romans really loved their games. The pompa was a regular fixture at them from the fourth century BCE to the sixth century CE, around 1000 years.[30]

In this most intriguing historical period there also arose several of the other major world religions, including Judaism, Taoism, and Buddhism.[31] They all had processions of one sort or another.

The exact origins of Judaism are complicated and imprecise. Suffice it to say that by the time of King David in the 10th century BCE, it was a well-established, monotheistic religion. The book of 2 Samuel in the Old Testament bible tells the story of King David—who reigned about this time—bringing the Ark of the Covenant to Jerusalem for the first time.[32] In abbreviated form, 2 Samuel 6 describes what must have been the procession that accomplished this (see color insert Figure 6-4).

Then David mobilized thirty thousand special troops. He led them to Baalah of Judah.... They placed the Ark of God on a new cart and brought it from the hillside home of Abinadab.... David and all the people of Israel were celebrating before the Lord with all their might, singing songs and playing all kinds of musical instruments—lyres, harps, tambourines, castanets, and cymbals.

Some biblical stories are understated and I think this is one of them. To begin with, 30,000 troops accompanying the Ark is no small number. Add to that probably thousands of singers and musicians—quite possibly participants and not just spectators—and this would have been a remarkable procession indeed. Upon their arrival in Jerusalem there was also public dancing and trumpet fanfares. Remember that this was the same Ark that led the Israelites as they wandered the wilderness in search of the Promised Land, also in a processional arrangement.[33] The enthusiasm of the crowd was very real and no doubt great emotion accompanied the Ark's settlement in its rightful home.

A semblance of this same procession is still a part of Judaism today and is called the Inauguration of a Torah scroll. It is "a ceremony in which one or more Torah scrolls are installed in a synagogue, or in the sanctuary or study hall of a yeshiva, rabbinical college, university campus, nursing home, military base, or other institution, for use during prayer services. The inauguration ceremony is held for new and restored scrolls alike, as well as for the transfer of Torah scrolls from one sanctuary to another. If the Torah scroll is a new one, the ceremony begins with the writing of the last letters of the scroll in the home of the donor. All scrolls are then carried in an outdoor procession to the scroll's new home, characterized by singing, dancing, and musical accompaniment. Inside the sanctuary, there is more singing and dancing, a short prayer service, placement of the scroll in the Torah ark, and a festive meal."[34] That would make this religious procession around 3000 years old, a true example of invariance.

Taoism (also known as Daoism) traces its roots to the sixth century BCE in China. It is both a philosophy and a religion. It "emphasizes doing what is natural and 'going with the flow' in accordance with the Tao (or Dao), a cosmic force which flows through all things and binds and releases them."[35] Within Taoist beliefs is the principle of yin and yang, the notion that all things exist as inseparable and contradictory opposites, for example, female-male, dark-light, and old-young. The Festival of the Nine Emperor Gods, celebrated by the Chinese in Malaysia, has two purification ritual processions that "lead the community from the state of yin to the state of yang, or, as the temple authorities put it, to 'birth beyond death.'"[36] The first one is the bridge-crossing cleansing procession on a hanging bridge some 20 m in the air.

> Devotees proceed to the bridgehead where a Taoist priest stamps a red seal on their foreheads to signify that they are crossing with the Divine Nine's blessings. The devotees cross the bridge in single file.... People believe that crossing the bridge without incident is a clear sign that their good fortune and their standing with the star deities are assured. As soon as the devotees have crossed the bridge the Taoist follows suit. Sword-wielding spirit mediums then "chop" their way over the bridge as if chasing after evil spirits attempting to cross in order to gain power. The spirit medium of the Emperor Gods is seen slashing his abdomen and bare back with his magic sword and flicking his demon-whip repeatedly across the bridge.[37]

The second purification ritual is the fire-walking procession.

> The procession is led by the entranced spirit mediums to the beat of the drum and gong. They are followed by the bearers of half a dozen sedan chairs laden with idols, charm papers, jewellery and other precious objects, packets of dried tea leaves, and bundles of garments. Following them are some fifty disciples in white shirts and pants and with yellow headbands. All participants are barefoot, and each carries a rolled-up yellow pennant of the Nine Emperor Gods to protect him from harm. They must be ritually clean, having abstained from sex and observed a vegetarian diet for the past nine days. They are not allowed to wear leather belts and metal objects, including rings and belt buckles, as these objects are highly repugnant to the spirits.[38]

In other Taoist processions in SE Asia, purification for this festival is taken to the extreme. "Images from the fifth day of the event in Phuket [Thailand] show followers piercing their cheeks with butchers' knives and firearms, while the Malaysian procession depicts devotees impaling their faces with four-metre spears."[39]

Buddhism has a fascinating procession that is part of the Festival of the Tooth, also known as the Kandy Esala Perahera (procession), where it is held in Sri Lanka. Legend has it that when Buddha was cremated in the fifth century BCE, one of his disciples took a tooth from the pyre, which eventually made its way to Sri Lanka. The purpose of the procession is associated with rainfall in that "the order of the procession is still defined by the belief that the Sacred Tooth Relic has the magical power to produce rain."[40] The actual tooth is held within its own temple, considered to be the epicenter of Buddhism in Sri Lanka. On the first day of the festival the main procession is held. A replica of the tooth relic is kept in a casket attached to the *Maligawa* or temple elephant. The blowing of a conch shell marks the start of the procession. Whip-crackers and fireball acrobats clear the path, followed by Buddhist flag bearers. Then, riding on the first elephant, is the official called *Peramuna Rala* (Front Official). Drummers and dancers who enthrall the crowd follow him, and are themselves followed by elephants and other groups of musicians, dancers and flag bearers. A group of singers dressed in white heralds the arrival of the Maligawa Tusker carrying the Sacred Tooth Relic.[41] All the elephants are highly decorated (see color insert Figure 6-5). Once again, an invariant procession, more than 2000 years old, remains important to believers.

Religious Processions in the Postclassical Period (500–1450 CE)

This period saw the rise of Christianity throughout the western world. Its story was captivating, and its hierarchical organization highly logical. The Catholic mass was the re-telling of a story of hope, along with its supernatural hero, a good vs. evil theme, and extensive symbology. "The Church was regarded as a purely superhuman institution. Men lived in an atmosphere of wonder; miracles were matters of everyday experience. Every epidemic gave rise to miracles. Every plague, every famine provoked extraordinary manifestations."[42] For several hundred years until the Late Middle Ages, most public parades and processions were Christian-themed.

Miraculous cures were often attributed to what is known as relics. These were any tangible evidence—such as body parts—that a holy person (e.g., a saint or martyr) or even Christ himself, lived (as with Buddha's tooth, above). Around these was constructed a culture of worship that bordered on fanaticism and that was, in part, formalized by processions that publicly displayed the relics. Even today, every Catholic Church in the world entombs a relic within the altar.

Unquestionably the most famous relics were the nails and cross used to crucify Christ. According to historians of the day, Empress Helena, mother of Emperor Constantine, traveled to the Holy Land in 326–328 CE, and there discovered the hiding place of three crosses that were believed to have been used at the crucifixion of Jesus and the two thieves.[43] In subsequent years, the story of the *True Cross* reads like a movie adventure, with the cross being broken and various parts captured and re-captured by Sasanids, Muslims, Crusaders, and others who took them to every corner of Europe and the Middle East.[44] Their entries into cities were usually pseudo-triumphal processions composed of ranks of clergy and a reliquary containing the holy relic. Detailed descriptions are scarce but one painting by the Renaissance Italian painter Gentile Bellini titled *Procession of the True Cross in Piazza San Marco* depicts hundreds, possibly thousands of participants and spectators (see color insert Figure 6-6).

Constantine subsequently ordered a church to be built on the site where Helena had discovered the True Cross. This church came to be known as the Church of the

Holy Sepulchre. The construction of the Church took nine years, and it was dedicated on September 13, 335 CE. A relic of the True Cross was processed into the Church the following day. This event and procession are still celebrated today in Catholic churches on September 14 with the Feast of the Exaltation of the Holy Cross.[45] The cross, of course, is the major symbol of the Christian religion worldwide, so much emotion and many powers are still attributed to it.[46]

The entries of other relics of saints and martyrs were similar.[47] Writer J.N. Hilgarth in describing the influence of Bishop Victricius of Rouen, France in the late fourth century CE, talks about the emotional effects of a procession of relics.

> He [Victricius] presents the Christian ideal, expressed in the martyrs and in the male and female ascetics who fill his procession and *are* the new martyrs, since their life is a daily martyrdom. He presents his ideal as *new*, in deliberate opposition to the glories of the Roman Empire, symbolized in the emperor's entry into a city, which Victricius contrasts with the entry of the relics of martyrs into Rouen, followed by a very different escort, the heroes of the new age. Camille Jullian observed, "This entry of Relics surpassed in emotional force, all spectacles and ceremonies which Gaul had yet seen." All those who took part believed that they now held at Rouen, in tangible form, the *power* of the martyrs, of Christ's saints, to heal men and to forgive sins.[48]

So empowering were relics of the True Cross believed to be that at least one Byzantine Emperor is said to have carried such a relic into battle and met with great success.[49]

In the Orient, we saw an example of complex religious processions with the Song Dynasty Grand Carriage processions in Chapter One

In the late Postclassical Period in central Mexico, between about 1300 and 1500 CE, the Aztec culture flourished (also known as Mexica or Nahua). Like the earlier Mayans, their religion was pantheistic and religious processions played a big part in their lives.[50] Most of these incorporated human sacrifice and cannibalism. The most famous ceremony was a dedication to the sun god Huitzilopochtli involving the sacrifice of prisoners of war.

In a lengthy dissertation in which she investigated psychological and biological responses to the violence of Aztec sacrifice, Linda Hansen speculated what the ritual would have been like.

> Naked prisoners of war, bound by ropes, would be dragged in procession by victorious warriors into the city of Tenochtitlan amid plumes of incense smoke placed in front of each miserable victim by shrouded priests.... A multitude of emotions would be experienced by onlookers when they heard the howling cries of these condemned war prisoners, along with the brassy calls of conch-shell trumpets and the deep throb of incessant drums.[51]

Unexpectedly, she concluded that "human sacrifice worked for the Aztec in every social station because it was biologically and psychologically satisfying to them. Each phase of their ceremonies promoted heightened emotional responses that correspondingly engulfed their bodies with pleasurable neurochemicals that created sensations of euphoria, well-being, pain mitigation, physical strength, and social connectedness."[52] In other words it would have produced similar moving encounters and feelings of belonging as I outlined in the Introduction, albeit incredibly misguided, as the Spanish Conquistadors were to learn. As to *why* so many humans were sacrificed, at least one scholar has postulated that it was to provide needed protein to the diet of a society that was mainly vegetarian and that had no domesticated animals for milk and meat. The rationale bought into by the populace was that it was to "appease the appetites of the gods."[53]

Further to the south, the relatively short-lived Inca Empire was on the rise in western South America, mostly in what is today's Peru, at the very end of the Post-classical Period. Their most important calendrical festival was the Inti Raymi, dedicated, as with the Aztecs, to the sun god (in this case called Inti—see color insert Figure 6-7). It is still celebrated today on the winter solstice and is a major tourist draw to Cusco, Peru. The original procession and rituals were described by a Spanish conquistador, Garcilaso de la Vega:

> The king always went in person, unless a war or some long journey kept him from doing so....
>
> The *curacas* [leaders of conquered tribes] came to the ceremony in their finest array, with garments and headdresses ornamented with gold and silver.
>
> Others, who claimed to descend from a lion, appeared, like Hercules himself, wearing the skin of this animal on their backs and on their heads, its head.
>
> Others still, came got up as one imagines angels, with the great wings of the bird called condor, which they considered to be their original ancestor....
>
> Others wore masks that gave them the most horrible faces imaginable ... with the heads and gestures of madmen or idiots. To complete the picture, they carried appropriate musical instruments, such as out-of-tune flutes and drums, with which they accompanied their antics....
>
> Each nation presented its weapons: bows and arrows, lances, darts, slings, maces and hatchets, both short and long, according to whether they used them with one hand or two.
>
> They also carried paintings, representing feats they had accomplished in the service of the Sun and of the Inca, and a whole retinue of musicians played on the timpani and trumpets they had brought with them....
>
> ...the Inca went out at dawn, accompanied by all his relatives, each one of whom was placed according to his age and rank. The procession walked in this order to the main square of the city, called Haucaipata, where they took their shoes off and, turning to face the east, waited for the Sun to rise....
>
> The procession next headed for the house of the Sun and, at two hundred steps from this building, they all took their shoes off, except the king, who only took his sandals off at the temple door. He then passed through it, with those of his blood, and began to worship the image of the star.[54]

Following this, many animals were sacrificed and roasted for the ensuing feast. The king then took his place on his gold throne and proceeded to launch a series of toasts. The festivities lasted nine days in all. This festival, including the procession, was full of color and entertainment, both comedic and musical, as well as much dancing, just as it is today.

Religious festivals and processions continued through the Late Middle Ages, but following the Reformation in the 16th century, secular festivals began to appear and religious processions diverged in their own separate direction.[55] When they did crop up again, as part of pageants and other events, they were mixed with secular rituals and entertainment, and these are covered in other chapters.

Seven

Days of Our Lives

Tradition is what often draws us to parades.

In the lexicon of ritual, traditionalism is one of the least understandable terms, because it is intertwined with other terms like nostalgia, heritage, and history. All these, for the most part, make up culture. It is further complicated by the fact that traditions may be viewed from either a personal perspective or a collective perspective. This chapter examines the personal perspective; Chapter Eight, the collective.

From a personal perspective, "tradition is an essential part of how one experiences the world, since without tradition, experience lacks those orientations to the past that enable one to be adequately situated. Tradition, in other words, is a necessary part of cognition and a vital part in managing, interpreting, and applying information to our lives."[1] It is, I would say, a "security of the known." It helps to ground us.

Personal tradition is frequently tied to what are known as rites of passage, a term first proposed by Dutch-German-French ethnographer Arnold van Gennep. These are celebrations associated with life's main events or transitions, such as coming of age, graduation, marriage, retirement, and death. Gennep theorized that these rites comprised three phases: separation, transition, and incorporation. A marriage, for example, has several separate rites. Going from adolescent or unmarried to betrothed, involves separation from the previous state (unmarried), then transition and incorporation to being betrothed. Going from betrothed to married involves separation from the previous state (betrothed), then transition and incorporation to being married.[2] As we know, both betrothal and marriage involve—or may involve—certain rituals and ceremonies, some that may well contain personal or family traditions. But why do we need rites of passage and their attendant ceremonies?

First, they provide a sense of renewal and belonging by marking the beginning of a new phase in our lives. They remind us that we are constantly evolving and that life is a transformative journey. On the other hand, they also provide a sense of belonging, since a rite of passage is always performed by and for a community.

Second, they form a connection with our past and herein lies the tradition. These ceremonies tend to be highly ritualized and are passed from one generation to the next, in a flow that evokes the continuity of life, and reminds us of our place in the great scheme of things.

Third, they place us in a sacred space. When we take part in a rite of passage, we usually find ourselves in a sacred space. There are rules and rituals regarding dress, place and time that must be respected. As humans, we need this sense of sacrality to feel more attuned to our individual journey.

Last, they help us make sense of change. A rite of passage can help us gain a deeper awareness of the transitions going on in our lives, while providing a sense of continuity with our own personal stories and of our connections with our community.[3]

Many rites of passage have processions as part of the ceremonies, even though they may be private affairs. Throughout history, some of these personal—and private—ceremonies have become public along with their processions. In general, these are the ones that are held by or for celebrities or royalty. Their timeless rituals still help us to feel more stable and grounded, even if we live them vicariously. We are familiar with most of them: circumcisions; coming of age; weddings; graduations; funerals; and coronations, inaugurations, and enthronements. Following from the last chapter, most of these originated as religious ceremonies but have veered away from that association in modern times. Some, though, still linger.

Let's take a short walk through life from beginning to end and see how some cultures have celebrated rites of passage with public processions.

Circumcision and Coming of Age

Although in most societies that practice it, circumcision is no more than a medical procedure completed when the child is a baby, occasionally it is also considered a form of coming of age completed ceremoniously when the boy is a teenager.[4]

Sultans of the Ottoman Empire that ruled modern-day Turkey and part of the Middle East from the 14th to the 20th centuries, used rites of passage to reinforce their legitimacy and lineage.[5] In the year 1582 CE, Sultan Murad III celebrated the circumcision of his son Prince Mehmed with a festival that lasted 55 days. It was the longest and most grandiose festival the Ottomans ever held. The 1582 festival was recorded in a festival book, *Surname-i Hümayun*, in which the celebrated court artist of the age, Osman, created 427 miniature illustrations that told the story. Most of the events took place in the hippodrome in Istanbul. There were daily processions in front of the Sultan, who watched from the balcony of his palace while honored guests, including foreign emissaries, were seated in three-tiered tribunes set up along sides of the hippodrome.[6] Uniquely, many consisted of the various guilds of the city creatively parading their own specialties on carts or wagons, often with entertainment. One group, the glassblowers, displayed a full glassblowing process, complete with a furnace on wheels and artisans showing off their products. Another group, the coffee-sellers, paraded a model coffeehouse on wheels, complete with customers sitting inside, and then proceeded to humorously act out scenes of serving the customers (see color insert Figure 7-1).[7] These were also wonderfully creative examples of float forerunners.

Other daily processions were acts of homage, but these were no less important. Invitations had been sent to all the major countries of Europe and the Middle East, and the fact that their representatives attended attests to the political importance of the festival. Furthermore, "the presentation, in a great public spectacle, of gifts to the Ottoman sultan by all the constituents of his state and country and by all the sovereigns of the world was clear evidence of the sultan's power."[8] A second, similar large circumcision celebration was also held in 1720 and beautifully illustrated in a second festival book.

Coming-of-age rites of passage are more universally found in societies—Bar/Bat Mitzvah (Jewish), Confirmation (Christian), Quince Años (Spanish-Catholic), Guan Li/Ji (Confucian), and similar ceremonies—many secular—have continued unchanged for centuries. They mark the transition from child/youth to adult. Most are private and even royalty seldom share these private moments. Also, most do not incorporate parades.

One interesting example, however, *is* public and has a procession. It is called the *Eunoto* ceremony, and marks the transition of young Kenyan male Maasai warriors, or *morani*, into senior warriors.[9] It is performed approximately every 10 years and is part of an *age-set* series of rites of passage. There may be hundreds of *morani* participating, all having left businesses and schools to return home to take part. Throughout a night they dance the *adamu* or "jumping dance" and some even enter trance-like states. At sunrise, the mothers of the morani shave off their sons' hair, then the young warriors, adorned in colorful cloaks and body paint, are blessed at a communal ceremony, completing the transition. There follows a joyous, singing, dancing procession around the village (i.e., a *circumambulation*) by all the new senior warriors (see color insert Figure 7-2).[10] After completing the ceremony, senior warriors are permitted to marry and to engage in the decision-making processes in the community, in order to prepare them to become future elders.[11] This is a perfect example of a combined personal and collective communal tradition that has been around for at least several hundred years. One can only imagine how such a ceremony would help to solidify communities in western societies if this were done today with say, proportionally thousands of participants and even more spectators, ending with a parade through city streets. It would be headline news and, I would guess, influence the belief system of all of us.

Graduations

In western societies, graduation from high school and university are both important milestones in a young person's life. University graduation is more steeped in tradition than high school and involves an elaborate procession into the ceremony by the graduating students and the institution's academic staff (see Chapter Three for details about academic regalia). While graduation ceremonies are usually only for graduates and invited guests, their history indicates a more public announcement of the achievements of the scholars. "The contemporary academic procession dates back to mediaeval times, when the procession was through public thoroughfares, so the public could bear witness to the status of the new graduates."[12] This may have been as early as 1088 CE when the University of Bologna opened in Italy, or up to 2000 years earlier in the Islamic world.[13]

Modern processions follow a generally standardized order. At the University of Glasgow, for example, the procession is led by a *Bedellus* carrying a ceremonial mace, the symbol of the university's authority.[14] Next comes the person conferring the degrees, usually the university Chancellor, followed by the Professor of Divinity, the Clerk of the Senate and the Dean of Faculties, then *individual* Deans of the Faculties, members of the Senate and other teaching staff—clearly a pecking order that still defers to the church origins of universities.[15]

Academic processions are always accompanied by stately music. In Europe the favorite seems to be *Gaudeamus igitur* ("So let us rejoice"), which is believed to have come from a 1287 CE Latin manuscript. It is in the tradition of *carpe diem* ("seize the day") and is a light-hearted endorsement of the bacchanalian mayhem of student life. In the USA, Canada, and the Philippines, the favorite is *Land of Hope and Glory*, taken from part of Edward Elgar's famous series of British patriotic military marches, *Pomp and Circumstance*, composed around 1901. Ironically, the motto of Elgar's entire suite had nothing to do with academia, but was "the naïve assumption that the splendid show of military pageantry—pomp—had no connection with the drabness and terror—circumstance—of actual warfare," a theme I discussed in Chapters Three and Five.[16] To be fair, the lyrics to *Land of Hope and Glory* are—thankfully for graduation ceremonies—tamer than the theme would suggest.

Weddings

Weddings are undoubtedly the most celebrated rites of passage in our lives. Sometimes even the very private, personal ones become communal, public affairs. In ancient Rome there was a public street procession as part of the festivities.

> After the wedding feast the bride was formally taken to her husband's house ... since it was essential to validity of the marriage.... It was a public function, that is, anyone might join the procession and take part in the merriment.... As evening approached, the procession was formed before the bride's house with torch-bearers and flute-players at its head. When all was ready, the marriage hymn (*hymenaeus*) was sung and the groom took the bride with a show of force from the arms of her mother.... The bride then took her place in the procession. She was attended by three boys.... Two of these walked beside her, each holding one of her hands, while the other carried before her the wedding torch of white thorn.... Behind the bride were carried the distaff and spindle, emblems of domestic life.
>
> When the procession reached the groom's house, the bride wound the door posts with bands of wool, probably a symbol of her own work as mistress of the household, and anointed the door with oil and fat, emblems of plenty. She was then lifted carefully over the threshold, in order, some say, to avoid the chance of so bad an omen as a slip of the foot on entering the house for the first time.[17]

It's interesting to see the very clear phases of this ritual, as outlined by Gennep, that complete the marriage: separation of the bride from her mother and family; the transitional phase of the procession to the groom's house; and finally, the incorporation into full married life by the groom's carrying of her over the threshold.

Things haven't changed much in 2000 years; they've just been modified. In our case today, the separation could be the horn-honking motorcade from wedding ceremony to the reception, which becomes the transition, and this would be followed by the bride and groom formally departing for their honeymoon—often in a car to which tin cans have been tied—in other words the incorporation into full married life. The motorcade could even be considered as temporarily transforming it into a public event.

Obviously, weddings can incorporate one or more *different* processions—one (private) within the confines of the sacred space used for the official ceremony (e.g., entrance of the bride in a church, or sandy beach for that matter), one that publicly takes the bride or the groom *to* the ceremony, and one that publicly takes the married couple *from* the ceremony, as above.

Medieval weddings, for example, began with a procession from the bride's home to the church. Minstrels led the way, playing bagpipes, six-stringed viol, flutes, drums, and trumpets. They were followed by the bride and groom, the best man on horseback, the groom's parents, and the bride's parents. Notably, the best man in those days was not necessarily the couple's best friend but the best swordsman they might know. Protection from thieves on the way was a priority.[18]

In modern Hindu and Sikh weddings, the groom is led to the marriage venue in a public procession known as the *Baraat*. The groom's transport is usually a well-caparisoned white horse, but could be an elephant. A retinue of singing, dancing relatives and friends, all formally attired, takes up the rear. Electronic music often accompanies the procession. "The music during a Baraat sets the mood for the rest of the marriage event, with upbeat and exciting songs.... Modern Indian weddings showcase a fusion of Hip Hop and Bhangra."[19] The procession may have to navigate through city streets full of traffic (Figure 7-3).

As with the wedding processions of royalty and celebrities, these modest events are a pronouncement to society at large that the couple has entered a formal arrangement from which children are the expected outcome. While some would argue that this is no longer the intention, tradition says otherwise, and I suspect it will be a long time before that tradition disappears, if ever.

When it comes to processions associated with royal personages and celebrities, it would take another entire book to analyze all of them. There are some reasons, however, why they are and always have been so popular. First, they provide a form of escapism.[20] What girl does not want to be Cinderella, or man the handsome

Figure 7-3: Hindu wedding procession through city streets. Note the groom on a horse (photograph by the author).

prince? When they are offered to us in real life we will travel across oceans and continents to see them in person. They also are more accessible through these very public processions and through live televising of the entire proceedings. Lastly, when literally beautiful people are involved, our interest increases even more. Some memorable weddings come to mind. Movie actress Grace Kelly and Prince Rainier of Monaco captured the world's attention with their fairy tale wedding in 1956. Three years earlier, the wedding of Jacqueline Lee Bouvier and John F. Kennedy was a similar public union of two extremely attractive, well-known people. However, its public reach was not as great as that of Kelly-Rainier partly because of the lack of television. By 1956 television sets occupied a pride of place in America. In 1953, 45 percent of American homes had a TV set; in 1956 that number had blossomed to 72 percent.[21] Of course we all know about recent weddings of royalty that generated so much interest that they are known only by first names—Charles and Diana, William and Kate, Harry and Megan, British royals all.

Other historical royal nuptials are worth a look, too.

A singularly gaudy and pretentious state wedding took place in Paris on April 2, 1810, when Napoleon Bonaparte married his second wife, Archduchess Marie Louise, the 18-year-old daughter of Emperor Francis I of Austria, head of the House of Habsburg. This was the last of three similar extravagant ceremonies comprising the single marriage. The procession was not unlike those associated with royal weddings we have seen up to the present. "The next day, Monday, April 2, the imperial couple rode to Paris in a procession led by the cavalry of the Imperial Guard, followed by other horsemen and their bands, heralds of arms, and many carriages. Napoleon and Marie Louise were in his gilded coronation coach, drawn by eight horses. They paused for speeches at the Arc de Triomphe. The bases of the arch, still under construction, were only about twenty feet high, but a full wooden mock-up had been hastily assembled and dressed in canvas for the occasion. The procession continued along the Champs-Élysées to the Tuileries Palace [see color insert Figure 7-4], where wedding guests had been kept waiting for about five hours in the Louvre."[22] The procession continued through the Louvre to a specially constructed chapel. Here the ceremony took place, but not before the contemptuous Napoleon famously did the unthinkable once again—placed his crown on his own head, a habit he acquired for his original coronation in 1804 for which the Pope himself presided. Although a brilliant military tactician, Napoleon was not brilliant at marriage. This one only lasted four years.

When we consider the physical attractiveness of royalty, there has been no modern couple that could beat Duchess Cecilie of Mecklenburg-Schwerin (part of Germany), and Crown Prince Wilhelm of Prussia, who married in 1905. Cecilie was a tall, dark-eyed, ravishing beauty with whom the equally handsome Prince Wilhelm became immediately smitten when they met in 1904 when she was 17. Before long, Cecilie became a favorite of the people, much like Lady Diana Spencer in the next century. Upon arrival in Berlin for her wedding, she was greeted at Bellevue Palace by the entire German Imperial Family and later made a joyous procession through the Brandenburg Gate, including a gun salute in the Tiergarten. Crowds lined the sides of the Unter den Linden (remember this was one of the grand boulevards mentioned in Chapter Two) as she passed on the way to the Berlin Royal Palace.[23]

Talking about bringing a wedding into the public eye, it would have been difficult to ignore the wedding of Hind Bint Maktoum to Sheikh Mohammed Rashid al

Maktoum in Dubai in 1979. The Sheikh, part of the ruling Al Maktoum Dynasty, did not scrimp on the affair. At $137 million USD, it holds the Guinness World Record as the most expensive wedding ever held. A 20,000-seat stadium was constructed especially for the ceremony and parades and processions abounded. "The Sheikh's Royal Guard presented a parade comprised of riders on horseback and on camels. During the wedding ceremony, the Sheikh delivered wedding gifts to his bride, which were carried on twenty camels decorated with jewels. Fifty Arab and African dance troupes provided a parade for the royalty in attendance…. The Sheikh also traveled by horseback during his wedding week to visit every town in the emirate. He distributed food, personally giving it to the residents in each town."[24]

Although the Sheikh's loyal subjects would no doubt have enjoyed the processions for what they were, simply a component of a massive public ceremony, his benevolence undoubtedly contributed to their connection with him and his bride.

Funerals

The last rite of passage, death, is often acknowledged by a public funeral, especially for well-known, beloved public figures. As with private funerals, these provide—at least in part—a sense of closure, an opportunity for one to remember that person the way they were known in life, and to say goodbye to their physical presence that no longer will be part of our lives.[25] Much of the populace can form highly emotional connections with such public figures, especially if they were respected and contributed significantly to their communities or countries during their lives. A funeral procession offers the opportunity for more of that populace to view them for the last time. Moving encounters often occur during such processions. Two examples, among many, were historically impactful.

After Alexander the Great died in Babylon in 323 BCE, he lay in state for two years while his incredibly elaborate hearse was under construction. During this whole time, no actual funeral was held—nor *ever* was. The hearse was the focal point of the subsequent procession intended to transport Alexander's body to its final resting place in Macedonia. It was one of the most elaborate funeral vehicles in history.

The hearse was covered with a golden vault, decorated with gold scales and precious stones, eight cubits wide and twelve cubits long.[26] Gold Ionic columns resembling acanthus sprouts supported the roof. The architrave was adorned with relief animal busts with golden rings, through which ran a colored festive garland. At the ends there were tassels that held large bells. Four gold Victories stood at the four angles of the roof, whose centre was decorated by a gold olive wreath. Furthermore, a thick gold net with four panels spread between the columns. The panels depicted Alexander with scepter on a chariot between Persians and Macedonians, as well as troops of his army. Two gold lions guarded the entrance to the chamber. Gold lion-heads adorned the wheels of the hearse, which was carried by sixty-four mules, wreathed with gold wreaths.[27]

Writers have suggested that the hearse—also called a *catafalque*—resembled a temple on wheels, indicative of the reverence that the countries of Alexander's empire held for him. Indeed, a great number of their inhabitants came out to witness the historic procession, which also included hundreds of soldiers and artisans accompanying the hearse (Figure 7-5). The hearse, though, never made it to Macedonia. Along

Figure 7-5: Mid–19th century reconstruction of Alexander's catafalque based on the description by Diodorus (© Andrew Michael Chugg, reproduced with permission).

the way Ptolemy I, the governor of Egypt and one of Alexander's former elite guards, hijacked it. Ptolemy had it directed to Egypt, where Alexander's body was placed in a tomb, but moved several times over the centuries. In fact, the location of his body remains one of the world's greatest archaeological mysteries to this day.[28] His funeral procession was thus extremely long and circuitous, probably more than 2000 km! This extraordinary outcome caused 40 years of war between the generals of Alexander's army, known as the Wars of the Diadochi. These, in turn, resulted in the disintegration and redistribution of the countries of what eventually became today's Middle East. The disposition of Alexander's body eventually led up to the Grand Procession of Ptolemy Philadelphus discussed in Chapter Four.

In 1852, another grand hearse was the centerpiece of the funeral procession of the Duke of Wellington, a statesman and the great English military hero who defeated Napoleon at the Battle of Waterloo in 1815. Beloved by his nation, his funeral procession drew more than 1.5 million spectators. It was one of the largest in the country's history.

Over the course of four hours, the procession wound its way from Horse Guards Parade through the streets of London, ending up at St. Paul's Cathedral for the funeral service. It was essentially a military parade with dozens of regiments and more than 10,000 soldiers. The royal family of Queen Victoria also formed part of the procession. The hearse—with a nod to that of Alexander the Great—was an "11-ton funeral car built upon six solid bronze wheels. 27 feet long by 11 feet wide, its heavy black velvet lavishly embroidered with silver trimming and surmounted by semblances of weapons and coats of arms; the car was pulled with difficulty by 12 sable horses."[29] It was variously described as everything from "abominably ugly" to "gorgeous and towering."

The procession and funeral itself also met with a range of reactions. It was considered a "mass catharsis," but Charles Dickens went so far as to call it a "palpably got up theatrical trick."[30]

However, the event, viewed by so many, was more. As one writer said, "The funeral, with its procession of the hero's body through the streets of Westminster and the City, stamped itself indelibly in England's cultural memory precisely through its spatial staging: it came to be perceived as a profound episode in the history of

London, in the ideological construction of that metropolis as the world's economic and cultural capital during the early Victorian era."[31]

Coronations, Enthronements, and Inaugurations

I have saved these events and their parades for last in this chapter because, while they are personal rites of passage for sovereigns and governing presidents, they also represent a collective tradition for the country or society in which they are found. In their execution and rituals, they are more standardized and inviolable compared to the previous rites of passage. Here is a simple example. Wedding vows in royal weddings can be changed easily, as they were in the wedding of Megan Markle and Prince Harry in 2018. However, the spoken rituals in a coronation are not as flexible. Most importantly, their occurrence is more predictable than the other rites of passage. Everyone knows, for example, that coronations and enthronements are held when the previous sovereign either dies or abdicates; an inauguration normally occurs at certain regular intervals after elections are held.

Coronations go a long way back. Anthropologist Sir James George Frazer, in his famous book *The Golden Bough*, theorized that religious and political leaders broadly evolved as follows. Initially, what was a shaman or traditional healer in hunter-gatherer societies at some point divided responsibilities into disease healers and others like rain-makers who dealt with the natural world. The one considered as the most powerful member of the order went on to take over roles as chief and eventually sacred king, who ruled within the well-known concept of divine right of kings. Still later, according to Frazer, this job further subdivided into a civil power (e.g., a king or political leader) and a spiritual power (e.g., a religious leader). Meanwhile, the remaining "magicians" eventually abandoned sorcery in favor of science.[32] It's a simplistic analysis but sufficient for our purposes.

What were the consequences of this evolution of leadership? The predominant consequence for most of human history was the complex marriage between state and religion, which, until relatively recently, meant that political leaders (e.g., kings, emperors) only ruled because either they were believed to *be* gods or they had been given the right to do so *by* gods (i.e., divine right of kings). Examples of this include Egyptian pharaohs, Roman emperors, Chinese emperors, Mayan kings, and the ancient Israelite kings. Today, this divine right is still alive and well with such institutions as the British constitutional monarchy, and unbelievably, another 30-plus constitutional monarchies around the world. Even democracies have incorporated a semblance of this in their formation, the United States being the most obvious example with their official motto, "In God We Trust." Indeed, coronation and inauguration ceremonies still include significant religious ritual components, so it is not hard to understand why the overall events—including the processions—are so sacrosanct.[33]

Writing shortly after the coronation of Queen Elizabeth II in 1953, Edward Shils and Michael Young argued that the event "was the ceremonial occasion for the affirmation of the moral values by which the society lives. It was an act of national communion.... The key to the Coronation Service is the Queen's promise to abide by the moral standards of society.... When she does this, she symbolically proclaims her community with her subjects who, in the ritual—and in the wider audience outside the Abbey—commit themselves to obedience within the society constituted by the moral rules which she has agreed to uphold."[34] They further went on to note that there was an "extraordinary stillness and tranquillity of the people on the [parade] route." In simple terms, the people of Great Britain understood and bought in to the collective bonding nature and meaning of the coronation.

Despite spectators camping out in order to witness the procession of that very coronation, the procession was not particularly memorable as coronation processions go. Save for the florid, horse-drawn golden state coach of the Queen, the entire procession was composed solely of marching military units, cavalry, and bands from various regiments of the British and foreign armed services, totaling some 30,000 men.[35] It was, however, especially memorable for the fact that it was the first time that a coronation and a major world event had been broadcast on television.

Five hundred years earlier, in 1559 CE, the coronation of her namesake, Queen Elizabeth I, was memorable for other reasons. She had to endure three processions. The main one, in which she officially entered the city, was a much more elaborate affair than Elizabeth II's. It took her from the Tower of London to Westminster on the eve of her coronation. Ironically, it was for a similar reason, and on the same route, that she had been carried in her mother, Queen Anne Boleyn's womb, some 26 years previously. It was, in fact, a royal entry like those described in Chapter Four. Elizabeth stopped at four points where tableaux vivants with distinctly Protestant-leaning themes were performed, which she received with aplomb and kind words. "'Her Grace, by holding up her hands and merry countenance to such as stood far off, and most tender and gentle language to those that stood nigh to her Grace, did declare herself no less thankfully to receive her people's good will, than they lovingly opened it unto her.' In return, 'the people again were wonderfully ravished with the loving answers and gestures of their Princess.'"[36] In short, Elizabeth conquered London.

Elizabeth knew what she was dealing with. The times were turbulent. Mary I, her half-sister and predecessor, had brought Roman Catholicism back to England and Elizabeth in her adroit handling of her coronation and processions—especially the royal entry—signaled that she might return the country to the more popular Protestantism. It presaged the *Elizabethan Religious Settlement*, the name given to the religious and political arrangements made for England during her reign that brought the English Reformation to a conclusion. The Settlement shaped the theology and liturgy of the Church of England and was important to the development of Anglicanism as a distinct Christian tradition.

Of course, there have been thousands of other coronation processions throughout history, some better documented than others. Some, too, were historically more important than others. To cover them all would take several books. However, two more, the coronations of Charlemagne as the first Holy Roman Emperor in 800 CE and Charles V as Holy Roman Emperor in 1530 CE, conveniently book-ended the role of the Pope in the ceremony and played important historical roles in the formation of Europe.

The Holy Roman Empire was a complex, political-religious entity set up in Western Europe during the Middle Ages that sought, in simplistic terms, to maintain the role of the church in politics. The coronation was a ceremony in which the ruler of Western Europe's then-largest political entity received the Imperial Regalia at the hands of the Pope, symbolizing both the pope's right to crown Christian sovereigns and the emperor's role as protector of the Roman Catholic Church, a sort of *quid pro quo* arrangement. Charlemagne (Charles the Great) and Charles V were the first and last emperors respectively to be so crowned. Charlemagne's coronation by Pope Leo III took place in Rome; Charles's by Pope Clement VII in Bologna more than 700 years later. Some scholars have suggested that Charlemagne's coronation was "the most important occurrence of the Middle Ages" and "indicated the beginning of Europe." Through his and his successors' reigns, the main emphasis was to maintain the unity of the Christian (i.e., Roman Catholic) realm in Europe, but by the time of Charles V, the territory of the empire had decreased considerably and the Reformation portended the first stage of failure.[37]

There is no evidence confirming that a procession was part of Charlemagne's coronation, although it would be unlikely that there would not have been one for a warrior-king such as he, at the very least into the church. History indicates that his successors had them as part of the ceremonies. Certainly, Charles V did. His coronation was "one of the most important ceremonial events of the sixteenth century.... It provided the context for a number of political agreements that were to determine the course of European history for the remainder of the century."[38] There were three processions—a royal entry into Bologna, a procession *to* the coronation, and a procession *from* the coronation (see color insert Figure 7-6).

For complicated political reasons, the coronation had been moved from its traditional location, Rome, to Bologna. In their enthusiasm to do well, the Bolognese decorated the city and the processional routes in the style of ancient Rome with its triumphal arches and statues of emperors.[39] Near the entrance to the city, a fountain was installed in the shape of a black eagle and two lions, all of which poured forth wine and water all day. For Charles's entry, he "was greeted by twenty cardinals and four hundred Papal guards. Preceded by light cavalry in red, ten pieces of artillery mounted on chariots, and fourteen companies of German foot soldiers, Charles rode in full armour under a gold canopy supported by four lords on foot, with twenty-five pages of honor from Bologna running at his side. Accompanying him were Henry of Nassau and Antonio de Leyva (carried in a chair because of gout). They were followed by Charles' household and Spanish infantry."[40]

The procession *to* the coronation was short, about 250 ft across a temporary, raised walkway that crossed the Piazza Maggiore, the large town square, from the Palazzo d'Accursio, where Charles and the Pope were temporarily living, to the Basilica of St. Petronius, where the coronation was to be held. The Pope led the way, followed by "pages, cupbearers, stewards, chamberlains, military officers, councillors, ministers, envoys from across Europe, and then Charles." All went well until a portion of the walkway collapsed just behind Charles, "throwing pike-wielding soldiers into the crowd of spectators in the square, some of whom were crushed." But the procession continued, leaving others to clean up the mess.[41]

Following the coronation ceremony, the popularity of the two main players was so great that they had to wait an hour to clear a path through the crowds to their waiting horses. The sovereigns rode in procession through the city under a single canopy followed by delegations of cardinals, ambassadors, princes, dukes, and German and Spanish soldiers. Magnificent though the ceremonies and processions had been, and though Charles set out on his reign to continue to unite the Christian world, it "was a world system that was about to disappear. In the words of Charles V's biographer,

Karl Brandi, this imperial coronation was the last ceremonial display of pre-modern concepts of empire."[42]

Enthronements are similar ceremonies to coronations except without the crown. They can be either religious or secular. In most, an oath has replaced a crown. The Pope is enthroned, although he used to be crowned. Countries whose monarchs now have enthronements include Belgium, Japan, Luxembourg, Malaysia, Spain, and Sweden. The last recent enthronement took place in Japan in 2019 when Emperor Naruhito was invested. Parades of performing arts groups and portable shrines were held and a motorcade with the Emperor and Empress Masako wound through Tokyo—actually a few months later—to the enthusiastic cheers of 120,000 flag-waving onlookers.[43] In fact, so popular was the couple that they inspired a buying rush on formal wedding gowns and tuxedos.[44]

Inaugurations, like coronations and enthronements, are installation ceremonies for a leader. No crown is involved. However, there is more commonality of ritual between coronations and inaugurations than one might expect. The swearing of an oath is an important one. Queen Elizabeth II—while holding a Bible at her coronation in 1953—had to affirmatively answer the following two questions posed by the presiding Archbishop of Canterbury.

- Will you solemnly promise and swear to govern the Peoples of the United Kingdom of Great Britain and Northern Ireland, Canada, Australia, New Zealand, the Union of South Africa, Pakistan, and Ceylon, and of your Possessions and the other Territories to any of them belonging or pertaining, according to their respective laws and customs?
- Will you to the utmost of your power maintain the Laws of God and the true profession of the Gospel? Will you to the utmost of your power maintain in the United Kingdom the Protestant Reformed Religion established by law? Will you maintain and preserve inviolably the settlement of the Church of England, and the doctrine, worship, discipline, and government thereof, as by law established in England? And will you preserve unto the Bishops and Clergy of England, and to the Churches there committed to their charge, all such rights and privileges, as by law do or shall appertain to them or any of them?[45]

The oath of office taken during the inauguration of the president of the United States, as an example, while simpler, has the same intent. The president must state, with his hand on a Bible, "I do solemnly swear (or affirm) that I will faithfully execute the Office of President of the United States, and will to the best of my ability, preserve, protect and defend the Constitution of the United States." If it is an "oath" then one question is also asked of the president at the end of the oath, "So help you God?" The president answers, "So help me God." If it is an "affirmation," the option to be the President's, then the last question is omitted. Most presidents over the last century have taken the oath and used a Bible.

Both articulations, the one for a coronation and the other for an inauguration, have two parts. The first obliges the monarch/president to uphold the laws of the land(s); the second to do so according to the laws of God.

What does this mean with respect to the ensuing processions? I believe it means that the citizens of either governing system—by their very citizenship—are obliged to give their tacit approval to what their leader has just sworn. This was implied earlier in the discussion about the meaning of the coronation. By their act of witnessing the ceremony and procession, they are, in fact, agreeing to that obligation. There are certainly those who would oppose this view, but citizenship comes with obligations, and this is an important one.

American presidential inaugurations are always followed by a procession, and these processions have a long history going back to George Washington (Figure 7-7).[46] Here are a few interesting historical facts.

- Some soldiers that Washington had commanded during the Revolutionary War escorted him through a few New York streets on the first inauguration day in 1789.
- Floats were used for the first time in Martin Van Buren's inaugural parade in 1837.
- Native Americans and African Americans participated in the inaugural parade for the first time in 1865.
- In 1881 for James Garfield's parade, 38 arches representing one for each state, were set up along the parade route on Pennsylvania Avenue. One is reminded of Medieval royal entries.
- Over the years, marching bands, herds of livestock, fife and drum corps, and minority groups were added.
- There were 40,000 participants in Woodrow Wilson's parade in 1913, the most ever.
- Women participated in the inaugural parade for the first time at Woodrow Wilson's second inauguration four years later.

Figure 7-7: Inauguration procession for U.S. President William Howard Taft along Pennsylvania Avenue in 1909 (from original real photograph postcard owned by author).

- Today the president parades to the White House and then reviews the remainder of the parade from a reviewing stand.[47]

Not all parades—or presidents—have been met with the full approval of the populace.

- The day before Wilson's inauguration in 1913, 8000 women suffragists protested.
- Anti-war protesters threw burning miniature flags and stones at police during the inauguration of Richard Nixon in 1969. The president's limousine was showered with eggs. During his second inauguration in 1973, 100,000 anti-war demonstrators protested at the Lincoln Memorial.
- President Bush's inauguration in 2001 was the recipient of 20,000 demonstrators against his thin election win.
- Protesters and supporters alike were in attendance at Donald Trump's parade in 2017 but a telling commentary was the *lack* of an audience in the temporary bleachers set up for the event.[48]

Other countries that have inaugurations include Brazil, Croatia, Ireland, the Philippines, and Russia, all of which have variations on the same theme.

We next look at parades that are collective traditions but have no predetermined personal expectations.

EIGHT

The Hero's Journey

Tradition from the collective perspective is more complicated but coronations, enthronements, and inaugurations provide a nice segue. In this chapter I am talking about parades that evince our relationship to a broader society—our city, our country, or our culture, sometimes all intermingled. While experienced on a personal level, they relate to how we fit within a specific culture or geographical location. In other words, they are about our common heritage and history and are not necessarily dependent on strict, predetermined rituals. They are both an expectation and an acknowledgment of who we are collectively.

In the Introduction I spoke about the human need for belonging and emotional connections. Such moving encounters are more easily achieved within groups of common heritage and history, as with Wellington's funeral, or the other coronations and inaugurations I mentioned. I have also shown how wearing a common costume can help establish these moving encounters. Now I am broadening the effects of that personal costume to include heritage and history. Let's look at a modern example, the Calgary Stampede Parade to which I briefly referred in Chapter Three.

To put the story in context, here is a short history of the city of Calgary and the stampede itself. Calgary is located in the eastern reaches of the foothills—and within sight—of the Canadian Rockies. Indigenous peoples have inhabited the area for more than 11,000 years and it is still a culturally relevant location for them. The actual city was founded in 1875, after "the site became a post of the North-West Mounted Police [now the Royal Canadian Mounted Police or RCMP]. The NWMP detachment was assigned to protect the western plains from US whisky traders, and to protect the fur trade.... Between 1896 and 1914 settlers from all over the world poured into the area in response to the offer of free 'homestead' land. Agriculture and ranching became key components of the local economy, shaping the future of Calgary for years to come. The world-famous Calgary Stampede, still held annually in July, was started by four wealthy ranchers as a small agricultural show in 1912. It is now known as the 'greatest outdoor show on earth.'"[1] Thus, since the beginning it has been a celebration of the city's historic past, particularly as a center for cattle ranching and cowboy culture, as well as for its Indigenous heritage.

The parade is the opening public event of the stampede. Like most large community parades in North America, it is of average length at 4.2 km and takes about two hours to pass any given spot. It typically draws around 300,000 spectators. About half of these spectators sport white Stetsons, the symbolic wardrobe accoutrement that represents the city worldwide. Indeed, many important visitors to the city are immediately given a Stetson by tourism representatives at the airport upon arrival.

As noted in Chapter Three, this small piece of costumery gives the wearer an instant implied and visible personal connection with the history and heritage of the city and the parade.

The major components of the parade are an interspersed amalgam of: Indigenous people in full regalia; uniformed members of the RCMP and military (Calgary is an important military center); large marching bands and color guards, many in western attire and even some from other countries; community floats; ethnic performers and dancers from different cultures who live in Calgary; dignitaries, celebrities, and famous sports figures; hundreds of horses used to carry participants; and cowboys and cowgirls. "The parade's finale comes with the flashing lights and whooping sirens of fire engines, police cars, and street sweepers scooping up the mounds of horse manure and other parade debris."[2]

For a long time in the early years of the parade this curious mixture was intended to represent a traditional history that narrated the arrival and success of European settler culture in the Canadian West and the suppression of First Nations cultures. Yet, in spite of this, the various groups managed to work in harmony for the parade to the extent that the parade did create moving encounters with spectators. The following observation from the 1935 parade shows to what extent.

> We enjoyed everything, but I could not help but notice the extra expression of heartfelt pleasure when the cowboys and old-timers' section of the parade came into view. One could … feel the vibration of good feeling running all through the crowd…. It vibrated along the side-walks, echoed and re-echoed from the tops of trucks and businesses and on up to the windows and roofs of the buildings that lined the avenue.[3]

Because the majority of parade spectators have always been local, this type of connection indicates that the spectators have an understanding of the importance of local history and the heritage of the people in the parade, some of whom may well have been related or relevant to the spectators (i.e., if the spectators were either of settler cowboy origins or First Nations origins). As numerous anthropologists have stated, parades have always acted as public spectacles intended to bring disparate communities together.[4] A parade, in helping to make sense of the past, creates a "collective autobiography."[5] Catherine Bell notes that events such as parades "draw together many social groups that are normally kept separate and create specific times and places where social differences are either laid aside or reversed for a more embracing experience of community."[6]

Parades, however, in mirroring society, are not static in their nature. In recent years, the stampede parade's emphasis has changed to reflect the public's desire to move on from the negative effects of European colonialism and to honor the country's First Nations heritage. At the same time, it has increased emphasis on the fictional—or Hollywood—version of the cowboy as well as the widespread fervor to embrace all things hero-related.

This has been exemplified in the stampede parade organizers' choice of parade marshals, those public figures who, as in parades everywhere, are celebrated for their work and given a place of honor in the parade—in this case as the leader of the parade.

In the more distant past, these figures tended to be politicians like governors-general, prime ministers, mayors, and military and police leaders. In other words, they reflected an apparent societal bias towards the white European males

Figure 8-1: Bing Crosby as Parade Marshal in the 1959 Calgary Stampede Parade (courtesy Peel's Prairie Provinces, a digital initiative of the University of Alberta Libraries, public domain via https://creativecommons.org/licenses/by/4.0/).

who dominated the "taming" of the Canadian west. In the mid–1950s this began to change with the appointment of entertainer Bing Crosby as a parade marshal (Figure 8-1). From then until now, marshals have reflected the public's growing interest in celebrities and heroes. Some of the more famous have included Bob Hope, Walt Disney, Mickey Mouse, Douglas Bader (World War II flying ace), astronaut Chris Hadfield, numerous Canadian Olympic medal winners and rodeo champions, actor Christopher Reeve, famous musicians, and even cancer fundraisers.[7] Although not marshals but definitely performers at the stampede, Hollywood cowboy/cowgirl stars Roy Rogers and Dale Evans rode in the parade in 1962, just a sampling of the many cowboy stars who participated in past decades. I remember as a boy being thrilled to see Roy Rogers in person at that very parade. Probably most noteworthy, though, of the changes in attitude toward the place of First Nations in the building of Calgary and the Canadian nation is the fact that seven of the 10 most recent parade marshals have been First Nations chiefs. Interestingly, the modern parade always ends with community first responders in a particular place of honor.

The Hero's Journey

The transformation of the Stampede parade into a modern event that honors heroes such as first responders and First Nations chiefs, brings us to the classic *monomyth* of the *hero's journey* and what it means when applied to parades.

American literature professor Joseph Campbell borrowed the word monomyth from James Joyce's *Finnegans Wake.* It has become a common model for a broad category of tales and lore that involve a hero who goes on an adventure, and in a decisive crisis wins a victory, then comes home changed or transformed.

According to Campbell it comes in two versions—a physical trial or a spiritual quest. Although the distinction between the two is not always clear, they both involve three main phases—departure, initiation, and return.[8] If these look like the three phases of rites of passage, there is good reason. Campbell was influenced by van Gennep's work, and simply renamed the phases for his purpose.

Departure deals with the hero's adventure prior to the quest and their reluctance to leave, initiation deals with the hero's many adventures along the way, and return deals with the hero's return home with knowledge and powers acquired on the journey.[9] Susanna Schrobsdorff, writing for *Time*, says Campbell "believed that people need these superhuman figures because they are 'the symbols that carry the human spirit forward.'"[10]

The earliest example of the hero's journey in literature is considered to be the *Epic of Gilgamesh*. Written in about 2100 BCE, it concerns the trials and tribulations of Gilgamesh, king of Uruk in ancient Mesopotamia. There is no end of other examples: ancient mythical heroes like Herakles (Hercules), Achilles, Jason, Prometheus, Odysseus, and Theseus; ancient real-life heroes like Alexander the Great (Greece), Cleopatra (Egypt), Julius Caesar (Rome), Ramesses the Great (Egypt), Moses (Israel), King David (Israel), Vercingetorix (France), and Cyrus the Great (Persia); Middle Age mythical heroes like King Arthur and the Knights of the Round Table, Robin Hood, Beowulf, and even Lady Godiva and the Pied Piper of Hamlin; Middle Age real-life heroes like Richard the Lion-Hearted and Joan of Arc; modern fictional heroes like Harry Potter, Hobbit Frodo Baggins, Luke Skywalker, Batman, Ironman, Wonder Woman, Superman, Spiderman, Tarzan; religious heroes like Christ, Buddha, and Muhammad; and modern celebrities such as astronauts, scientists, first responders, athletes, and even the occasional politician.

With the exception of religious heroes and modern celebrities, it is worth noting that almost all of the heroes mentioned, whether mythical or real, underwent a physical trial that involved a war or battle. Is it any wonder, then, that some of the earliest recorded parades were military victory parades? I think not, because, taking our cue from myth and legend, it has been humanity's proclivity through the millennia to endow certain members of our species with the definition of hero. What better person than a conquering military general? And what better form for embodying collective cultural tradition than a victory parade?

Victory Parades

Real military victory parades run deep through history.

Near the entrance to the Egyptian Museum in Cairo is an unimposing glass case resting on a wooden plinth. Inside is housed what has been described as the "first historical document in the world" by Egyptologist Bob Brier.[11] Called the Narmer palette, it's a grey-green siltstone palette about two feet high that records what some believe to be the union of Upper and Lower Egypt into a single country around 3150 BCE. The union of Egypt appears to have been the result of a battle between the kings of Upper and Lower Egypt, with King Narmer of Upper Egypt (i.e., the south) the victor. On one side of the palette is recorded a small parade or procession of the king and standard-bearers marching in step toward decapitated prisoners (Figure 8-2). It could be one of the first recorded victory processions in history.[12]

Another artifact, the Victory Stele of Naram-Sin, housed in the Louvre in Paris, shows the god-king Naram-Sin leading a victory procession atop a mountain with his troops behind him and trampled enemies underfoot. Naram-Sin was a ruler of the Akkadian Empire in the 23rd century BCE.[13]

The British Museum in London has several carved victory parade scenes from early Assyria. One, that of King Ashurnasirpal, dates from about 865 BCE and shows the king, accompanied by a god, returning to camp in his chariot. The scene includes other chariots with the standards of Assyrian gods. Soldiers march behind and in front,

Figure 8-2: The Narmer Pallette. Note victorious soldiers in upper right (from original real photograph postcard owned by author).

some holding or playing with the heads of the enemy. Decapitated bodies line the route and a vulture carries another head away. Musicians celebrate with harps and a tambourine.

A second large artifact, a large, four-sided stele called the Black Obelisk of Shalmaneser III from Nimrud in northern Iraq dated about 825 BCE, records tribute processions paid to King Shalmaneser from subdued kings of five countries. Two of the subdued kings can be seen prostrating themselves before Shalmaneser as their tribute bearers follow them in the processions. The details are described in cuneiform script on the stele.

A third series of carved scenes of a victory parade for Assyrian King Tiglath-pileser III around 728 BCE, comes from the king's palace in the city of Nimrud and shows shackled men *and* women prisoners, along with captured camels, sheep, and goats.

These three significant events of the day were understood to be so because they constitute surviving records. That they *did* survive makes them the equivalent of modern history books that shape society. Like other societies such as the Maya, stelae were erected in public places, often the center of a city as in the case of the Black Obelisk of Shalmaneser III. Other scenes like those from Assyria were carved on public buildings or on the walls of palaces. They were the early monuments and monumental buildings discussed in Chapter Two.

The first *written* account of a victory procession in any detail is found in the writings of Xenophon (430–354 BCE) who described the celebrations that followed the capture of Babylon by Cyrus the Great of Persia in 539 BCE.[14] Cyrus dressed his officers and high-ranking officials in purple, scarlet, and crimson garments then formed a procession that led from the palace to the temples. It was led by bulls of sacrifice and sacred white horses, then a white chariot with a golden yoke, hung with garlands and dedicated to Zeus, after that a white chariot of the Sun, wreathed like the one before it, and then a third chariot, the horses of which were caparisoned with scarlet trappings. Behind the chariots walked priests carrying sacred flames. Finally, Cyrus appeared in a chariot, wearing a tiara and diadem on his head plus a purple and white tunic, scarlet trousers, and a purple cloak. Following Cyrus marched his army and his military allies in the thousands. The procession ended at sacred precincts—probably temples—where sacrifices were made to Zeus, Ahura Mazda, and the Sun. Prisoners-of-war *may* have been sacrificed as part of the rituals.[15]

In 331 BCE, Alexander the Great and his army entered Babylon following the Battle of Gaugamela on a street carpeted with flowers and with silver altars heaped with frankincense and perfumes set up at intervals on both sides. A short mention of this was made in Chapter Two. The procession, in order, included: gifts of horses, lions, and leopards; priests; musicians; the Babylonian cavalry; Alexander in a chariot; the Macedonian army; and finally whatever townspeople wanted to follow.[16]

The most historically influential and enduring example of a military hero undergoing a trial may be found in the Roman Triumph. The Roman Republic, and later the Empire, flourished because it was funded in part by the spoils of war, and the spoils of war were immense. Indeed, *successful* war was encouraged by this singularly significant procession that was both public spectacle and personal award. The first one was held around the founding of Rome in approximately 753 BCE; the last around 403 CE.

Of the literally hundreds of triumphs, only a handful were truly memorable. One, that of General Lucius Aemilius Paulus against the Macedonian army and King Perseus, stands out as a story that encapsulated the man as hero, the rituals, and the politics of the Republican era in their totality (see color insert Figure 8-3—note that in the painting the captives come after Paulus; in reality, they preceded him).

Because of the importance of the triumph in later parade history, it deserves a comprehensive analysis and the writer Plutarch's description of the event is the best one.[17]

> The people erected scaffoldings in the theatres for equestrian contests, which they call circuses, and round the forum, occupied the other parts of the city which afforded a view of the procession, and witnessed the spectacle arrayed in white garments. Every temple was open and filled with garlands and incense, while numerous servitors and lictors restrained the thronging and scurrying crowds and kept the streets open and clear. Three days were assigned for the triumphal procession. The first barely sufficed for the exhibition of the

captured statues, paintings, and colossal figures, which were carried on two hundred and fifty chariots. On the second, the finest and richest of the Macedonian arms were borne along in many waggons. The arms themselves glittered with freshly polished bronze and steel, and were carefully and artfully arranged to look exactly as though they had been piled together in heaps and at random, helmets lying upon shields and breast-plates upon greaves, while Cretan targets and Thracian wicker shields and quivers were mixed up with horses' bridles, and through them projected naked swords and long Macedonian spears planted among them, all the arms being so loosely packed that they smote against each other as they were borne along and gave out a harsh and dreadful sound, and the sight of them, even though they were spoils of a conquered enemy, was not without its terrors. After the waggons laden with armour there followed three thousand men carrying coined silver in seven hundred and fifty vessels, each of which contained three talents and was borne by four men, while still other men carried mixing-bowls of silver, drinking horns, bowls, and cups, all well arranged for show and excelling in size and in the depth of their carved ornaments.[18]

On the third day, as soon as it was morning, trumpeters led the way, sounding out no marching or processional strain, but such a one as the Romans use to rouse themselves to battle. After these there were led along a hundred and twenty stall-fed oxen with gilded horns, bedecked with fillets and garlands. Those who led these victims to the sacrifice were young men wearing aprons with handsome borders, and boys attended them carrying gold and silver vessels of libation. Next, after these, came the carriers of the coined gold, which, like the silver, was portioned out into vessels containing three talents; and the number of these vessels was eighty lacking three. After these followed the bearers of the consecrated bowl, which Aemilius had caused to be made of ten talents of gold and adorned with precious stones, and then those who displayed the bowls known as Antigonids and Seleucids and Theracleian, together with all the gold plate of Perseus's table.[19] These were followed by the chariot of Perseus, which bore his arms, and his diadem lying upon his arms. Then, at a little interval, came the children of the king, led along as slaves, and with them a throng of foster-parents, teachers, and tutors, all in tears, stretching out their own hands to the spectators and teaching the children to beg and supplicate. There were two boys, and one girl, and they were not very conscious of the magnitude of their evils because of their tender age; wherefore they evoked even more pity in view of the time when their unconsciousness would cease, so that Perseus walked along almost unheeded, while the Romans, moved by compassion, kept their eyes upon the children, and many of them shed tears, and for all of them the pleasure of the spectacle was mingled with pain, until the children had passed by.

Behind the children and their train of attendants walked Perseus himself, clad in a dark robe and wearing the high boots of his country, but the magnitude of his evils made him resemble one who is utterly dumbfounded and bewildered. He, too, was followed by a company of friends and intimates, whose faces were heavy with grief, and whose tearful gaze continually fixed upon Perseus gave the spectators to understand that it was his misfortune which they bewailed, and that their own fate least of all concerned them. And yet Perseus had sent to Aemilius begging not to be led in the procession and asking to be left out of the triumph. But Aemilius, in mockery, as it would seem, of the king's cowardice and love of life, had said: "But this at least was in his power before, and is so now, if he should wish it," signifying death in preference to disgrace; for this, however, the coward had not the heart, but was made weak by no one knows what hopes, and became a part of his own spoils.

Next in order to these were carried wreaths of gold, four hundred in number, which the cities had sent with their embassies to Aemilius as prizes for his victory. Next, mounted on a chariot of magnificent adornment, came Aemilius himself, a man worthy to be looked upon even without such marks of power, wearing a purple robe interwoven with gold, and holding forth in his right hand a spray of laurel. The whole army also carried sprays of laurel, following the chariot of their general by companies and divisions, and singing, some of them divers songs intermingled with jesting, as the ancient custom was, and others paeans of victory and hymns in praise of the achievements of Aemilius, who was gazed upon and admired by all, and envied by no one that was good.[20]

Other sources for at least partial descriptions of Paulus's triumph come from Livy and Siculus.[21] As a body of information, they, along with Plutarch, provide the most of any triumph.[22]

The reason for the triumph has long been debated and there is no consensus on a single one. They range from the triumph as celebration of good fortune, to a reflection of how Romans saw themselves, and one scholar acknowledges after lengthy analysis that the "why" question is unanswerable.[23]

However, previous analyses were done without considering the triangular link amongst the key stakeholders of the event mentioned in the Introduction—the sponsor, the participants, and the spectators. The sponsor/organizer of the triumph was in reality the Senate of Rome, of which the victorious general at the time of the Republic was by decree a member, and one of two leaders (consuls). With few exceptions, he did not go to war nor was he awarded a triumph without the sanction of the Senate. They had a much simpler reason for the triumph—economic.

From earliest times, Roman victories brought into the country massive amounts of booty and huge numbers of slaves. It was said by Livy, for example, that just the gold and silver coinage from Paulus's triumph brought in the equivalent of at least $65–70 million USD (in today's money) and probably as much as $250 million considering the weights of the carrying vessels.[24] Plutarch tells us that the spoils from Paulus's campaign provided so much income that no special taxes were levied until the time of the first war between Mark Antony and Octavian, well over 100 years later.

Therefore, from the Senate's point of view, why not make a public statement about the value of this influx and how it is a good way to fund state affairs? To me, the main reason for the triumph throughout its history was political/economic, pure and simple. War—that is *successful* war—equaled fortune. It opened up trade routes and gave easy access to raw materials and precious goods from distant countries, thereby increasing the Romans' standard of living. Their persistence and resilience had proven they were good at war. It made ultimate sense. This was the real meaning *and* the message that was delivered.

What about the hero aspect? Strangely, throughout the long history of the triumph, the curious social mores of the Romans demanded a certain reticence from the triumphator to take on a role that held such power. Because of this, the triumphator was forced into a peculiar tug-of-war between the intoxication of fame and the feigned false modesty of not being worthy of such an award. In the end, those who played the game did well. Paulus was one of them. According to all the source writers, he, of all too few, maintained his integrity and his unflinching dedication to the Roman Republic, choosing to remain poor rather than take a larger share of the spoils for his personal gain and the loss of the state. To the populace, he was revered right up to his death, according to Plutarch and others, despite continuing as a member of the aristocracy. He was a true hero, achieving greatness in spirit and in action.

Not all to follow modeled themselves after him, and by the time of the Empire the "popular hero" in the form of the army general was far too greedy and self-absorbed. Finally, Augustus, the first Emperor, put a stop to the competitive nature of the triumph by permitting only Emperors to parade victoriously before the people. By then, though, the triumph had become firmly entrenched as a defining feature of Roman culture.

A legacy of the triumph, then, is the implantation into an entire civilization's culture of the concept that a *human being* could complete a hero's journey and achieve success. He—and the fact that the hero is male is noteworthy—could leave home for a distant land, battle enemies, strange foreigners, or evil forces, and return home to be rewarded. From thence forward it was to be a dominant theme in *all* western culture.

As author Margery Hourihan states, "It [the hero's journey] is a story about superiority, dominance and success. It tells how white European men are the natural masters of the world because they are strong, brave, skilful, rational and dedicated. It tells how they overcome the dangers of nature, how other 'inferior' races have been subdued by them, and how they spread civilization and order wherever they go.... It tells how their persistence means that they always eventually win the glittering prizes, the golden treasures, and how the gods—or the government—approve of their enterprises. It is our favorite story and it has been told so many times that we have come to believe that what it says about the world is true."[25]

Of course, since the era of the triumphs, countless military victory parades have been staged throughout the world, and many corroborate Hourihan's statement. Two notable and historically significant examples from the Middle Ages and Early Modern historical periods, are worth explaining.

The first comes from the First Crusade of 1095 to 1102 CE, which was conceived by Pope Urban II, with the goal of capturing Jerusalem and regaining Christian control of the city from Fatimid Shiite Muslims. After besieging the city for a month in the early summer of 1099, the combined crusader forces broke through the gates on July 15. They proceeded to slaughter many of the inhabitants, including non-combatant Muslims, Jews, men, and women. While there was no victory parade per se, 88 years later the famous warrior king, Saladin, a Sunni Muslim Kurd, recaptured the city and famously entered it in triumph with little bloodshed, having agreed—for a price—to allow many of the remaining crusaders to leave the city unharmed. Although the real story is much more complicated than this brief explanation, the comparison of the treatment of the conquered inhabitants of Jerusalem has gone down in history as a black mark against Christians and the crusades in general.[26]

A second example relates to the Spanish conquistador and conqueror of Mexico, Hernán Cortés. As Cortés and his forces approached the Aztec capital of Tenochtitlan (today's Mexico City) in 1519 CE, Moctezuma, the Aztec ruler, stalled for time, thinking that it would be better to have Cortés and his few hundred Spanish mercenaries and thousand or so Indigenous allies within the city and under his (Moctezuma's) control. Moctezuma went out and greeted Cortés with gifts and then allowed the Spanish to enter the city, in a similar fashion to the royal entries described in Chapter Four. While being hosted by the Aztecs, Cortés managed to capture Moctezuma in an attempt to gain full control of the city by proxy through the Aztec emperor. In short, this ploy failed, Moctezuma was mysteriously killed while in captivity, and the Spanish had to flee from the city. They regrouped and returned with more allies in 1520 to finally defeat the Aztecs and occupy their capital. Cortés returned to Spain in 1528 and was honored with a triumphal entry procession through various towns and into Toledo along with many Aztec chieftains "in their barbaric finery." It was for Cortés a vindication of sorts, since he had been admonished for his methods in New Spain. It was said, "The houses and streets of the great towns and villages were thronged with spectators, eager to look on the hero, who … had won an empire for Castille, and who, to borrow the language of an old historian, 'came in the pomp and glory, not so much of a great vassal, as of an independent monarch.'"[27]

Moving forward 300 years, closer to our own time when more records were available, I want to emphasize several noteworthy victory parades. We begin in the USA with the Grand Review of the Armies in 1865 in Washington, D.C., to celebrate the Union victory in the American Civil War. For six hours on each of two consecutive days, the victorious armies paraded along Pennsylvania Avenue to adoring

Figure 8-4: Grand Review of the Armies, 1865, on Pennsylvania Avenue, Washington, D.C., USA (Library of Congress).

crowds. On the first day, May 23, 80,000 infantry, artillery, and cavalry trod past President Andrew Johnson and General Ulysses Grant, often breaking out into patriotic song (Figure 8-4). On May 24, another 65,000 men followed the same route, this time trailed by freed blacks, laborers, adventurers, scavengers, and a vast herd of cattle and other livestock that had been taken from Carolina farms.[28]

Paris's Avenue des Champs-Élysées with its famed Arc de Triomphe has been the site of military victory parades since its construction in the early 19th century. Thousands of troops from both sides of conflicts have marched through the arch's portal. The first was in 1871. Thirty thousand Prussian, Bavarian, and Saxon troops held a victory parade in Paris on March 1, 1871, following the Siege of Paris in the Franco-Prussian War.

In 1880, France began its national Bastille Day Parade along the Champs-Élysées, and on July 14, 1919, detachments from all of France's World War I allies (except Russia) took part in the parade, together with colonial and North African units from France's overseas Empire. It was one of the most glorious ever held, and the first time since the day of infamy in 1871 that military men had marched through the arch. On the eve of the parade, more than 100,000 spectators already waited expectantly along the sidewalks of the great boulevard. The parade was led not by generals, but by "three young men, or what remained of them, unspeakably crippled by war, still in uniform, but trundled by their nurses in primitive chariots like the prams of deprived children. Immediately behind them came a large contingent of more *grand mutilés*.... The totally blind came led by the one-legged or armless; men with their destroyed faces mercifully hidden behind bandages; men with no hands; men with their complexions still tinted green from the effects of chlorine; men with mad eyes staring out from beneath the skull caps which concealed some appalling head injury.... As they passed a stand filled with 150 Alsatian girls in national costume, flowers rained

Figure 8-5: Victory parade in Paris, July 14, 1919. The American Army marches through the Arc de Triomphe (from original real photograph postcard owned by author).

down upon them. For a brief moment, the terrible spectacle of the broken men was met with a kind of stunned silence. Then an 'immense cry, which seemed to spring from the very entrails of the race, arose from the vast crowd, a cry which was both a salute and a pledge.'"[29] The generals followed and then the many men of the Allies, all accompanied by their own lively marches—the Americans with *Over There*, the British with *Tipperary*, and so on (Figure 8-5). Talk about moving encounters!

Other victorious armies strutted down the famous boulevard. In June 1940, the German army marched down the Champs-Élysées after the fall of France. Four years later, things had changed, and on August 29, 1944, the U.S. Army's 28th Infantry Division, which had assembled in the Bois de Boulogne the previous night, paraded 24-abreast up the Avenue Hoche to the Arc de Triomphe, then down the Champs-Élysées. Joyous crowds greeted the Americans as the entire division, men and vehicles, marched through Paris. The tradition continues today with the Bastille Day military parade honoring French and allied troops marching on the Champs-Élysées each July 14.

Allied victory parades after World War II were everywhere. Russia held the Parade of Victory, the longest and largest military parade ever held on Red Square in the Soviet capital Moscow. It involved 40,000 Red Army soldiers and almost 1900 military vehicles and other weaponry. The parade lasted just over two hours on a rainy June 24, 1945, more than a month after May 9, the day of Germany's surrender to Soviet commanders. That victory is still commemorated annually, but on May 9.

Sports victory parades are another version of the hero's journey, and can be seen for World Cup winners, Stanley Cup winners, Super Bowl winners, World Series winners, NBA winners, and the list goes on. An estimated two million people viewed the Toronto Raptors' victory parade on June 17, 2019, as it passed through the city, a number similar to other professional sports victory parades (Figure 8-6). There is no doubt that emotions run high at these modern versions of the triumph as spectators hail their conquering heroes. The parades establish a common bond between spectators and participants, achieving that magical moving encounter. One reporter at the Raptors' parade noted the following.

> The atmosphere was simply electric. Everyone was grinning like mad. Everyone was feeling part of something big. Canada's 150th birthday was a church tea compared with this blowout.... Packs of whooping young dudes spilled out of the subway stations into the streets. About half of the city's school children seem to have played hooky. Old folks, toddlers, teenaged girls in ripped jeans, businesswomen in heels—everyone was wearing some article of Raptors merchandise in black, purple, red or grey.... Not just the whole city, but the whole country came together over the Raptors.... Sometimes, people say Canada has no personality, no identity. It is merely a hotel country—a comfortable place to live, nothing more. That seemed foolish and cynical amid Monday's happy madness. Whatever their origins and differences, all hearts were as one on the streets of Toronto, united in pride and jubilation. For a day at least, we were family. It was a sublime feeling. Let's hold onto it.[30]

Victory parades are not limited to sports or the military. New York's Canyon of Heroes, mentioned in Chapter Two, has seen ticker tape parades for modern heroes such as aviator Charles Lindbergh following his solo transatlantic flight, explorer Rear Admiral Richard Byrd following his expedition to Antarctica, politician Winston Churchill, religious leader Pope John Paul II, and astronaut John Glenn. Since 1886, there have been 206 such parades.

Figure 8-6: Spectators at the Toronto Raptors Victory Parade (photograph by Andrew Scheer, CC0 1.0).

At this point it's fair to say that the concept of the traditional hero's journey is clear. What may not be so clear is the notion that the journey also mirrors the trajectory of our own lives. We subconsciously want to be like the hero, able to overcome the challenges along the circuitous path that is our real life, in order to become successful and to become better human beings. That's why we attend such parades.

The problem with all these hero figures, including celebrities, is that they are flawed (except for Christ). In the case of mythical and fictional heroes, their characters are purposely flawed in some manner in their creation. They are vengeful, lustful, arrogant, proud, greedy, or all of these. Why? Because like real humans, they operate in a morally grey area (e.g., should the hero kill one person to save many?) Writer Laura Studarus says succinctly, "Perhaps it's a worldview we're hardwired into.... In flawed heroes exists a noble version of ourselves—willing to go the extra mile, willing to make the right choice, regardless of the personal cost, even if it may take some cajoling to get there."[31]

Real-life heroes are flawed from birth, thanks to the phenomenon known as concupiscence, the propensity of humans to transgress divine law (i.e., sin). The crusaders, along with Saladin and Cortés, all mentioned previously, were prime examples. While honored as heroes, they were ruthless conquerors, no matter to which side of history one might ascribe, and would just as easily slit your throat as give an inch. Cortés, for one, was hated both by his leaders (for disobedience) and by the Aztecs (for treachery). Not only that, but he was a selfish, manipulative adulterer to boot.[32] Neither he nor any of the others were truly worthy of being emulated on the personal level.

The question that thus confronts us is that if we enjoy relating to heroes and may indeed have moving encounters with them, as in a parade, how should we treat them? My answer is simple—and some readers may disagree, but that is their right. Emulating heroes may be of questionable benefit because of the moral implications, but they can and should be appreciated for their lofty goals and perseverance and for what has allowed them to successfully complete the hero's journey.

NINE

Marching for Change

U.S. Army General Douglas MacArthur was known for the saying, "Rules are made to be broken," though we seldom hear the second part of his expression, which is, "and are too often for the lazy to hide behind."[1] The full expression seems to be an incitement to break *any* rules regardless of what they stand for. But believing this should only be done with caution, because the statement has broad interpretational possibilities. Some have taken the word "rules" to mean physical or societal *barriers*, such as, for example, "handicapped people cannot climb Mt. Everest," or "a black person will never be the president of such and such company." In these cases, sure, why not break them (i.e., burst through the barriers)? Other rules like "please line up here," or "smoking only in designated areas" allow us to live less stressful lives. Simply put, not all rules are created equal.

While most people normally obey rules—sometimes begrudgingly—it is understood that doing so is for the greater good of our fellow humans. Rules accomplish two goals. First, they protect the weaker members of our society by ensuring a stable environment in which to live. Second, they keep people safe and protect us from ourselves.[2] They are successful because we are motivated by the fear of getting caught and being punished.

Like most human activities, parades need rules, both for spectators and participants. Rule governance, in fact, is a characteristic of ritual. Parades are also subject to laws, which tend to be stricter and have more substantial consequences. For example, a parade might have a rule for spectators that says, "Do not throw garbage on the parade route." There might also be a municipal law that says, "Nudity is not allowed." Disobeying the first might attract the ire of one's fellow spectators; disobeying the second might put one in jail. From here on, I am going to use rules and laws interchangeably and just call them rules.

Why We Break Rules

When it comes to parades, most people, whether participants or spectators, will obey the kinds of rules laid out for them by organizers. If they didn't, things would quickly become chaotic. With chaos, a sponsor's message will fail to be delivered and emotional connections may never be made. The parade, in other words, will be ineffective.

Today, cities have rules for parade participants. Some are quite simple, such as those for the Rose Parade in Pasadena, California, which state, among other things, "every inch of every float must be covered with flowers or other natural materials, such as leaves, seeds or bark."[3] There are also rules for marching bands and equestrian units. Other parades have rules covering permits. Rules covering security. Rules covering behavior. The list goes on. The New Orleans City Council has more than 45 pages of regulations for the conduct of the annual Mardi Gras Parade(s) in their city.[4]

But rules don't stop with participants. There are both written and unwritten rules for spectators. They are great examples of "protecting us from ourselves" in order to have a more positive experience. For the Rose Parade, the City of Pasadena has promulgated a list of 23 Safety Tips for spectators. New Orleans has a set of mostly informal rules.

- Personal effects must be six feet from the curb
- No "saving" spots
- Don't move other people's stuff
- Don't interfere with the parade
- No nudity
- No glass containers
- Plan wisely for transportation and parking
- Respect the authority.[5]

Most of these are just common sense, but they bear putting in writing because, unfortunately, common sense is not as common as it should be. In society at large, some will choose to occasionally break rules, and the connections and sense of belonging that we spoke of in the Introduction will be fulfilled for them by taking this action.

For those so inclined, there are parades which do exactly that, provide a form of comfort and, dare it be said, exhilaration, in disobedience. I am talking specifically about protest marches and carnival parades.

These are two sides of the same coin. Protests seek to right social injustices; carnivals seek to free individuals from moral slavery, if only temporarily. Protest marches encourage a person (occasionally) to break civil law or other rules; carnival parades encourage a person (occasionally) to break their own or society's moral code (i.e., whatever happens in Vegas stays in Vegas).

Who, then, is inclined to break the kinds of rules we are talking about for protest marches and carnival parades, and why? The short answer to the first part of the question is all of us, at least at some time or other, and to the second part, it depends.

Having a moral code is the first hurdle to breaking rules and the real problem arises when we try to differentiate right from wrong. Today's western society is awash in moral ambiguity, thanks to the rise of humanism, the belief that an individual creates their own moral code as opposed to being forced to follow religious teachings. Without a gold or absolute standard of morality, breaking rules becomes easier, especially easier on the conscience.[6]

More than anything, social and situational forces are really what drive our decisions. In fact, there appear to be five factors that affect how we will behave.[7]

The first is creativity. The more creative one is, the easier it is to concoct a believable defense for breaking a rule, which seems to be particularly applicable to criminals.[8]

The second is what is known as a *cheater's high*. This is a feeling of euphoria provided by the sense of accomplishment at having dodged the rules.[9] It is likely also the reason why the threat of getting caught in a compromising situation can be a huge turn-on for sex, thanks to the flood of survival-mode stress hormones to the brain.[10]

The third is status. "The more people care about power and winning, and the more they feel threatened by competition, the faster their values fall to the wayside."[11]

The fourth is bonding. Bonding ties us to one or more social groups with whom we feel connected, a tribe if you will—females, scientists, musicians, lovers of Starbucks coffee, etc. You will do what your tribe does. "If your tribe downloads pirated music, cheats on tests, sells dubious stocks, flouts the no-smoking ban, or accepts bribes, then you're likely to go with the flow or at least cover up for peers."[12] Bonding is also known as our *social identity*, or "that part of a person's self-concept that relates to his or her awareness of belonging to a specific group or category and that has a certain value and emotional meaning."[13]

The last factor affecting how we behave with respect to rules is fairness. This is the thinking that leads to, "If they can get away with it, why can't I?" Typical of the kind of people who fall into this thinking are those who believe themselves to be entitled. In a study done for Cornell University, it was found that "entitled people do not follow instructions because they would rather take a loss themselves than agree to something unfair."[14]

Crowd Psychology

If rule-breakers join with enough other rule-breakers, they become a crowd, and crowds have their own psychology.

Parade audiences are considered to be crowds, whether or not they are rule-breakers, and for most parades they are *passive*. The audience members watch the parade and follow the rules of good social behavior that are either written down or expected, as mentioned earlier. However, for protest marches and carnival parades, the audiences usually begin as passive but at any moment could transform into *active* crowds or mobs, in essence becoming rule-breakers and changing from spectators into participants.[15] Active crowds can be: aggressive (violent and outwardly focused); escapist (panicked people trying to escape a danger); acquisitive (desperate people fighting for limited resources); or expressive (any other group gathering for an active purpose).[16] Protest marches and carnival parades fall into this latter category. Protest marches, especially, have the potential to incite spectators to join and possibly become aggressive.

What is it about the crowd that would entice someone to change from passive spectator to active participant? We have already discussed the type of *individual* who would be so inclined, so there must be something about the crowd itself that would act as a catalyst. I believe it is the fact that they engender bonding and a sense of belonging that are so important for people to get their emotional fixes. In crowds, people take on the *collective identity* of the group. "Collective identity is a learning process that leads to the formation ... of a social movement.... Collective identity concerns shared beliefs."[17] One fairly recent theory on crowd behavior called *deindividuation*, "argues that in typical crowd situations, factors such as anonymity, group unity, and arousal can weaken personal controls (e.g., guilt, shame, self-evaluating behavior) by distancing people from their personal identities and reducing their concern for social evaluation. This lack of restraint increases individual sensitivity to the environment and lessens rational forethought, which can lead to antisocial behavior."[18] This is akin to "The Devil made me do it" excuse—also called *disinhibition*—and is ultimately applicable for the parades we are talking about.

There we have it. A great many people are morally confused and, given the opportunity to flout rules, especially if they are in a crowd, will probably do so. When it comes to parades, these opportunities present themselves in protest marches and carnival parades, occasionally as spectators but most often as participants.

Protest marches and carnival parades are the two types of parades in which the line between spectator and participant is often blurred. There is more likelihood that spectators, moved by the *communitas* of the moment and a sense of belonging to the collective identity, will subdue their normal persona of reticence and join in the parade. In fact, the very nature of these parades in that they are *by* the people and *for* the people, effectively demands that the two—spectator and participant—become one.

I will deal with carnival parades in the next chapter; the remainder of this one is devoted to protest marches.

Literally marching for a cause (i.e., a protest), however, is not for everybody. Although moral outrage and anger may abound in all or parts of a populace, it is generally not until a significant number of the silent majority can successfully identify with the cause that they will take action. This is called a *tipping point*.[19] Even when this point is reached, a proportion of the population will probably not make a show of disobedience. "According to the World Values Survey, fewer than one in five citizens of North America, Western Europe, Australia, and New Zealand report having participated in a political demonstration; more than a third say they would 'never' do so."[20] More about this later.

Historical Examples of Protest Marches

Protest marches are not what we think of when we think of parades. They are loosely organized, non-homogeneous, moving gatherings of like-minded people. There is not much in the way of ritually meaningful components within them or ceremonies at either end of them. There is some, of course, if we can realistically call them rituals: the trite symbology of crude, homemade signs; the performance of rudimentary chants and rhythms; the "ceremony" of politically charged views spoken over cranky microphones. They are social statements that scream "LISTEN TO US!" in their nescience and homage to the common person. Most begin peacefully; many end catastrophically. Their record of achieving their goals, usually seen as the instigation of social change, is spotty. The ones that do succeed tend to be the ones that are repeated, that have put thought into organization, that are very large, that have a silent majority of the populace on their side, and that have a sympathetic ear from some or all of those in power. Disruption to everyday life is one of the useful tools in their toolbox, as is the breaking of laws (e.g., ignoring curfews, blocking rights of way, and occasionally fighting and looting, although these last two are usually not intentional, at least at the beginning). For those participating or spectating, the experience can be emotionally stirring.

Protest marches have a long history, and this section is only going to give a very brief overview of a handful of the most famous.

In the 12th century BCE, toward the end of the New Kingdom in ancient Egypt, the most favored of state employees, the tomb-builders and artisans of the Royal Necropolis in the Valley of the Kings, went on strike. This was the earliest recorded strike in history and likely the first recorded protest march. With food rations and wages nearly three weeks overdue, they marched en masse from their village of Deir el Medina on the west bank of the Nile, shouting, "We're hungry!" and temporarily invaded the sacred enclosure surrounding the king's [Ramesses III] mortuary temple.[21] Several months, sit-ins, and demonstrations later, they finally won their back wages, but regular strike action continued as the New Kingdom slid slowly into decline. Although an active crowd, this protest did not tip them over into an aggressive one.

Even ancient Rome had its problems. "We have not kept our women individually under control, we now dread them collectively," said Cato the Elder, as women took to the streets of Rome in 195 BCE. Their march was in protest to laws forbidding women to wear fine dresses and excessive gold jewelry, which at the time was important for them since it exhibited their social status. From far and wide they streamed into the city and blocked streets and approaches to the forum. They even did the unthinkable in a patriarchal society—"approached and urged men, consuls and officials for their support and votes."[22] In their day, this would have been an instance of breaking a social norm. They were successful in their efforts and the *lex Oppia*, the offending law, was repealed. Once again, the crowd remained active expressive, which helped them achieve their goal.

In late Middle Age Europe, peasant revolts occurred in several countries as a result of the socio-economic and political tensions generated by the Black Death pandemic in the 1340s, coupled with high taxes. Most of the revolts expressed the desire of serfs to share in the wealth, status, and well-being of those more fortunate. They almost always ended badly with the nobles defeating the peasants. One representative, famous example was the Peasant's Revolt in England, especially that in London. On June 13, 1381, a massed group of rebels entered London where they attacked jails, destroyed a palace, and burned books and other buildings. The next day they marched to the east end of the city where they met with the then 14-year-old King Richard II (see color insert Figure 9-1). He acceded to most of their demands, including the abolition of serfdom. This would have been a fitting and historically significant end to the revolt but thanks to lack of organization, similar uprisings continued in London and southeastern England. This led to the deaths of many royal officials and the eventual defeat of the rebels and their execution, as well as repeal of the law to end serfdom.[23] This was a good example of a protest march that had the wrong intentions to begin. The participants formed an active aggressive crowd whose purpose was to use violence as the way to succeed.

Moving forward several hundred years, we start to see protests aimed at achieving equal rights for all peoples within democracies instead of monarchies. One of the early ones was women's suffrage.

The first women's suffrage protest march in the United States was held in Washington, D.C., on March 3, 1913. It was an excellent case in point of how spectators could be incited to break social norms by taking advantage of the anonymity of the crowd.

The procession began late, but all went well for the first few blocks. Soon, however, the crowds—mostly men in town for the inauguration of Woodrow Wilson the following day—surged into the street, making it almost impossible for the marchers to pass. Occasionally only a single file could move forward. Women were jeered, tripped, grabbed, shoved, and many heard "indecent epithets" and "barnyard conversation." Instead of protecting the parade, the police "seemed to enjoy all the ribald jokes and laughter, and part participated in them." One policeman remarked that the women should stay at home where they belonged. The men in the procession heard shouts of "Henpecko" and "Where are your skirts?" As one witness explained, "There was a sort of spirit of levity connected with the crowd. They did not regard the affair very seriously."[24]

Worth noting is the statement that there was a spirit of "levity" within the crowd. This meant they had connected with each other and felt a sense of belonging. They did not, in other words, identify with the participants but with other spectators who broke rules. Women's suffrage was finally won in the United States in 1920, thanks in no small part to these marches but also to the work contributed to the World War I effort by women.

Shortly after, the fight for equality with men took an unexpected twist. At this time, smoking was considered inappropriate for women, even immoral. Cigarettes were perceived as props for prostitutes. As women began to take the jobs of men who were fighting in World War I, they also began to smoke, thus challenging social norms in an effort to gain equal rights. Eventually, this defiant act turned the cigarette into a symbol of rebellious independence and sexual allure. It did not take long for cigarette companies to understand the profit potential. In 1928, George Washington Hill, the president of the American Tobacco Company, hired public relations expert Edward Bernays to help recruit women smokers. Bernays came up with a brilliant scheme. He paid women to smoke their "torches of freedom" as they walked in the 1929 Easter Sunday parade in New York. The event was seen as a protest march for equality and became an instant newsworthy item around the world. Cigarette sales boomed, going from 5 percent sold to women in 1923 to 18 percent by 1935, and they continued to grow.[25]

The template for modern peaceful civil disobedience was the *satyagraha*, a nonviolent resistance focusing on truth and love, initiated by Indian lawyer and anti-colonial nationalist Mohandas Karamchand (Mahatma) Gandhi. He first rose to fame when he led the famous 24-day Salt March or Salt Satyagraha from Sabarmati Ashram to Dandi on the northwest coast of India in 1930 (Figure 9-2). The march was to protest Indian salt laws that were established during colonial rule. These laws taxed salt produced in India so that inferior-quality salt produced in Britain could be imported and sold more cheaply. With 78 volunteers, mostly young men, all clad in white *khadis* (hand-woven cloth), Ghandi, at 61 years of age, and his followers marched about 10 miles a day. All along the route in every village, the marchers were greeted by tens of thousands of sympathetic onlookers. They were followed by the international press and soon word of the march spread all over the world. When they reached their destination on April 6, 1930, Ghandi famously raised a lump of salty mud and declared, "With this, I am shaking the foundations of the British Empire."[26] He then boiled it in seawater, producing illegal salt. He implored his thousands of followers to likewise begin making salt along the seashore, "wherever it is convenient" and to instruct villagers in making illegal, but necessary, salt.[27] He continued his march south to the Dharasana

Figure 9-2: Gandhi leading the famous 1930 Salt March. This peaceful resistance was part of Gandhi's Non-violent opposition to British rule in India (Photo: akg-images / World History Archive).

Salt Works where another protest against British rule was planned but Ghandi was arrested and imprisoned before it began. He was released about a year after the action at Dharasana had drawn worldwide attention and more satyagrahas had been staged.

Although the march innocuously protested the salt tax, it was actually aimed at eliminating British rule, and the Civil Disobedience Movement in India needed a strong inauguration that would inspire more people to follow Gandhi's example. His satyagraha would be used in many demonstrations that would follow throughout the 20th century. It strongly influenced Martin Luther King.

On August 28, 1963, the full impact of that influence was felt as King led more than 200,000 people in the March on Washington for Jobs and Freedom that culminated with his famous "I have a dream" speech. The march was a major part of the American civil rights movement that aimed to end racial discrimination in voting, jobs, and marriage. The movement, taking its cue from Gandhi, advocated for nonviolent action. The march was two years in the planning and thanks to this, was accomplished almost flawlessly. More than 2000 buses, 21 chartered trains, 10 chartered airliners, and uncounted cars converged on Washington on August 28.[28] All regularly scheduled planes, trains, and buses were also filled to capacity.[29] Thousands of professionally made signs were provided for participants, most of whom were conservatively attired. The march took place on the National Mall. Participants marched from the Washington Monument to the Lincoln Memorial, where various musicians performed and speeches were made, with King's being the last. The march provided an outstanding example of moving encounters and the sense of belonging for participants. Some first-hand comments bear witness.

• "You couldn't help but get swept up in the feeling of the March. It was an incredible experience of this mass of humanity with one mind moving down the street. It was like being part of a glacier. You could feel the sense of collective will and effort in the air."[30]

• "You could see nothing but this landscape of people, nothing but people. It was really incredible. We were giddy. I can remember it."[31]

• "For me, and so many others, the event itself was redemptive and personally transforming.... It was as if a Norman Rockwell painting had come alive."[32]

The march was arguably considered a defining moment for black activism. It was credited with propelling the U.S. government into action on civil rights, creating political momentum for the Civil Rights Act of 1964 and the Voting Rights Act of 1965.[33] It became an improved template for protest marches of the future. However, it could have gone another way, had things not been so well organized.

"The Washington, D.C., police forces were mobilized to full capacity for the march, including reserve officers and deputized firefighters. A total of fifty-nine hundred police officers were on duty. The government mustered two thousand men from the National Guard and brought in three thousand outside soldiers to join the one thousand already stationed in the area. These additional soldiers were flown in on helicopters from bases in Virginia and North Carolina. The Pentagon readied nineteen thousand troops in the suburbs. All of the forces involved were prepared to implement a coordinated conflict strategy named 'Operation Steep Hill.'"[34]

Fortunately, these forces did not have to work that day. This mobilization does prove, though, how concerned officials can get over the threat of anarchy.

This fear of anarchy was nowhere more prevalent than in the totalitarian regime of communist China in 1989. Heads butted between the regime and student protesters who were calling for greater accountability, constitutional due process, democracy, freedom of the press, and freedom of speech. They were inspired by the Chinese elite intellectual community and other people-power movements occurring around the world at that time. Small protests in 1986 began the movement, which blossomed into serious civil disobedience upon the death of Communist Party General secretary Hu Yaobang, considered a sympathizer to the democratic cause, in mid–April 1989. On the night of April 17, 3000 Peking University students marched from the campus towards Tiananmen Square, and soon nearly 1000 students from Tsinghua University joined them. On April 27, in response to a *People's Daily* editorial that branded the protests as anti-government, some 100,000, banner-waving students from all Beijing universities marched through the streets of the capital to Tiananmen Square, breaking through lines set up by police, and receiving widespread public support along the way.[35] Another massed march of more than 100,000 occurred on May 4 (see color insert Figure 9-3). From then until early June, Tiananmen Square remained peacefully occupied, sometimes with what estimates claimed to be as many as a million or more people. The government, trying to save face, declared martial law and on June 3 the army's tanks rolled down Chang'an Avenue toward the square, killing thousands of protesters and civilians along the way. By June 5 the protests were over, but as a symbolic exclamation point, a single protester defiantly faced down a column of tanks on Chang'an Avenue. His brave stand was immortalized in a press photo. It seemed to be silently saying, "We were here. We marched for freedom, and even though we did not succeed this time, we will eventually."

Like the London Peasant's Revolt, Tiananmen might have ended successfully were it not for poor organization, lack of skilled leadership, and knowing when to quit. When one studies the sequence of events for Tiananmen and other protests, there are obvious small windows of opportunity that could have allowed for meaningful dialogue or that should have indicated the time was right for pausing protest action. The fact that this did not happen is an indication that the sense of belonging and connection that I have been discussing may have gotten out of hand. Could the propensity to break rules really have led to caution being thrown to the wind in favor of an entitlement mentality and a continuous fix of emotional highs through disobedience? While I have no empirical proof, I suggest that this may well have been the case—and continues to be the case today.

Protest Marches in the 21st Century

Since the turn of the century, the face of protest marches and of protesters has changed.

Fifty or 60 years ago, a large protest was an unusual event. However, since 2000, the number and size of protests globally have increased exponentially. Between 2010 and 2020, there were at least 900 protests around the world with more than 10,000 participants. Since 2016, there have been at least 10 mass protests with well over a million participants.[36] In 2019, more protests were recogized as occurring than at any other time in history, and between 2009 and 2019, mass protests increased annually by an average of 11.5 percent.[37]

Protests have been for a variety of reasons.

Political reform is one of the most prevalent reasons. Under this would come the Arab Spring series of Middle East protests. It began in 2010 starting with protests in Tunisia in response to oppressive regimes and a low standard of living, then spread to another 17 countries. Of all the protests, only the one in Tunisia resulted in a lasting solution that brought in a constitutional democracy, but as a result of all the protests, more than 61,000 people paid with their lives.

Likewise, protests in Hong Kong against the heavy hand of the Chinese Communist regime have continued to foment since 2014 as the Chinese government has increasingly taken away more democratic rights. Similar protests have sprung up in dozens of countries around the globe.

Equality has always been at the forefront of protest march reasons. Recent years have provided numerous examples of two of the most prevalent forms—equality of race and equality of sex, or as some may prefer, gender. Racial equality and treatment have been a part of the national culture in the United States in particular, for more than a century. Coming in waves of protests and tensions beginning in 1919, the race question has never been far from the surface of daily life.[38] The latest protest in 2020, the largest one ever, with up to an estimated 26 million participants in more than 60 countries, was a Black Lives Matter (BLM) movement in protest against the murder of civilian George Floyd at the hands of police in Minneapolis, Minnesota, USA. The

BLM movement began in 2013 to advocate against violence towards black people. The 2020 protest morphed into a general, ongoing protest against racism in many countries, for what are now known as BIPOC (Black, Indigenous, and People of Color).

Sexual equality, also known by the more familiar term feminism, has been with us since the days of the suffragists, who were mentioned earlier. Although that movement attained the right to vote for women, there was still a lot more to do to achieve equality with men. The path to this goal took an interesting turn in 1968 in a protest that provides a humorous story. In the summer of that year, a handful of women marched in protest on the boardwalk in Atlantic City, New Jersey, USA, against the Miss America Beauty Pageant and its objectification of women. In their press release inviting women to participate, the organizers said that "the protest would feature a 'freedom trash can' into which women could throw away all the physical manifestations of women's oppression, such as 'bras, girdles, curlers, false eyelashes, wigs, and representative issues of *Cosmopolitan, Ladies' Home Journal, Family Circle*, etc.'"[39] This seemed innocent enough until the press got hold of it and erroneously stated that the contents of the trash can would be burned, giving rise to "one of the great misrepresentations of the women's liberation movement [i.e., burning of bras]." But the image had already been implanted in the public's mind—and it got lots of attention. Although this minor protest did nothing to change the Miss America Pageant at that time, it did manage to propel the fledgling Women's Liberation Movement into the public's consciousness.[40] The movement continues today with recent iterations such as: the March for Women's Lives with more than a million participants in 2004, advocating for abortion and reproductive healthcare rights; the 2017 and 2018 Women's Marches, prompted by what some considered to be misogynistic comments by the then U.S. president, Donald Trump, and advocating for a general list of rights for women, LGBTQ, disabled, different races, religion, and others; and the #MeToo Movement, a global protest against sexual harassment and abuse of women.

One other subject that has been simmering along since the first Earth Day in 1970, is environmental protection and climate change.[41] Thanks to seven major reports by the United Nations Intergovernmental Panel on Climate Change (IPCC) since 1990 assessing the science related to climate change, major world leaders are now taking the subject seriously. While these leaders have taken steps to begin to both mitigate and adapt to climate change, the cost to do so is unbelievably expensive in economic and societal terms, so debate continues. Meanwhile, protesters, particularly younger protesters such as activist Greta Thunberg from Sweden, have taken up the cause in an effort to focus on the urgency of taking corrective action. The result has been an ever-increasing number of large protests, mostly by the young who seem to be almost fully tuned in to the prospect that they will be the ones having to deal with the problems. In 2019, more than 170 countries hosted climate change protests. In the USA alone, also in 2019, monthly environmental protests rose by more than 400 percent from a year earlier. Ironically—and not unexpectedly—one of the predicted results of actual climate change such as the displacement of populations due to drought and flooding, will be *more* protests.[42] See Figure 9-4.

The sheer number of protests since 2000 inevitably begs the question as to how many have been successful, and why. The answer may be surprising. According to at least one study, of 565 civil resistance campaigns that began and ended over the past 120 years, nonviolent protests succeeded by a margin of two to one over violent

Figure 9-4: "Fridays for Future"—30,000 participants protest against climate policy in Munich, Germany (©foottoo/123RF.COM).

ones.[43] In fact, nonviolent resistance has expanded across the globe within the last 50 years thanks to Gandhi and King, and it has proven to be highly effective. Most recent protests, including those for women's rights, climate change, and even BLM—despite sensational media reports—have been nonviolent. Governments know this. It is better for them if protests fail because of violence. In fact, it has been suggested that some purposely infiltrate the protesters with violent members in order to *start* such violence so that the protest *will* fail.[44]

The root causes of protest as well as the ability of movements to remain nonviolent are both concerning. This brings us to the new face of protesters themselves. This chapter began with explanations of the type of personality that would be inclined to break rules. Indeed, such personalities would be more suitable for protests that *did* break rules, perhaps violently, but definitely for breaking lesser rules such as blocking rights of way or causing noise disturbances. We now turn to the reasons why people choose to participate in protests, rather than concentrating on their personality traits.

The first is grievances. These can be such things as "illegitimate inequality, feelings of relative deprivation, feelings of injustice, moral indignation about some state of affairs, or a suddenly imposed grievance."[45] Today, one of the root causes of protests is global youth unemployment and underemployment. More than 42 percent of the world's population is under the age of 25 and the global unemployment rate for that group has grown to almost 13 percent.[46] Since the group makes up most mass protesters, it is little wonder that any protest that promises potentially more work is going to be popular.

Another root cause is environmental stress and climate change, the consequences of which, as mentioned earlier, will be inherited by youth, so they are more invested in this cause and more likely to join their friends who feel the same way.

A third root cause is the perception of inequality and corruption. Since the 1980s, the top 0.1 percent of earners globally captured more money than the bottom 50 percent. Global corruption is on the rise and "linked to this is a crisis of confidence in major institutions around the world." In many cases, this includes established democracies.[47] Trust in government has been severely eroded and people want change.

A second reason why people choose to participate—and a root cause of protests—is social media. These have only been around since the first decade of the 21st century; they were not around for Gandhi, or King, or protesters in the 1980s—or even 1990s. They spread information to a broader range of people—and faster—than ever before. They also create networks on which individuals can discuss a protest and instantaneously spread politically activating information with perceived anonymity. Global data indicate that social media users are the most likely to show up initially at a protest. And these users are younger, more educated, and more politically engaged in general.[48]

Two more reasons for participation are efficacy and mobilization.[49] Efficacy refers to the individual's expectation that it is possible to alter conditions or policies through protest, and mobilization refers to how well the protest is organized and how easy it is to participate. Some protest organizations today are very sophisticated. Black Lives Matter and Extinction Rebellion are two examples of full-time, professional protest "machines" that are lubricated by persuasive marketing and savvy Internet and social media use. This guarantees that any potential protester will be more likely to join a cause that they know will be professionally organized, in these cases respectively, protesting violence against blacks, and climate protests. Not only that, but these organizations exchange information with others around the globe to determine the most effective, best practices for protest.[50]

The final reasons for participation are identity, emotion, and social embeddedness. Taken together, they refer to the importance a potential participant places on being a member of a protest group, in other words the social bonding discussed at the beginning of the chapter. Membership often means having a stronger identity and feeling of self-worth. This membership can generate stronger emotions than going it alone. Being embedded in a protest group allows for more information to flow amongst members, thereby making a decision to participate much easier.[51]

There is one other disturbing aspect to recent protests/protest marches. Many that end in or incorporate violence and looting are no more than riots, plain and simple, and they do a disservice to legitimate protests. The media, according to at least one expert, has been reluctant to call them riots because it brings into the open the moral degradation that I mentioned earlier or, as he put it, a "crisis of moral authority."[52] I suspect it is as much about all governments' complete inability to replace the moral gold standard by which western societies used to live, with anything that can reasonably be followed by the populace. Not to be a doomsayer, but things may get a lot worse.

To sum up, potential protesters in a contemporary setting will be drawn to physically march if they believe in a cause that affects them, if they are more connected with others via social media, if an efficient organization is running the protest in the background, and if they can achieve strong social bonding with other protesters.

There is no question that today's nonviolent mass protests can shape—and are shaping—societies more than any other type of parade.

TEN

The Lure of Carnival

Throughout history, carnival has been the social equivalent of a bad penny. It will be enthusiastically embraced for a period of time only to be restricted or eliminated for another period, with the cycle repeating itself continuously. It lives on because it is one of the few acceptable human activities that acts as a communal stress-reliever.

All carnivals, almost without exception, have incorporated—and still incorporate—a parade of some sort. Often the parade is the highlight of the carnival.

What Is Carnival?

Carnival is not—to get this out of the way at the outset—our modern notion of a midway with rides and games. Rather it is a period of time set aside each year, typically in mid- to late winter, in which social norms and boundaries no longer exist, a time when people have an opportunity to break moral and social codes.

Two main themes permeate all carnivals. The first is the removal of class barriers through masking and role reversal. Masking can involve donning no more than a basic eye or face-covering mask to as much as cavorting in a body-enveloping, elaborate costume. With these, the wearer becomes unidentifiable and free to pursue the activities of carnival with supposed impunity. The mask/costume enables the wearer to temporarily become someone else of higher or lower status, of greater or lesser morality, and even of real or imagined character; in other words, role reversal. King becomes pauper, boss becomes employee, nerd becomes superhero, priest becomes village drunk, prostitute becomes nun, and vice versa for all.

The second theme is one of hedonism. It was—and still is—believed that for the period of carnival, gluttony, drunkenness, and licentious behavior were morally and socially acceptable. Part of the reasoning, in the case of medieval carnivals when Christianity provided a moral gold standard, was that they were a last hurrah before Lent in which confessions of one's sins had to be made to obtain forgiveness and pave the way to eternal life. In other words, party now and ask forgiveness later.

To sum up what carnival is, one of the world's foremost authorities on the subject, Mikhail Bakhtin, compared it to theater.

> In fact, carnival does not know footlights, in the sense that it does not acknowledge any distinction between actors and spectators.... Carnival is not a spectacle seen by the people; they live in it, and everyone participates because its very idea embraces all the people. While carnival lasts, there is no other life outside it. During carnival time life is subject

only to its laws, that is, the laws of its own freedom. It has a universal spirit; it is a special condition of the entire world, of the world's revival and renewal, in which all take part.[1]

I have to interject here, though, a personal and skeptical view of the amount of scholarly ink that has been spilled trying to prove the origins of carnival and the inclusion of these two themes. This is because the two themes are not *purposely* made a part of carnival; they are ubiquitous in all societies regardless of the festival or celebration or lack thereof. Here is a case in point. When I was in the military for my first career, without exception at every posting I had there was at least one day per year when roles were reversed. The highest-ranking officer switched places with the lowest-ranking enlisted man/woman, including switching uniforms. There was no aforethought that this little ritual had a history of any sort. Neither did it unleash the hounds of misrule. It was done purely and simply to increase bonding.

Likewise, with hedonism. This is, as I have mentioned before, no more than the propensity of humans towards concupiscence. It will happen whenever and wherever the opportunity presents itself. Was there a conscious decision at some point ages ago when a carnival celebration was initiated to include this? Possibly. More often than not, however, I posit that it became part of such a celebration not because of any relationship to ancient rites but because there was a party going on. Certainly, there are uncountable parties per year around the world where this occurs; they are just not publicly acknowledged. It's all just a question of which came first, the carnival or the role reversal, the carnival or the hedonism.

How and where did carnival originate? There are two evolutionary theories. One is that it emerged as a result of a complex series of mutations from the fertility celebrations of early and classic civilizations. The other is that it began later in the Middle Ages and emanated from pre–Lenten Christian holidays. I believe it was a combination of the two. But let's go back in time and try to trace just what happened.

A Brief History of Carnival Parades

Carnival-like activities have been documented as far back as the Mesopotamians in the 22nd century BCE (on cylinders written in cuneiform from the city-state of Lagash) and the Persians in the seventh century BCE (with a festival called the Sacaea).[2] However, details are scarce and interpretations varied, so they cannot be reliably considered as forerunners.

Things do get interesting, though, in ancient Greece, beginning around the sixth century BCE when descriptions of the Dionysia start appearing. The procession of the Great Dionysia (see also Chapter Six) took place in mid- to late March, the beginning of spring. Although it was a springtime fertility celebration, the timing also represented the beginning of the sailing season, and in Athens, a port city, it was thus designed to attract merchants and foreign visitors. It was an early example of a parade partly staged for tourism.

The main procession or *pompē* included a large wooden statue of Dionysus, cattle for sacrifice and phalloi (both of which were probably brought from allied cities and might have numbered in the hundreds), large loaves of bread, wine, weapons, displays of gold-spun clothing and gold jewelry in woven baskets, more than 150 dancers, more than 1000 actors and singers in ornate costumes, and up to 500 men carrying gold and silver tribute money.[3] The procession ended at the Theater of Dionysus where *dithyrambic* competitions were held.[4]

There was much more to this procession than meets the eye. It was far from being a somber affair, but more an ebullient burst of creativity and interactive nonsense focused on the dozens—or more likely hundreds—of large phalloi being carried by choruses consisting of 12–50 singers, actors, and dancers each, often masked or costumed as satyrs or *silenoi*, who came from the allied cities in the surrounding area. Likely there were also costumed maenads or female followers of Dionysus.[5] Using depictions of the parade on Greek vases of the period, Eric Csapo has determined that there were all manner of phalloi, varying in size and shape, some of which were so large as to need wagons to transport them. There were even individual clowns sporting a variety of phalloi just about everywhere on their person save the most obvious place (e.g., from their foreheads, noses, shoulders, etc.). Csapo has further calculated that there were at least 3000 phallus-carrying participants.[6]

Inspired by the fact that the erect penis was the symbol for the divine madness inflicted on the Athenians by Dionysus, and which excused licentious behavior, one can imagine the chaos of this wild procession. Erect penises, some so large that they were ridden (see color insert Figure 10-1), or carried by 15 or more men, would move helter-skelter along the procession route and interact with the crowd, sometimes quite aggressively, all to a background of lively music, dancing, and singing. No doubt a goodly amount of wine lubricated participants and spectators alike, further reducing inhibitions and emotionally connecting them. It would have been, more than anything, a grand exercise in physical comedy. That things could get out of hand is apparent in reports that armed guards were deployed in order to prevent riots.[7] The procession itself probably contained as many as 8000 participants and spectators could have numbered 200,000 or more.[8]

Some scholars have suggested that most of the ribald, drunken behavior occurred at a smaller uncontrolled, torchlight parade through the streets in the evening after the main pompē, but no well-researched, legitimate references are available. Likewise, there seems to be little valid study that proves any sort of role reversal as part of the Greater Dionysia, although there is a suggestion that the maenad, in that she was also a hunter, usurped the role of the male, thus putting her in a position of authority.[9]

Today, smaller versions of the Dionysia still exist—or more appropriately have been reborn—in Greece and Japan. In Athens and the Greek town of Tyrnavos, revelers dress up in phallic costumes and parade in similar fashion to the ancient Dionysia. In Tyrnavos, whose parade is part of the Buorani Festival, penis-shaped food figures prominently. There the festival has been going on since 1898.[10] In Japan, the Shinto Kanamara Matsuri (Festival of the Steel Phallus) is held each spring in Kawasaki near the Kanayama Shrine. Three giant enshrined penises are paraded through the streets, carried on palanquins (Figure 10-2). The origins of the festival can be traced back to the 17th century. The shrine has long been a place where couples have prayed for fertility and marital harmony. The phallus is glorified and loved in this setting as a symbol of creation.[11] This festival is not as wild as the Dionysian resurrections in Greece.

By the late third century BCE, the worship of Dionysus had migrated to Italy and Rome.[12] There it gathered steam as a libertine celebration called the Bacchanalia,

Figure 10-2: Kanamara Matsuri in Japan. A phallus is being paraded (©Brandon Fike/123RF.COM).

after the god Bacchus, the Roman version of Dionysus. It was said to have been started, according to Livy, "under the inspiration of a priestess, Paculla Annia, a native of Campania, who introduced men into what hitherto had been an exclusively female ritual, and altered the time of the celebration of the rites from the day to the night. It was then that licence and debauchery became rife at the nocturnal orgies held five times every month instead of three times a year. So contagious was the Bacchanalian frenzy that it spread rapidly throughout Italy, and even those of noble birth did not hesitate to embrace the esoteric movement."[13]

However, in 187 BCE, a ritual involving both men and women got out of hand one night in a wooden grove beside the Tiber River. According to sources, allegations of illicit heterosexual and homosexual behavior, as well as murder, were made. The Senate was extremely concerned, and widespread limitations on the rituals were imposed, although according to one scholar, it would have been next to impossible for them to not know that this ritual had probably been going on for some time prior to 187.[14] It was from about this time that the writer Livy believed that the seeds of moral decline were sown in the Republic. Since the Bacchanalia was conducted in private and at night, there was no known public parade, and thus little clear evidence that it was any sort of precursor to Carnival, other than the implicit acceptance of licentious behavior.

What does have some potential as a carnival ancestor was the Saturnalia, a Roman festival that occurred in mid–December. Again, although there was no parade, there was an emphasis on role reversal. The Saturnalia was a seven-day event dedicated to the Roman god of sowing and seed-corn. This was a joyous, though mostly private affair within households, during which social distinctions were held in abeyance, businesses were closed, and war was avoided. Gambling and feasting were encouraged. Also, gifts were exchanged, leading some to suggest it was a precursor to Christmas.[15] It is the role reversal that was the most prevalent. "Slaves were served by their masters and sat at table with them, railing at them, wearing the *pil-leus*, the badge of freedom, and clad in their master's clothes.... In the eastern provinces lots were cast for a mock king who was to exercise his rule in the role of Saturn during the festival. He performed his functions by issuing comic injunctions and behaving in a ludicrous manner, as by carrying a flute-girl on his back around the house."[16] In the lexicon of carnival, this character would later become known as the Lord of Misrule.

Between the breakdown of the Roman Empire in the fifth and sixth centuries CE and the Late Middle Ages, there is almost nothing in the way of descriptions of carnival-like activities, although some have tried to make connections.[17] Nevertheless, it was during this period that the actual word "carnival" came into use.[18] By the Late Middle Ages (1250–1500 CE), there is lots of information. For example, "on 12 March 1445, the Faculty of Theology at the University of Paris issued a letter to the bishops and chapters of France, deploring clerical behavior during seasonal festivities.

> Priests and clerks may be seen wearing masks and monstrous visages at the hours of office. They dance in the choir dressed as women, panders, or minstrels. They sing wanton songs. They eat black puddings at the horn of the altar while the celebrant is saying mass. They play at dice there. They cense with stinking smoke from the soles of old shoes. They run and leap through the church, without a blush at their own shame. Finally they drive about the town and its theaters in shabby traps and carts; and rouse the laughter of their fellows and the bystanders in infamous performances, with indecent gestures and verse scurrilous and unchaste."[19]

This obvious case of role reversal happened during the Christmas season and similar shenanigans had been going on for centuries before this. While it did look like a carryover from the Saturnalia and even spring festivals, no reliable documented evidence has been found to prove it. It was more likely a continuation of the Feast of Fools, a Middle Age Christmas tradition in which participants would elect a false Bishop, false Archbishop, or false Pope (see color insert Figure 10-3). Ecclesiastical ritual would also be parodied and higher- and lower-level clergy would change places. "The reversal of hierarchies had an explicit theological justification. 'Its legitimation ... was a line from the *Magnificat*.... He hath put down the mighty from their seat and hath exalted the humble.'"[20] The Magnificat was the prayer of the Virgin Mary during her visit to her cousin after she became pregnant. It was the proclamation that a new reign was to begin that would make all people equal: a true reason for happiness and celebration.

Although the church finally suppressed the Feast of Fools, it became immensely popular with the laity and easily spread into the streets as a secular celebration, as well as moving closer to the springtime pre–Lenten celebrations. In Dijon, France for example, in 1553,

> Several hundred uniformed fools regularly marched through the city streets, *marotte* (fool's sceptre) in hand. Elegant horse-drawn wagons followed, on which members of the company performed plays designed "to correct the bad habits of society" through faithful (and comic) public imitation. Husbands who beat their wives were special targets, being mounted in effigy on the back of an ass and led through town by "a troupe of fools disguised in hideous masks and fantastic costumes." The company was known by the name of its leader, the Mère Folle, no longer a bishop of fools but now a cross-dressed "prince of Mardi Gras."[21]

While carnival acted as a communal stress release mechanism through its inversion of political or clerical hierarchy, it also inverted sexual morality. Medieval carnival, with its elaborate and occasionally erotic masking and costuming provided ample opportunity for liaisons. As one Swiss observer to a carnival in Barcelona wrote with respect to women in masks, "They put on masks and run the streets in complete freedom [presumably this could refer to a parade].... So for more than one husband, the cuckoo sings before Spring comes."[22] A story is told of a German "married couple who, both masked, met unwittingly at Carnival time and 'indulged their sudden fancy on their way in the penumbra of a cloth-worker's shop ... and never did the hallowed joys of matrimony taste like the forbidden fruit of infidelity; at any rate so each imagined.'"[23]

Modern Carnival

Today's innumerable carnivals carry on these traditions of masking, costuming, and, frequently, questionable behavior. They are far too numerous to detail individual histories here since much can be found on the Internet. Most modern carnivals and their parades are outright sheer fun, and highly representative of their respective cultures. However, many also stray into excesses, offering—perhaps unintentionally—too much of that fun atmosphere, calling into question whether it is the hedonism that attracts tourists or the culture. They become magnets for those people inclined to break moral or social codes that we referenced early in Chapter Nine.

The immensely popular New Orleans Mardi Gras, with a history going back to the early 18th century, has had its share of problems. The early carnivals were more representative of those in the Middle Ages with extensive cross-dressing, costuming, racial mixing, and promiscuity. However, in the late 18th century this was effectively sanitized by krewes, who were "self-appointed arbiters of culture." Although their fanciful floats, costumes, and orchestrated parades proved to be a boon for tourism, there was a lack of spontaneity, so they changed course. From then until now, the krewes—themed teams of organizer/participants—added more creativity and brought in what were previously unacceptable ideas and people, including in 1999, a contingent from Playboy Enterprises who took up a balcony on Bourbon Street and helped to propel the act known as *flashing for beads* into the stratosphere. By baring their breasts (i.e., flashing), the Playboy bunnies encouraged those on parade floats to throw beads at them. "Beads and other trinkets, known as 'throws,' have been tossed from floats since as least 1910—transforming parades into a participatory experience, as spectators beg and scramble for treasure"[24] (see color insert Figure 10-4). Attempts to suppress the promiscuity failed, and to this day there continues to be sexual misbehavior amongst spectators and participants, some of whom presumably take part for no other reason than to get laid.[25]

The massive Carnival in Rio de Janeiro, Brazil, dwarfs all other such celebrations with its four-million-plus annual attendance. Its history traces back to the 19th century, with the dance form *samba* being introduced in 1917. This has become the backdrop for the elaborate floats and thousands of costumed performers that parade through the famous Sambadrome every night, as well as less formal street parades around the city. Even more blatantly obvious than those in New Orleans, the skimpy costumes and risqué dance moves can provide sexual titillation to the point that similar problems have arisen in Rio. One writer, Nicole Froio, has observed the following.

> Parading down the Marquês de Sapucaí naked or very nearly so is common practice, and it has always been this way. The "sexier" you look the better; a big butt, generous breasts and flat stomach are practically mandatory—especially for the drum queens who dance in front of the samba bands, keeping them motivated with their dancing and yes, their bodies.... Complete nudity is acceptable, sometimes desirable. But even the least revealing outfits for this position are as small as thong bikinis.... Men often feel up women as if it's nothing and kiss them against their will, because they feel they have the right to. Perhaps they consider it a joke, or an expression of their "freedom" but this behavior can escalate to something far more serious.[26]

Froio goes on to point out that sexual violence and abuse against women increase during carnival, including rapes, which in 2012, grew 24 percent over the previous year. Interestingly, in 2007 a report in Britain's *Guardian* newspaper stated that U.S. soldiers on leave from Iraq were planning to attend the carnival for "recreation," meaning sex tourism, which upset the Brazilians to no end. To them, the carnival "isn't all about sex. It is, they say, a celebration of the body, closer in spirit to the Olympics than a strip bar." One is left to wonder, then, why the government goes out of their way to distribute millions of free condoms and provide frank discussions about sexually transmitted diseases.[27]

Another of the major carnivals on the western side of the Atlantic is in Trinidad. Carnival migrated there from Europe and Africa in the 18th century. Similar to Rio, it is home to some of the most spectacular carnival costumes in the world, most of them leaving little to the imagination. Parades are fuelled by highly rhythmic *soca* and steel drum music and provocatively close dancing known as *wining*. Along with the usual excessive alcohol consumption, this has led local poet La Borde to actually refer to it as a Bacchanalia. It is a well-known fact that "'the celebrated sensuality and freedom of Carnival inspire more sexual activity.' This annual sex explosion, in Trinidad for example, creates the Carnival baby phenomenon. The Central Statistical Office reports that there is an approximately fifteen percent increase in live births, nine months post Carnival (i.e., November and December). Thus, also packaged with the Carnival season, is an exponential growth in abortion rates and STIs."[28]

Moving north, even the innocuous Quebec Winter Carnival with its creepily happy Bonhomme Carnaval (a giant, red-toqued snowman acting as the king) has had excesses. Staged in the minus 20 C mid-winter chill of Canada since 1894, and re-branded unashamedly in 1955 as a tourist attraction showcasing the French Canadian culture of the past, it has been highly successful. It has the usual inspired costumes—at least as much or as little as can comfortably be worn at those temperatures—a unique giant ice castle, and patently French Canadian sports such as a boat race across the frozen St. Lawrence River, axe-throwing, tobogganing, ice sculpture-building, snowshoeing, and skating. As well, a unique souvenir plastic trumpet, about a meter long, has found its way into carnival tradition. It's also hollow, so in addition to blaring out a single note at an ear-piercing 114 decibels, it acts as a handy container for alcohol. Thus, while there may be no serious, explicitly sexual behavior on the streets (who would want to?), there is drunkenness everywhere. Having been a visitor to the carnival a couple of times, I can attest to this fact. Indeed, there is ample evidence that drunkenness had been a problem with the earlier Mardi Gras celebrations preceding the 1894 carnival, and some hint that the well-known brothels of old Quebec were quite active at that time.[29] However, in the present day, other than a few indoor parties that occasionally get out of hand, there is nothing like the behavior that accompanies carnivals in the warmer climes of the Americas.

Quebec has a massively popular carnival parade, but in 2019 organizers tried to change its much-loved format. Scathing reviews followed. "The criticism focused on lengthy delays, choice of location and a new format where spectators waited at designated 'stations' for music, theatre and dance troupes to arrive and perform. Other reviews noted the 'sombre' costumes and makeup and the fact that the celebrated snowman was placed on the first float instead of his usual position at the parade's conclusion."[30] The message was basically, "Don't mess with the invariance of our parade—as mentioned in Chapter Six—and never take our Bonhomme from the place of honor."

Finally, looking briefly at modern carnivals in Europe, there is a noticeable difference from those of the western Atlantic which seem to "appropriate the precedent of classical Bacchanalia as a license for present excess." In contrast, some northern European Carnivals "incline more to bourgeois respectability than to dissipation or religious challenge. Eschewing all but the mildest social satire and keeping transgressive behavior well in bounds, they reinforce rather than contest the prevailing standards of morality and status."[31] If wild partying is your thing at carnivals with lots of booze and free sex, don't expect to find much in Europe—although it can be found without too much effort if one is so inclined.[32]

Mind you, Europe used to be party central. After all, it started in Greece, spread to Italy, and then throughout Europe in the Middle Ages as noted earlier. Yes, they all had their years of scandalous behavior but are much tamer now. Let's look at two examples.

In Venice, some might say the senior carnival of them all, the first use of the word "carnival" was in 1094 CE in a document issued by the then Doge (the chief of state of the Italian Republic), Vitale Falier. By the 13th century, the carnival lasted from December 26 to Ash Wednesday, a period of six weeks, but festivities began in early October, inducing the use of masking by all inhabitants. The almost continuous use of masks all year long led naturally to an abundance of profligate behavior, including by the city's most famous son, Casanova, whose liaisons in 18th-century Venice were the stuff of legend. "Bianca Mazzarotto, a historian of Venice, describes 18th century carnival as 'indescribable for its orgiastic madness' when 'all regarded themselves as equals in their heedless exuberance.'"[33]

Today it is a mere shadow of its ribald past. Reinvented in 1979, it has become famous worldwide for its beautiful, *commedia dell'arte*-styled masks. Tourists throng to see them—the estimated number of annual visitors is in the order of three million—but most of the carnival events are comparatively staid affairs. There are expensive masked costume balls and parties and numerous parades, usually around or on the Piazza San Marco. The parades are often historical re-enactments with lots of costumes and symbolism. There is an opening water parade along the Grand Canal. The water parade is watched by thousands and consists of creatively decorated boats and gondolas (how close to floats can you get?), manned by costumed gondoliers and performers. The official opening event is a water show on the Rio de Cannaregio, another main canal. It resembles a water-born Cirque with acrobats and performers on floating stages.

Further north in Germany, masking takes on different forms. Groups of fantastically costumed and masked fools skip, jump, and carouse along parade routes, teasing and scolding spectators. In some places such as Gengenbach, to become a fool requires an internship and formal job interview. Witches, like fools, seem to be prevalent in almost all the German parades. Replete with brooms and ugly, hooked-nose masks, they snatch children, only to reward them with candy, conjuring up images of Hansel and Gretel. The city of Mainz is famous for its gigantic papier-mâché characters meant to ridicule public figures. In Munich, large community organization floats full of members in themed costumes seem to dominate, as do modern dance troupes and acrobats. In Cologne, the kissing of strangers is the norm. Pretty well all the carnival parades showcase the ubiquitous German brass bands, some playing traditional march music, others preferring more modern tunes. Depending on the city, the celebration could be called Karneval, Fasching, or Fastnacht, each occurring on different dates but all meaning essentially carnival or Mardi Gras.[34]

The European audiences seem much less boisterous than their warmer counterparts in Latin America and the Caribbean, perhaps because of weather that is still very much wintry. After all, it's hard to do any *wining* (see next section on Trinidad Carnival) with a head-to-toe costume and mask that reveal not a square inch of flesh. European audiences' appreciation moves from a polite clap to more shouts and cheers when an upbeat and "poppy" band comes on the scene, but still not to the same extent as in say Rio or Trinidad. It's not that they don't love their parades; it's just that they are more inclined to go for the culture and tradition than for the party vibe. Do European audiences connect emotionally with participants? The apparent but not proven conclusion that I would posit is that yes, they do if they understand the culture, which can be rather obscure. In other words, it is more likely that local audiences will make emotional connections than foreign visitors. In the warmer parts of the Americas, the obvious party culture and relative lack of clothing means that *everybody* gets it.

But to paint all modern carnivals, especially those on the western side of the Atlantic, with the same hedonistic brush would be disingenuous. There is no question that many visitors to carnivals and parades go for this reason (i.e., to break personal/moral codes of conduct), although the exact percentage is unknown.[35] The remainder attend to experience new culture, to which I alluded in the Introduction when discussing general reasons why spectators attend parades and events.

Let's revisit the Trinidad Carnival and its parades in order to understand what this means. It is considered to be a model for numerous other carnivals throughout the Caribbean diaspora (e.g., many Caribbean carnivals and festivals in the USA, Great Britain, and Canada, plus other countries) and is the largest in the Caribbean.

The Trinidad Carnival evolved from a complex history of sociological upheaval brought about by colonization. Today it retains some of its original roots in masking (or masquerading, known in Trinidad as *mas'*), role reversal, and sexually suggestive behavior, not unlike most other carnivals everywhere. While events happen for several weeks and preparations (e.g., costume design and construction) begin well in advance, the main activities are concentrated into about a five-day period, and specifically into two main days of parades.

The first of these is called *J'Ouvert*. It is devoted to more traditional role reversal with the representation of characters arising from Trinidad's storied past, like *jab jabs, blue devils, bats, midnight robbers,* and *Dame Lorraines,* the latter being a man in a dress with enormously stuffed bosom and bottom, as one example. Apart from these characters, most participants in this loosely organized, pre-dawn parade use oil, mud, clay, body paint, and even chocolate as their costumes. This is more pure culture and less pure party.

> "Ole mas," an essential part of J'Ouvert, is street theatre. Ole mas competitions pit rival masqueraders—dressed in their own or borrowed old clothes, often incongruously composed and cryptically elaborated by a satirical placard (usually of something socially or politically topical)—against each other for the prize. Puns are a mainstay for the placards and costumes. These cheeky and clever costumes and characters often reflect public sentiment on current affairs, and also reflect Trinidadian's playful creativity (some of the other islands actually refer to us as *Trickidadians*).[36]

The second and most famous of the carnival parades is *Pretty Mas',* more pure party and less pure culture. Pretty Mas' is a competition among *bands,* which are organizations of designers, costumers, musical groups/DJs, and participants or players. There can be more than 100 of these groups who, on the final day, must parade up to 10 km and pass several judging points, the last one being a large main stage. Rules for the competition are strict and to break them can result in complete disqualification (note the relevance to rule-governance).[37]

Pretty Mas' derived from origins that focused on wearing elaborate body-enveloping costumes that represented everything from historical figures to superheroes. *Big costumes* as they are known, still exist today within bands. They are elaborate, fantasy creations that a single performer manipulates but which must be moved along the parade route with the help of small wheels because of their weight. Other previously large *individual* costumes have now become minimalist and are known generically as *Bikini and Beads* (see color insert Figure 10-5). A point of contention for some older locals is that players (participants) originally had to use their own creativity to act out the characters of their costumes, a clear form of street theater, whereas today they only "play themselves."[38]

The Bikini and Beads form of costume is a reflection of the influence of Las Vegas showgirls and the Brazilian Carioca style of attire. It has had the effect of stripping away the older form of costume to reveal the person underneath, who has now *become* the costume and who must act out however, whatever, or whoever she pleases. I use the word "she" here because the playing of mas' has now been largely overtaken by females who have adapted it as a form of freedom and empowerment.

One participant in Pretty Mas', fashion psychologist Shakaila Forbes-Bell, found her skimpy costume liberating. She said, "In the Caribbean, the woman's form is celebrated. I didn't experience the lustful looks or hear the tsking of an older person when I had more skin on show than they would have liked. My body was decorated as if it were a prize to be celebrated and being among other women, who were all dressed similarly if not the same, can heighten that freeing feeling."[39]

This type of playing for some time has also incorporated a dance form known as wining (*winin'* in the vernacular) that is done against an aural backdrop of constant soca music played at a frenetic 160 beats per minute.[40] To wine is basically to wind or grind one's hips in a circular motion. It is usually done either alone or in very close proximity to one or more other people of either sex in any and all locations along the parade route.

> Winin' ... is intimate (whether danced individually or as a couple) and collective. Facial expressions and eye contact form part of the body-dance, and, to an extent, parody it. The movements and expressions usually highlight the feelings of the person dancing. Sexuality is not part of the dynamic, even if there is a grotesque simulation of it during carnival. Sexual encounters can be initiated in verbal exchanges during the dances or right after, but the dance itself is not—despite the media misrepresentation which leads to misunderstanding on the part of many foreign tourists—a subversive dynamic linked to sexuality.[41]

Unfortunately, the subversive dynamic should not be unexpected. Participation in Pretty Mas' as a player in the present day involves joining a band, which anyone can do who has the money. This includes a basic costume which can be accessorized, food and drinks, the comfort and sense of belonging that group participation brings, and not least, paid security to prevent unwanted behavior. The paid security has become necessary because of the type of costumes and dancing, and also because of the attention sought by participants. The vernacular phrase "Watch meh nah! I is pretty!" is heard frequently and demands that the player be watched or photographed. The result sought by participants is to have their photo or video show up in mainstream or social media. Obviously, the more outrageous the performance the more likely that popularity will be gained. "It seems that *Bikini and Beads* players must choose between the possibility of being portrayed in a decontextualized, sexualized way, or being invisible and anonymous in the main carnival."[42]

What does this all mean with respect to carnival parades and rule-governance? I think mainly it highlights the enigma that has always been carnival. The historical tug-of-war between individual desire to break—or come very close to breaking—societal and personal moral codes, and the establishment's desire to remain outwardly decent and lawful, is still present. Likewise, it poses questions. Must standards of decency be sacrificed in order to attract tourist dollars? Can there ever be a middle ground, and if so, will participants still be able to make the powerful emotional connections that present-day carnivals like Trinidad's generate? Let's hope so, because today's carnival parades are some of the largest and most popular types of parades in the world, in no small part thanks to their color, portrayal of local culture, and boisterous party atmosphere.

ELEVEN

Onto the Water and Into the Air

It would be hard not to acknowledge that parades on streets have extended onto the water and into the air. Boats, ships, and aircraft, all symbolic in their own way, have their own forms of parades.[1] For boats the form of parade is known as a water procession or water parade. For ships the parade takes the form of a sailpast or ship parade, and occasionally, a unique event called a fleet review. For aircraft the form is known as a flypast, flyover, or flyby. For all of these, the main similarity when compared to land parades is linear movement. Except for aircraft aerobatic maneuvers, they all take place in only two horizontal dimensions and of course, they have a starting and ending point, often the same. The synchronous movement of these large machines can influence people as much as any land-based parade.

Water Processions and Parades

The difference between a water procession and a water parade is the same as for regular parades and processions. A water procession will usually have rituals or a ceremony at one end or the other; a water parade is done only to exhibit the boats.

Symbolically there are differences between water parade participants and land parade floats. Unless a land parade is structured as a protest march or possibly a carnival parade, there is seldom any possibility of spectators spontaneously joining it as participants. Not so with a water parade. Typically, boats of all shapes and sizes may join a water parade simply because it is exciting. Rules are usually minimal or non-existent, except for general maritime rules that should be known by all boaters, but there can be problems. In September 2020, a boat parade in Texas in support of President Donald Trump got out of control and several boats sank, thanks to lack of overall control.[2]

The mere fact that a boat is participating in any water parade or procession is symbolic in that it represents support and validation for whatever reason the event is being held. In this same way, if the spectators are also in tune with the reason for the event, then seeing a large participating contingent may in turn emotionally affect them and create a moving encounter.

One example from my own experience goes back to 1962 when the movie *Mutiny on the Bounty* was released. That summer the Canadian-built, movie replica ship, *Bounty II*, sailed into Vancouver harbor on a tour of North American west coast ports to promote the movie. I was on a small naval vessel that sailed out to greet and escort the *Bounty* as she entered the harbor. We were one of scores of boats. As one media observer wrote, "Wherever the ship goes, it is greeted with much fanfare, from the platoon of official and unofficial water craft accompanying the ship into the harbor, to the list of local dignitaries attending the official ceremonies, to the throngs of fans who are lining up to take a tour of the vessel."[3] I was personally thrilled at seeing the *Bounty* not only because I enjoyed seeing the movie but also because the ship was unusual. I had never seen an old sailing ship under sail before. Whether the tour was successful is questionable. The movie was nominated for seven Academy Awards but won none. It was the fifth highest-grossing film of 1962 but was considered a box-office flop. However, it did help to make Marlon Brando, the leading man, into a superstar.

Historically, there are numerous examples of water parades and processions, beginning in ancient Egypt. The Opet Festival procession from Chapter Six provides the first example, in which the magnificent river barge carrying the sacred statues of the gods was pulled upriver in procession to the Luxor Temple, accompanied by the pharaoh's barge and dozens of ordinary boats of the common people. There are carvings of this and other similar water processions in temples throughout Egypt.

The National Archaeological Museum in Athens holds another example, a fresco scene of boats in what appears to be a parade or procession, taken from the town of Akrotiri, on Thera (modern-day Santorini), one of the Aegean islands supporting the ancient Minoan civilization (Figure 11-1).

> Eight large ships and three smaller vessels, all powered by oarsmen, travel from one port to another with centre stage taken by the flagship of the fleet…. The scene may be a representation of a seasonal maritime festival or even a scene from a lost epic poem. The ships are decorated with flowers, butterflies, swallows, and symbols of nature which all suggest a religious festival as more likely.[4]

The town was destroyed sometime between 1650 and 1550 BCE by an earthquake, so this scene was probably older than that of the Opet Festival in Egypt. To have it recorded at all indicates that this type of water event was of great importance to the Minoans.

Water processions were popular during the Renaissance with the monarchs of the day. One particularly spectacular but little known one was the Thames River procession that transported Queen Anne Boleyn, the wife of Henry VIII, to her coronation in May 1533. Britons love their royalty, and it was no different then, when

Figure 11-1: Part of an Akrotiri ship procession circa 17th to 16th century BCE (photograph by the author).

thousands cheered Anne and her water procession as it made its way from Greenwich to the royal apartments in the Tower of London.

There were more than 300 river barges that took part, with as many as 120 being 60 to 70 feet long. All the barges, both large and small, were completely outfitted with colorful banners, streamers, and metal shields, and onboard had minstrels playing. There were separate barges for the Mayor of London and all city officials. Rules dictated that barges were to keep away from each other by at least twice the length of their own barge, with every one having an officer aboard to keep their order. In the lead barge was a "great red dragon continually moving and casting wild fire and round about the barge stood terrible monsters and wild men casting fire and making hideous noise."[5] The Mayor followed and then other barges of the various guilds and liveries. On one of these there was a live falcon sitting on a gold tree stump around which sat "virgins singing and playing sweetly."[6] After an hour the Queen's barge joined them and from there to the Tower, barges along the shoreline fired off gun salutes as they rowed by. Upon their arrival at the Tower, all the Tower's armaments were let loose. The Queen alighted and was greeted with a kiss by the King at the waterside.[7] Ironically, three short years later, Anne Boleyn awaited her execution in the same royal tower apartment in which she had awaited her coronation.[8]

The Thames has been a popular route for numerous historical processions. As examples, one was held to begin the coronation of Elizabeth I in 1559, and in 1454, another took the place of a land procession for the annual inauguration of the Lord Mayor of London. It has been held intermittently on the water ever since.

These were typical of the efforts that went into creating waterborne entertainment components as part of the land-based royal entries in the rest of Renaissance Europe, some of which were discussed in Chapter Four. Sometimes monarchs traveled by water and sometimes they watched from the shore as entertainment proceeded to unfold on the water (i.e., usually rivers). As an aside, one of the more elaborate performances was a *naumachia* or staged mock sea battle, in which great galleys with soldiers and seamen would literally battle each other. It was started by the Romans who did it in flooded arenas as a blood sport, but by the Renaissance it was not so gruesomely real.[9]

Another long-standing water procession tradition is the Royal Barge Procession that takes place on the Chao Phraya River in Bangkok, Thailand, for rare state occasions. Dating back to the 14th century CE, the last one took place in 2019 as the final ritual in the Thai King's coronation ceremony (Figure 11-2). The King and Queen traveled in the royal barge *Suphannahong*. One of the most beautiful of the four main royal barges, it has a bow resembling a mythical swan, or *hong*, adorned with gold lacquer and glass jewels, with a crystalline ball and tassel dangling from her mouth. This 46 m-long craft was carved from a single trunk of teakwood, and was launched November 13, 1911. There is a golden pavilion on board to house the king and his immediate royal family.[10]

The procession involved fifty-two ceremonial barges with twenty-two hundred oarsmen, and travelled for 3.4 kilometres. Yellow-clad spectators crowded the banks of the river hours before the event began in a show of loyalty to the King and Queen. The procession of barges was about twelve hundred metres long, and ninety metres in width. Monks at six temples along the river began chanting ceremonies for Their Majesties as the procession approached them. Officials estimated 10,700 spectators flocked to six official viewing

Figure 11-2: Part of the Royal Barges Procession, the last ceremony of the Royal Coronation Ceremony of the King, in Bangkok, Thailand, 2019 (Nopwaratch Stock / Shutterstock.com).

locations on the river banks, and millions more watched the live broadcast of the ceremony at home and abroad.[11]

No matter where or when the event, if royalty is involved, there will always be people who are emotionally attached to water processions.

National heroes can be just as popular. I discussed the land funeral procession of the Duke of Wellington in Chapter Seven and now turn to the water funeral procession of Admiral Lord Horatio Nelson, the British naval hero who vanquished Napoleon's maritime forces at the Battle of Trafalgar in 1805. Nelson died in the battle and his funeral was held a few months later in January 1806.

The first part of it consisted of a water procession that travelled upriver on the Thames from Greenwich (as with Anne Boleyn) to the Admiralty in London.

The coffin, banners and accoutrements left Greenwich at about half past eleven so that everyone could be at their stations by noon. A gun was fired from one of the boats of the River Fencibles to announce the departure of the procession. A strong south-westerly wind, gusting to gale force, made rowing difficult.... The banks of the river at Greenwich were thick with crowds, and, despite the weather, the river was thronged with boats. The barge bearing the coffin was rowed by sailors from the Victory. At the stern was a specially constructed canopy adorned with black ostrich feathers. At each corner were shields depicting the four coats of arms of the deceased.... At the bow a naval lieutenant held an enormous Union flag from the Victory. This was another potent symbol of a new sense of Britishness. The Union flag incorporating the cross of St Patrick had been introduced only after the union of the Dublin and Westminster parliaments in 1801. Bringing up the rear came the barge carrying the chief mourner with his two supporters, six assistants, four supporters of the pall and six bearers of the canopy, all admirals. Before the cabin door stood Captain Thomas Masterman Hardy of the Victory, holding a banner of emblems commemorating Nelson's victories. Immediately behind came the royal barge with the Prince of Wales and his brothers, then that of the lords commissioners of the Admiralty, the city state barge with the Lord Mayor and aldermen, and lastly the barges of the livery companies and other dignitaries.

Despite the strong wind and the occasional squally showers of sleet and snow, there were crowds of silent spectators all the way up to Westminster. The Reverend Alexander Scott, who was in the first barge, was deeply moved: "the very beggars left their stands, neglected the passing crowds, and seemed to pay tribute to his memory by a look—many did I see, tattered and on crutches, shaking their heads with plain signs of sorrow. This must be truly the unbought affection of the heart." At a quarter to three the barges arrived at Whitehall Stairs, where they were welcomed by trumpets and muffled drums, playing the death march from Handel's Saul.[12]

It is apparent from this account how emotionally moved were people of all stations in life. This is no doubt attributable to the combination of symbols used in the water procession—as in others like Anne Boleyn's—that were highly effective in their choice and placement at the right times and places. For example, the shields and coats of arms, the new Union flag, the banners chosen, the design of the canopy for the coffin, the trumpet fanfare, the muffled drums, and Handel's death march—all were staged for maximum effect (see color insert Figure 11-3).

In terms of emotional reaction, it's hard to top the final Thames water component of the 1965 funeral of Sir Winston Churchill, Britain's wartime Prime Minister. As the coffin made its way downriver, 15–20 of the Port of London's huge dockside cranes lowered their booms in succession, leading one observer to remark, "It undid us all."[13]

One modern, less formal water parade concludes this section, and that is lighted boat parades, although they are commonly and incorrectly called ship parades. In many coastal cities around the world water parades are held annually to celebrate "something." Most often this is Christmas. In Vancouver, Canada for example, my home town, there is such a parade in which small boats of all shapes and sizes, both engine- and wind-powered, for the two weeks preceding Christmas, parade nightly to one or more waterfront communities. Each boat is decorated with festive lighting and most that are large enough have onboard choirs who perform along the route. While not as spectacular as the processions already described, they are, nevertheless, a tradition to which the waterfront communities look forward. Indeed, many people have shore parties to coincide with the appearance of the carol ships as they are known. It is always a let-down when wintry weather prevents their sailing.

Sailpasts and Fleet Reviews

Sailpasts are parades of ocean-going vessels. Fleet reviews are large events, often international in scope and associated with an important date such as the anniversary of a naval force. A political VIP will review the capabilities of a nation's navy firsthand, typically from aboard a single vessel that sails amongst the navy ships.

Symbolically, sailpasts and fleet reviews are deliberately designed displays of power. Depending on who the spectators are, the emotional reaction may be different. If it is a naval review, for an enemy force it may be cautious respect; for the country presenting the display it is undoubtedly pride and nationalism. For a non-naval sailpast, such as tall ships, it might well be a sense of wonder or awe.

The great navies of the ancient Greeks and Romans with their warships propelled by multiple banks of oarsmen, would occasionally sail in a parade-type formation (i.e., a sailpast) for a populace to see. Setting sail from a port to go to battle, for example, would be a prime time for this. There is the occasional written reference. In 305–304 BCE, Demetrius I Poliorcetes, a Macedonian nobleman, military leader, and later king of Macedon (294–288 BCE), launched a siege against the mercantile island republic of Rhodes. Prior to the siege, he paraded his warships for all the Rhodians to see, a purposeful display of power, as described by the writer Diodorus Siculus.

> And so Demetrius, having drawn up his fleet as if for a naval battle in a way to inspire panic, sent forward his warships, which had on their prows the catapults for bolts three spans in length; and he had the transports for men and horses follow, towed by the ships that used oarsmen; and last of all came also the cargo-ships of the pirates and of the merchants and traders, which as we have already said, were exceedingly numerous, so that the whole space between the island and the opposite shore was seen to be filled with his vessels, which brought great fear and panic to those who were watching from the city. For the soldiers of the Rhodians, occupying their several positions on the walls, were awaiting the approach of the hostile fleet, and the old men and women were looking on from their homes, since the city is shaped like a theatre; and all, being terror-stricken at the magnitude of the fleet and the gleam of the shining armour, were not a little anxious about the final outcome.[14]

Artistic depictions of sailpasts remain scarce for anything up to modern times, although depictions of maritime warfare are plentiful. The so-called Age of Sail when windjammers and man-o'-wars plied the world's oceans for exploration, trade, and warfare between 1571 and 1862, has provided a few. Dutch artist Hendrik Cornelisz Vroom was a prolific painter of sailing ships, with several of his works depicting ships returning to or departing from ports in formations that implied sailpasts (see color insert Figure 11-4).

Today, the Age of Sail lives on in international events that exhibit re-built replicas of these magnificent ships. SAIL Amsterdam is one of the largest and features a sailpast of tall ships on the North Sea canal (Figure 11-5). A quinquennial event, the 2015 edition attracted close to three million spectators, thousands of small boats, and 44 tall ships from all over the world.[15] Even back in 1976, the United States bicentennial waterborne celebrations in New York City harbor attracted seven million people and 30,000 participating spectator craft, as well as 18 of the world's largest sailing ships. As one writer has commented on the increasing public interest in these ships, "their compelling charm is a rich mixture of beauty and romance tempered by their vulnerability to wind and water, the very elements they were built to exploit."[16]

As for sailpasts of modern or near-modern naval vessels, one of the most famous examples is the expedition of the Great White Fleet. Between 1907 and 1909, 16 battleships of the United States Navy, divided into two squadrons, circumnavigated the globe on orders from President Theodore Roosevelt. Roosevelt sought to demonstrate growing American military power and blue-water navy capability (Figure 11-6). The fleet, all painted white, sailed line astern (i.e., single file) into 28 ports around the world to the enthusiasm of thousands of onlookers.[17]

Figure 11-5: Colombian navy tall ship ARC *Gloria* participates in SAIL 2015 in the North Sea canal near Amsterdam (Photo 58253157 © VanderWolfImages | Dreamstime.com).

One final type of ship parade is a fleet review—or naval review in the United States. This is a traditional gathering of ships from a particular navy to be observed by the reigning monarch/president or his/her representative, a practice allegedly dating back to the 15th century. It is done to mark special occasions. Nowadays a fleet review often includes vessels from other countries and is called an International Fleet Review (IFR). A few examples include:

- 1415—Generally acknowledged as the first fleet review on record, by King Henry V, at Southampton, England, before sailing for his first French campaign that ended in the Battle of Agincourt
- 1700—Peter the Great's visit to England as a show of strength
- 1897—Queen Victoria's Diamond Jubilee
- 1936—Royal Australian Navy 25th birthday review
- 1953—Coronation of Queen Elizabeth II
- 1959—Opening of the Saint Lawrence Seaway, held at Montreal, Canada
- 1976—International Naval Review for the United States Bicentennial in New York City Harbor
- 2016—International Fleet Review in Visakhapatnam, India.

International Fleet Reviews are held infrequently, but when they are, they are major events. The 2016 review in India included a total of 90 ships from 50 navies, plus more than 70 aircraft. The review was aimed at assuring the country of the Indian Navy's preparedness, high morale, and discipline.[18] Fleet reviews are not like a typical ship parade in which the ships sail line astern past a shore location, but actually

Figure 11-6: The Great White Fleet at Port Said, Egypt, approaching the Mediterranean Sea, January 5–6, 1909 (Everett Collection / Shutterstock.com).

the opposite. They anchor in place in pre-arranged formations and the reviewer (e.g., monarch or president) sails through the formation on a single craft. Part of the display may include a sailpast and other military entertainment. For example, the 2016 IFR included demonstrations of the landing and capture of a beach, the firing of aircraft guns, several aerial firepower demonstrations from helicopters and fighter aircraft, as well as onshore parades and live musical and dance entertainment. A special song was even written for the occasion!

The variety and excitement of the overall military and non-military entertainment of a fleet review is a big tourist draw. While the economic impact of the 2016 IFR is unknown, other reviews have garnered large sums. A much smaller review in 2010 in Victoria, Canada was expected "to generate $8 million in direct spending and to have an overall economic impact at more than twice that much."[19]

Flypasts and Formation Flying

Noisy. Fast. Scary. People have loved displays of aircraft in flight for more than a century. Grace and beauty combined with danger is somehow uniquely attractive. When more than a single aircraft participates in a flypast, both the beauty and the danger are amplified.

The basic ingredient of a flypast is a formation. "Formation flying developed in World War I, when fighter aircraft escorted reconnaissance aircraft over enemy territory. Fighter squadrons soon discovered that fighting in pairs reduced their losses and increased their victories."[20] Also in World War I, British squadrons on the Western Front sometimes overflew their airfields after their missions so the men on the ground could count the number of surviving aircraft.[21]

A formation consists of "two or more aircraft traveling and maneuvering together in a disciplined, synchronized, predetermined manner. In a tight formation, such as is typically seen at an air show, aircraft may fly less than three feet (one meter) apart and must move in complete harmony, as if they are joined together."[22] There are five standard formations, with large numbers of aircraft simply forming larger formations out of the basic ones.

- Line abreast—side by side or wingtip to wingtip
- Line astern—like ships, nose to tail
- Echelon—angled so that one wing of the trailing aircraft is behind the opposite wing of the aircraft in front
- V or Vic—inverted-V shape with a single lead aircraft and two or more off each side as in an echelon (like a five-pin bowling setup)
- Box—A diamond shape.

The largest mass flypast in history occurred on the signing of the *Japanese Instrument of Surrender* that formally ended the war between Japan and the allied powers in Tokyo Bay on September 2, 1945. Four hundred B-29 bombers and 3000 carrier aircraft participated (Figure 11-7).[23]

A flypast like this would have been, and is, awe-inspiring, complete with all the

Figure 11-7: Surrender of Japan, September 2, 1945. Navy carrier planes fly in formation over the U.S. and British fleets in Tokyo Bay during the surrender ceremonies. USS *Missouri* where the ceremonies took place, is on the left; USS *Detroit* is on the right. (National Archives and Records Administration).

psychological effects of awe that were explained in Chapter Two. The combination of fear-inducing sound with the knowledge that these powerful machines of destruction would never again have to be used for that very purpose would have been cathartic for those viewing the 1945 flypast.

Both simple and mass formations are used these days for flypasts at funerals, unique holidays, national days, major sporting events, and other special state occasions. Most flypasts occur at altitudes above 500 ft.[24]

One formation not mentioned but that is highly emotional is the *missing man* formation. The missing man is a single aircraft that is removed from one of the basic formations, typically a Vic of five aircraft thus made into four. It is most often used at funerals of aviators. An even more emotional version is sometimes flown in which the missing man starts the flypast as part of the formation but then at the last moment rolls away.[25]

One singularly spectacular type of flypast is known as a high-speed flyby. Technically it is not a "parade in the air" like a formation, because it is usually done by one aircraft, but bears mentioning as it can literally get the adrenaline pumping in spectators. When allowed and done safely, it is a low altitude maneuver by a jet fighter that breaks the sound barrier directly as it passes the audience. There is nothing quite like seeing a jet approaching silently at more than Mach 1 (the speed of sound) with shock waves attached to its wing trailing edge surfaces. Then suddenly as it passes, the crash of the shock wave hits the crowd, blowing away tents, toupees, and other loose items. Unforgettable!

An interesting recent development that has arisen out of formation flying has to do with the saving of energy to be gained by flying in formation like geese do, usually in a Vic formation. This phenomenon has long been seen as the reason geese fly in this formation, to take advantage of the energy-saving, altered airflow in the wake of the bird ahead. Now it is actually being considered for commercial airliners in order to save fuel. We may soon see two or more jumbo jets flying together in formation across the Atlantic, or elsewhere.[26]

Aerobatic Demonstration Teams

Flypasts are now mostly carried out by a nation's one or more military aerobatic demonstration teams, although some are performed by civilian teams. What they have done is bring the exhilaration of aerobatics into flypasts. Aerobatics takes the two-dimensional level formations into a third dimension through an aircraft's ability to maneuver around three axes. They use six basic maneuvers: the loop, aileron roll, barrel roll, stall turn, snap roll, and spin.[27] Any air display by a team consists of the coordinated use of all or some of these maneuvers, thus turning a simple flypast into a three-dimensional aerial parade.

Aerobatics and aerobatic teams have a history going back more than 100 years to the first major international aviation meeting in Reims, France in 1909. Called the Grande Semaine d'Aviation de la Champagne—because it was in champagne country—it was the first time that the world realized that aviation was a viable form of transportation. It was also the first time that pilots inadvertently realized that flying close to each other would not cause them to fall from the sky. This eight-day-long, extremely popular show—it was actually a series of competitions around a fixed course—had a wet and muddy first day. Once the rain stopped, all the waiting aircraft from several countries came out for a flight. A reporter from the *London Daily Mail* newspaper made a colorful observation.

> The sky is black with airplanes.... They whirl, tack, sting, disappear and come back with insane speed and grace. They put on a spectacle unlike anything seen in the history of the world. It was certainly a fabulous spectacle, but a dangerous spectacle and it was a miracle that no aviator or spectator was killed there, for, apart from experienced pilots, there were many novices among the competitors.[28]

Without the usual restraints of flying in close proximity we have today, there were many close encounters. It's no surprise. The aileron and other control surfaces were not yet perfected. From here on, aerobatics and formation flying were only to get more impressive.

Pilots, being intrepid, adventurous souls, did not waste time in experimenting with the capability of aircraft, partly because of competition in trying to market new aircraft designs, and partly because it was a challenge, much like mountain climbing. As with a lot of early aviation firsts, it started in France.

Essential to aerobatic technique is the ability to fly an aircraft inverted (upside down), which was first demonstrated on September 1, 1913, by the Frenchman Adolphe Pégoud, a test pilot for aviator Louis Blériot.[29] Eight days later, Russian military pilot Petr Nesterov, became the first pilot to perform a loop. During World War I, with the development of successful fighter aircraft, pilots began to engage in serious aerial combat, discovering in the process that aerobatic skills could give them a significant advantage in a dogfight.[30] After that, aerobatic skills and maneuvers rapidly developed.

Following the war, a lot of pilots, especially in North America, were out of work. They became what was known as *barnstormers*, itinerant ex-military pilots with surplus combat aircraft who toured rural areas performing stunt-flying demonstrations. These demonstrations eventually morphed into *flying circuses*, which took the idea of daredevil to a whole new level. "Wing-walking, air-to-air transfers, and parachutists were the window dressing, but aerobatics were the stock-in-trade of these early air shows. New maneuvers began appearing almost weekly, as pilots competed for reputations and a bigger share of the public wallet."[31]

Meanwhile in Europe, aerobatics took a different direction. "The most proficient war pilots were employed by aircraft manufacturers, displaying their skills and the manufacturers' products at public air shows. Competitions between pilots ensued, and these led to the development of rules, notations, and judging criteria. The first and only World Cup of Aerobatics was held in Paris in June 1934, with nine entries from six countries (all European)."[32]

Both approaches, however, eventually led to the same place, the formation of aerobatic demonstration teams. In 1931, the first ever team became a reality when the forerunner of the Patrouille de France air force team gave an aerial demonstration using three Morane-Saulnier MS.230 aircraft.[33] Over the years, more air forces got on the bandwagon. There are now some 84 demonstration teams worldwide. Many of these teams put on shows lasting 20 to 40 minutes, with some accompanied by carefully chosen music, usually at public airshows.

Figure 11-8: Patrouille Acrobatique de France (French Acrobatic Patrol) flying over a Bastille Day parade in Paris (Collections École Polytechnique, photograph by J. Barande, CC BY-SA 2.0, https://creativecommons.org/licenses/by-sa/2.0/deed.en).

Like any land-based parade, these can generate a lot of emotion in both spectators and participants (display pilots). Most people attend to see the flying displays and the overwhelming favorites are the jet fighter display teams. For example, in a 2002 study, one interviewed spectator was unequivocal. "If showmanship was the criterion, I'd vote for the F-16 displays which are ten times more exciting than a bunch of aerobatics [meaning slower prop displays]. I tend to find prop stuff very boring, I like the whole spectacle of a jet display—the noise, the afterburner flame, the car alarms going off." Quoted another, "I for one KNOW I'm risking my life anytime I let a 400 mph aircraft within about half a mile of me and pointed in my direction, even if it eats dirt that instant. I would sign any waiver and consider it worthwhile. Let all the wimps listen to the news broadcasts about 'dangerous airshows' and stay at home!"[34] Unfortunately, unlike a street parade, aerobatic display team flying does produce a risk of aircraft crashes which, for a certain percentage of the public, is an attraction and even an adrenaline high. Fortunately, most attend because the teams represent a strong visible and audible symbol of power and patriotism (Figure 11-8).[35]

These emotional fixes continue to fuel this increasingly popular form of entertainment. As of 2002, there were 350 airshows held annually in the USA, entertaining more than 24 million spectators. This put them second only to major league baseball as the most popular family-type event.[36]

Throughout this book I have taken pains to demonstrate the effects of parades from the viewpoint of both spectator and participant. Therefore, to end this chapter here are some quotes which clearly explain the draw for participants in airshows, the display pilots themselves.

> There is a thrill of vulnerability at all airshows. There is no way of making everything completely safe. When the machines are being thrashed to capacity and the pilots are flying at their limits to dazzle, things are bound to go wrong sometimes. There have been some historic disasters, but the danger is a part of the attraction.
>
> —Alex James, bass player of the group Blur, and a private pilot. *Bit of a Blur* (2007).

> We contrive to make the invisible air support us, we relinquish the security of feet on the ground because flying is demanding, delightful, beautiful: because we love it. Very few of us are actually crazy, and nearly all of us manage the risks as well as we can, but we all willingly trade some of our security for the immeasurable beauty of the sky.
>
> —Paul J. Sampson, writer and pilot.

Twelve

The Modern Parade

Throughout this book, history has been a constant through-line, appearing occasionally to provide some perspective on how and why certain parades developed. Part of the reason for using history to tell the story of parades was to illustrate the ingenuity of our ancestors in crafting meaningful spectacles. It is history to which I return for this final chapter.

What is termed the Long 19th Century by historians, the period from 1750 to 1914 CE, had profound effects on parades—and the world in general. This historical period had at its core the Industrial Revolution and a concomitant social upheaval. Not only did new inventions affect parades, so did societal changes. The Contemporary Period, from 1914 to the present, was icing on the cake, especially in terms of technological changes. This chapter is about how those technological and societal changes of the past 250+ years have continued to make parades enticing and influential in our lives and societies.

To put things in perspective, I am going to have my mother make a guest appearance. She was born in 1910 in England, at the end of the Long 19th Century and nine years after the puissant Queen Victoria's reign ended. At the time of her birth, societies on both sides of the Atlantic were beginning to reap the rewards of the Industrial Revolution. For individual families, electricity was being distributed to homes for the first time. Vacuum cleaners, refrigerators, air conditioners, and washing machines, all new life-altering conveniences, were starting to be sold (although I can remember my mother using an ice box in the early years of my own childhood and not having a washing machine until the 1950s). The telephone was the hot new ticket for communication and no doubt provided endless food for gossip at afternoon teas. On a broader scale, in her lifetime she witnessed: the introduction and growth of air travel; the introduction of the automobile; the Spanish Flu pandemic; two World Wars; the Great Depression; the development of consumer still and video cameras; the birth of television and movies; humans on the moon; and the widespread use of personal computers. Although she did not live to see the 21st century, she did witness the birth of the Internet. Could there have been any time in recorded history with more astonishing changes in such a short period?

Let's take a look at how some of these affected parades.

Societal Upheaval

The Long 19th Century unquestionably laid the foundation for western culture as we know it today.

Fueled by humanist leanings of such Enlightenment polemicists as Voltaire in France, governments around the world began to undergo wrenching transformations. The separation of church and state along with the notion that man alone should be able to control his own destiny, were guiding principles.[1] Monarchies yielded to democracies in the Age of Revolution.[2] Some colonies became self-governing but kept ties with their masters. Borne of this period were the democracies of the USA (1776), France (1789), Mexico (1821), Brazil (1822), New Zealand (1853), Canada (1867), Australia (1901), and others. Near the beginning of the subsequent Contemporary Period, some societies chose a darker, more extreme direction; Russia (1922) and eventually China (1949) became communist.

What was the effect of the establishment of new democracies on parades? On or near their founding dates, most of these countries enthusiastically began official annual celebrations, including parades, to celebrate their birth or new-found freedom. It has been interesting to see how the different countries and cultures have since treated their national days. Australia, for example, does not celebrate their Foundation Day, January 1, 1902. Instead, they have chosen to focus on the day that the British Fleet first landed in Botany Bay to establish a penal colony, January 26, 1788.

Some other countries, as noted in Chapter Five, chose to make their days all about military displays. China, France, Brazil, and Mexico commemorate with parades comprising almost 100 percent active military units. Russia does the same but their official day is Victory Day to celebrate victory in Europe in World War II, rather than any date marking the relatively recent end of communism. Canada, Australia, New Zealand, and the USA have national day parades without any significant military presence, focusing more on community and the multicultural aspects of their cultures.

Not only were countries politically rebuilt, but they were socially rebuilt, turning from primarily agrarian to urbanized societies in a short span of time. Technological advances led to the rapid production of goods and an assembly line factory system, which in turn required labor. In Great Britain, the epicenter of the Industrial Revolution, the population in 1700 was 14 million, of whom 25 percent lived in cities. By 1851, the overall population had grown to 27 million, of whom 54 percent lived in cities.[3] In that 150-year timespan, the overall population had approximately doubled but the urban population had quintupled.

What was the effect of urbanization on parades? The increased population meant more spectators and participants for urban parades. A prime example in this regard was the emigration of about a million Irish citizens to England, the United States, Canada, and other countries due to persistent potato crop failures between 1845 and 1850.[4] In the United States, most settled in coastal cities and ended up working in menial construction and factory jobs.[5] As a result, the St. Patrick's Day Parade in New York City quickly transformed from several modest processions marching from parish churches in the city to the original St. Patrick's Cathedral on Mott Street, to a large raucous affair that took over one of the city's largest thoroughfares, Fifth Avenue. It remains there to this day and is essentially the same as it would have been in the 1890s, with thousands of people marching, accompanied by bagpipe bands as well as brass bands, but in keeping with its original rules, no wagons or floats (see color insert Figure 12-1).[6]

As in our world today, the Victorians of the 19th century were a religiously conflicted lot. At the beginning of the period most people were regular church-goers and were the willing recipients of a punishing Protestant work ethic. As cities expanded and country towns languished, secularism grew. Church attendance figures garnered from regular censuses showed this to be the case. The cause was considered to be two-fold. First, an undersupply of churches in urban areas meant that existing churches could not accommodate the increased demand. Second, the culturally pluralistic nature of the new urban populations led to people being conflicted by the new reality of mixing with those who had different opinions. "Personal religious beliefs, in whatever denominational form, were constantly confronted to the point of scepticism by options and alternatives."[7]

Aggravating the impact of secularization and creating a Crisis of Faith were new scientific theories, the most obvious being Charles Darwin's popular book *The Origin of Species*, published in 1859.[8] But it did not stop there. "Geologists began to discover concrete evidence of earth's processes which did not add up to the events written about in the book of Genesis."[9] There would be no turning back.

With increasing secularization, moral ambiguity would not be far behind. As the era drew to its end, entertainment took more risqué forms. Music halls, burlesque, and spectacle went from censured low-brow to respectable high-brow art forms.[10]

What was the effect of secularization on parades? Although I can offer no concrete direct proof, I suggest that the rejuvenation of carnival and carnival parades in many western countries as seen in Chapter Ten, was one of the results. Although hampered by morally abstruse, on-again, off-again civic sanctions, some took a while to grab a permanent foothold, but eventually did. The struggles began in the late 19th or early 20th centuries as secularization was on the rise. A few examples of successfully revitalized carnival parades include: Cologne, Germany (1823); Basel, Switzerland (1835); New Orleans, USA (1837); Nice, France (1873); and Quebec, Canada (1894). All of these, and many more, continue to this day.

Another far-reaching societal advance of the Victorian era was improved education. "The years before Victoria's accession (1838) saw significant shifts in attitudes toward education. Suspicions of educating the poor 'beyond their station,' still very powerful in the 1820s, were in rapid retreat by the mid 1830s."[11] In 1879, The Education Act in Britain made basic schooling compulsory. "In colonial America, the Protestant determination to create a literate laity had provided elementary education for girls.... The census of 1850 showed the literacy rate of women equal to that of men, making the United States the first country where this was true."[12]

What effect did improved literacy have on parades? It gave access to information about them to a much larger potential audience than would have previously been possible. Advertising, stories, and eventually photos about parades would now be seen and understood by the masses. Increasingly popular were cheap newspapers and magazines. To this end in Britain, for example, "by 1900 daily papers were read by one adult in every five, Sunday papers by one in three."[13]

This neatly brings us to commercialism, tied inextricably to education and communications. From this period emerged the whole concept of mass media. It began with the invention of the paper machine, first patented by Sealy and Henry Fourdrinier in Britain in 1801. Working machines came into use beginning in 1804 in Britain and in 1827 in the USA.[14] This machine enabled the production of continuous rolls of paper versus the previous individual sheets. Of course, this improved both the quantity and production time for newspapers and magazines. Once again, statistics tell the tale. It is estimated that in 1851 there were 563 newspapers in Britain and by the end of the Victorian period around the turn-of-the-century, there were about 2,000.[15]

With production costs decreasing, advertising could be had for low costs, too. A survey of the proportion of advertising space to editorial space in the London Times between 1788 and 1888 shows an increase from 30 to 44 percent, considered the general minimum figure at which more profit could be obtained from advertising than from subscriptions.[16] Not only was advertising cheap and readily available in publications, but advertorials started to become popular, so that advertising for such things as special events like weddings or plays cost nothing. It would not be unreasonable to assume that a large community parade would likely receive the benefit of this type of advertising. As well, handbills and posters became increasingly popular, thus adding to the multiplicity of advertising formats available to parades.

Other advanced forms of media as we know them today did not become widespread until the 20th century, specifically radio (1920 onward), television (late 1940s onward), and latterly the internet (1980s onward), which put the finishing touches on what we now regard as globalism.

What was the effect on parades of this abundance of media? As mentioned, it became easier for parades to gain visibility in the eyes of the consumer. By the time that radio and TV made their way into the living rooms of most western nations, the stage was set for large parades to re-invent themselves as major national and international tourist attractions. The sheer size of the potential spectator base, as we have seen elsewhere, thus also provided a no-brainer reason for parade organizers to use advertising in the form of parade and float sponsorships to pay for ever-larger productions.

As a conclusion to this section, an illustrative case in point of how Industrial Revolution changes affected parades can be found in the Winter Carnival in Quebec City, Canada.

> On the night of February 2, 1894, twenty-five hundred torch-bearing snowshoers and militiamen wearing *tuques*, blanket coats and the *ceinture flechèe* of old Quebec, participated in one of the grandest spectacles seen in Quebec City. The occasion was the storming of the ice palace at the Quebec Winter Carnival which had begun at the beginning of that week and which was to last a few days longer [Figure 12-2]. The night's show was definitely considered to have been the high point of the celebration. From a balcony of the neighbouring Quebec Legislative Assembly building, Lord Aberdeen, the Governor-General of Canada and his party, watched the torch-lit procession as it approached the massive walls of the ice palace and observed the ensuing firework display, as each side filled the air with multi-colored fireworks for three-quarters of an hour. Thousands of spectators were thrilled by the impressive sight of the attack upon and the capitulation of the ice fortress and the later torchlight procession through the streets of the city. The organizers of the revived celebration of the carnival in Quebec City could well congratulate themselves.[17]

The rebirth of the Quebec Carnival and attendant parade was well documented in a 1982 thesis by Frank Abbott, mentioned in Chapter Ten.[18] In 1894, the year of the carnival's resurrection from its previous coarse, rural form, Quebec society was still largely controlled by the Catholic Church. The 1894 carnival was successful because it was marketed not as a celebration of immoral excess—which earlier local carnivals

Figure 12-2: Storming of the ice palace at the 1894 Quebec Winter Carnival (Engraving published in *Le Monde illustré*, vol. 12, no. 613 [février 1896], p. 607).

were, and which would have provoked church rebuke—but rather as a celebration of the traditional French-Canadian way of life. In a sense, in this form it provided—and this is my own opinion—a kind of foot-in-the-door opportunity to remove any semblance of association between carnival and the church and thus put a stop to potential moral objections. It was a subtle means to secularize the celebration.

But the reasons it was resurrected were really economic, and directly a result of the Industrial Revolution. The lumber industry was in decline because wooden-hulled sailing ships, built at the Quebec City shipyards, were being replaced by iron-hulled sailing ships and later steel-hulled steamships. In the 1860s, immediately prior to this upheaval, Quebec City was "the greatest shipbuilding port in British North America," as journalist Frederick William Wallace opined. In addition to the smaller consumer goods production that eventually replaced some of that income, there was recognition that the French-Canadian culture could be a money-making, serious tourist attraction for the winter season. More than anything, the decision to move ahead with a carnival was made because of the expansion of the American railway system up to, and across, the Canadian border.[19]

Printing advances played a large part in advertising for the new carnival. Numerous newspaper editorials helped to spread the word. However, it was the mass production and distribution of 21,000, 36-page carnival program booklets—that included merchant advertisements—all over the province and country that was most effective. "Ready-to-print articles were also mailed to newspapers in every town and city throughout Canada and the Eastern and Middle states."[20] It proved to be a worthwhile effort as some 22,000 visitors arrived by train for the six-day event.

After a successful repeat in 1896, the carnival and its well-known parade became dormant partly because of the sheer magnitude of the task of organizing it, but also because of a proliferation of other similar events in nascent stages throughout the country. It arose again as a permanent tourist attraction in 1955.

Technological Advances

The story of the Quebec Carnival highlights several technological advances that indirectly affected parades.

Invented in 1860, the *Bessemer* steelmaking process facilitated the inexpensive mass production of steel. It was supplanted around 1890 by the *open-hearth* process. These inventions enabled trains, railway tracks, and ships to be built easily and cheaply. Of course, none of *them* could have worked at all without the invention of steam power. While steam power goes back to Roman Egypt in the first century CE, it was not until the Industrial Revolution that it would become practical. The invention of a commercially successful steamboat by American Robert Fulton in 1807 and a working steam railway locomotive by Briton Richard Trevithick in 1804 became two of the most life-changing technological advances for humans in recorded history.

What did they do for parades? The 1894 Quebec Carnival experience proved that certainly trains were now a viable means by which tourists could travel long distances to attend an event. In fact, as early as 1851, the Great Exhibition in London, the first real world fair, had an attendance of more than six million, of whom at least 58,000 were foreigners. Most of these foreigners would have had to cross the English

Channel—if not the Atlantic—by steamship and upon landing take a train to London. Thomas Cook even began his famous travel agency just 10 years before the exhibition and by 1851 his tours were so famous that he organized train excursions to the exhibition's Crystal Palace for 150,000 visitors from all over the country.[21] What better proof that railways—and steamships—had become two of the main travel modes to successful public events?

As a side note, it was thanks to trains that modern suburbia developed in the mid–19th century when citizens of the increasingly populous cities of the Victorian era bucked the trend and decided they wanted to get out of town. Railways enabled them to become the world's first real commuters.[22] But all this influenced parades *indirectly*. What about technology that was applicable to them *directly*?

Answers started to come in 1876, when Nicolaus August Otto invented and later patented a successful four-stroke engine, known as the *Otto cycle* engine.[23] It was this engine that was widely adopted for liquid-fuelled vehicles to follow (except diesels and two-stroke engines). The first internal combustion engine-propelled truck originated in 1896 in Germany and was designed by automotive pioneer Gottlieb Daimler.[24] In 1908, Henry Ford introduced the Model T automobile.[25] By 1920, flower-covered automobiles were seen in the Tournament of Roses Parade in California.[26] Not long after, cars and trucks had morphed into ubiquitous self-propelled—or towed—floats in parades. Horses were put out to pasture. Street sweepers were put out of work!

The introduction of macadam and later asphalt road surfaces in the late Long 19th Century period helped to keep the dust down and allowed those cars and floats to glide smoothly along parade routes.[27]

Floats benefited the most from technological advances besides cars and trucks, and here we continue what we started in Chapter Four. Naturally, as engines grew more powerful, larger float superstructures could be constructed and chassis joined together to eventually craft the behemoths we see today. But they would not be behemoths without the right materials. First of all, the float chassis used today are no longer simple truck beds but complex, load-bearing custom frameworks made of steel plate and tubing. Steel also acts as "the main support and framework for the float's characters and backgrounds. The various shapes are formed with steel rods that are welded to the main supports and covered with aluminum wire screen. The screen is sprayed with a polyvinyl plastic 'cocooning' liquid, originally developed to cover and protect ships laid up in inactive reserve. The plastic hardens on the wire screen to form a hard, durable skin."[28] According to Tim Estes, President of the float-building company Fiesta Parade Floats in Pasadena, California, also used extensively on float decorations are lightweight foam products like Styrofoam (invented in 1947), flex foam, urethane foam, and bead board foam.[29]

Let's pause and look at the materials mentioned in this last paragraph.

We've already talked about the use of steel in ships and railways, but its use in cars and trucks has remained steady and today accounts for about 55 to 60 percent of the vehicle's structure.[30] It's the only material that can adequately support the weight of today's floats.

So that the weight does not become too cumbersome, elements of the float need to be strong yet lightweight themselves. Aluminum, famous for its light weight and durability, emerged in 1886–1887, when Charles Hall and French engineer Paul

Heroult, and then Austrian engineer Karl Josef Bayer, developed methods to extract aluminum from aluminum oxide and bauxite respectively. By World War II, it was used in a host of applications and later in cars and trucks.[31] Today it accounts for about 15 percent of total car parts.[32] Using it as part of a float is no surprise.

The famous movie line, "There's a great future in plastics" uttered to Benjamin Braddock (Dustin Hoffman) in the 1967 movie *The Graduate*, proved to be very prescient. Since that time, the use of plastics in every aspect of our daily life has taken off. But plastic is not a recent invention. *Parkesine* (nitrocellulose) is considered the first man-made plastic. This material was patented by Alexander Parkes, in Birmingham, England in 1856, again in that key time period of the Industrial Revolution.[33] Today, plastic components make up about a third of all car parts.[34] They are essential for floats.

But there are yet more inventions that have come out of the Industrial Revolution that have affected float design.

Although it is remotely possible—but not proven—that crude hydraulic technology helped to control the automata of floats as early as the third century BCE (remember Ptolemy's procession), sophisticated designs for movements only came following the invention of the hydraulic press by Joseph Bramah in 1795.[35] This is the fluid equivalent of a lever, so that a small force applied to one end of a hydraulic system can move very large and heavy objects with relative ease at the other end of the system. Hydraulic systems are essential today for such things as aircraft control surfaces and undercarriages, construction equipment, elevators—and floats. "If the float incorporates parts or figures with extensive or complicated animation, the motion is usually provided by means of hydraulic cylinders and motors powered by hydraulic pumps driven off a second engine. To make the motion appear smooth and realistic, the hydraulic cylinders and motors are actuated by a complex array of valves that are controlled by a computer."[36]

And that brings us to computers. In 1833, Charles Babbage, an English mechanical engineer and polymath considered the father of the computer, originated the concept of a programmable computer. While he did not live to see his concept take over the world, his son gave a successful demonstration of its use in 1906.[37] The technology eventually made its way to parade floats. In large parades like the highly commercialized Rose Parade in California, more bang for your buck means turning to movie animation and special effects experts for dramatic action. As with any complicated system, such animation nowadays requires computer controls. Expert computer programmers develop the programs required to properly sequence the motion. In fact, "many floats have three or four separate operators surrounded by an array of gauges, manual controls, and computers to monitor the animation effects."[38]

To reiterate, *all* the above inventions originated during the Long 19th Century and the Industrial Revolution. Let's look at some of the results.

Unique Modern Floats

Technology from the last 200 years has resulted in floats of record-breaking size and astonishing creativity.

In 2020, in an endeavor to promote tourism to Phuket, Thailand, the Kamala Carnival Parade featured the world's longest parade float, *Lyarawan*, at 72 m long (almost 240 ft) and sponsored by the Carnival Magic Theme Park. It broke a Guinness World Record as the "Longest Single Chassis Parade Float," beating the previous record by more than 30 m. That previous record was held by a float in the 2017 Rose Parade in California.[39]

In that year, a float created by the Lucy Pet Foundation for the Rose Parade broke a Guinness World Record as the "Heaviest Single Chassis Parade Float" ever built, at 67,222 kg (148,200 lb).[40] The float was basically a giant wave pool for surfing dogs. The wave pool tank alone was 90 ft long and contained 8,000 gallons of water. The dogs were transported back and forth at the end of their rides in a mini cable car system.[41] Until the Thai float, it was this float that also held the record as the longest.

Driving and operating this kind of self-propelled float is all done from inside the float itself where the "cockpit" resembles something out of a *Mad Max* movie. Surrounded by steel superstructure, the driver cannot see outside except via a TV monitor above the dashboard, if it can be called that. Controls consist of a steering wheel, gearshift—mercifully the transmission is automatic—a hand brake, a few gauges, an accelerator, and brake pedal. Directions are given over an intercom from a spotter who leads the float along the parade route. There can be as many as four or five other people in the cramped belly of the beast operating various movable float components, which means it's also hot. Driving a float has been described as everything from "a hideous experience" to "amazing" and "super cool."[42]

The Rose Parade is famous for the fact that every square inch of the exterior float surface must be covered with flowers, especially roses, or natural material. Other parades also have similar aspirations, notably the Jersey Battle of Flowers on the English Channel island of Jersey, and the Zundert Flower Parade in the Netherlands, perhaps the better known.

In Zundert, being the hometown of post–Impressionist artist Vincent van Gogh, floats often have an Impressionist or post–Impressionist theme. In fact, many floats are three-dimensional sculptures of the artist's paintings. Others are wildly creative (see color insert Figure 12-3). However, instead of roses covering the floats, the Dutch use dahlias since Zundert is the "Dahlia Capital of the World." Floats are sometimes human-powered and many support musical groups and animated figures.[43]

For sheer outlandishly creative designs, there is probably no parade more renowned than the Viareggio Carnival Parade in Tuscany, Italy, in existence since 1873. When we talk about size, some of the floats in these parades (there is one parade every day for six days) are arguably the tallest in the world, towering some 30 m (100 ft) into the air. Part of the reason this height is achievable is that the floats are constructed of papier-mâché, making them very lightweight. Even with this, they still weigh around 40,000 kg (more than 88,000 lb). Most floats are allegorical, adorned with giant, animated monsters and strange creatures, but many also reflect the political machinations of the day, often satirically.[44] Propulsion seems to be inconsistent, with some being towed by humans or tractors, and some self-propelled. Superstructures allow for massed choirs, bands, and dancers to perform on the floats, the larger ones accommodating more than 200 persons.

When talking about massed performers on floats, our thoughts usually turn to the Mardi Gras Carnival in Rio de Janeiro. For sheer mind-blowing entertainment value (see Chapter One), there is little else in the world that can beat the parade of samba school floats through the Sambadrome. Designed and built by individual samba schools, the floats encompass themes as diverse as religion, political satire, saving the rainforest, Indigenous culture, mythology, ancient civilizations, and the list goes on. Each enormous float is multi-tiered, often with several platforms or stages for dancers (see color insert Figure 12-4). Special effects (e.g., smoke, water, lighting, pyrotechnics) and animation of float components bring it alive and help to tell a story relating to the theme. More choreographed and vividly costumed dancers *not* on the float augment the whole theme and stop periodically along the route to perform their routines to non-stop samba music.

Inside, beneath all the exterior glitz, a Rio float is a marvel of mechanical advantage. A veritable jungle of steel rods, cranks, pulleys, cranes, ball bearings, and hydraulics works to bring the story together. Each float also has a motorized platform with a driver in the front and a large generator in the back to power lights and moving parts.[45] Externally, it's all about color-coordinated materials like Styrofoam, plastic paint, varnish, glass wool, and different fabrics—mostly post–Industrial Revolution inventions—to build effective adornments.[46]

Certain modern parades have flying elements. Helium, an inert gas, was first discovered in 1868 during the Industrial Revolution. In 1921, the first airship to use helium for buoyancy, the U.S. Navy blimp C-7, lifted off from Norfolk, Virginia, in the USA.[47] From that time on, its popularity as a lifting medium grew. Today, it has many uses, one of the most well-known being to inflate and keep aloft the giant balloons of the annual Macy's Thanksgiving Day Parade in New York City, one of several similar American events. This is a much-beloved parade and the balloons—each really just a huge symbolic float—are the main reason. Featuring children's popular characters such as Spiderman, SpongeBob, Yogi Bear, Snoopy, and dozens of others, the balloons are truly colossal. To date, the tallest has been more than 100 ft, the longest more than 178 ft, and the widest more than 45 ft.[48] Each balloon uses 300,000 to 700,000 cu ft of helium, and merely filling each one costs at least half a million dollars.[49] All balloons must be controlled from the ground by a team of handlers with support ropes. The parade is blatantly commercial, sponsored solely by the department store Macy's, and wildly successful, with roughly 3.5 million people attending each year in person.[50]

The Fascinating Case of Circus Parades

It would be unpardonable not to include the phenomenon of circus parades in a book about parades. The circus parade, part of that universally cherished form of variety entertainment, the circus, has a long history. Carvings from the Han Dynasty in ancient China (206 BCE to 220 CE) depict acrobats performing on poles extending from moving, two-wheeled horse-drawn carts.[51] Jugglers and acrobats in parades may even go as far back as 1500 BCE or earlier in Egypt although these performances were usually associated with religious festivals (e.g., the Opet Festival procession described in Chapter Six). The first mention of the term "circus parade" would appear to be the pompa circensis that led the contestants and numerous dancers, musicians, and costumed characters into the Circus Maximus in ancient Rome for chariot races (also described in Chapter Six).

These early forms of circus parades did not last and eventually were re-invented some 1,500 or so years later as part of what was to become the *railroad circus*. The railroad circus conveniently fits squarely into both the Long 19th Century and the Contemporary Periods of history.

It became the quintessential show to which every child dreamed of running away. There was wonder—wild animals, equestrian prowess, clowns, beautiful ladies, daring trapeze artists, crazy characters. Exotic travel. Adventure. Who could resist? This array of attractions was what drew entire cities across America and Europe to vacate their homes and offices for days for no other reason than to watch the circus and its accompanying parade.

It began in England. British ex-cavalry Sergeant-Major Philip Astley, the "father of the modern circus," opened a riding school near London in 1768 where he also performed feats of horsemanship. He enlarged the presentation in 1770 by adding acrobats, rope-dancers, jugglers, musicians, and a clown, and so was born what we consider the modern—or traditional—circus. By the late 18th century, the circus phenomenon had spread throughout Europe and over to the USA and Canada, and by 1872 was the most popular form of entertainment in America. In that year another innovation was to thrust the circus to ever-greater heights, the railroad.[52]

In the spring of 1872, famous entrepreneur and shameless promoter P.T. Barnum and his partners loaded their *Greatest Show on Earth* onto 65 railroad cars and thereby gave birth to the age of the giant railroad circuses.[53] A railroad circus could travel farther and visit more towns than the previous horse-drawn productions. In short, they would soon become massive revenue-producers for the likes of promoters such as Barnum and his partner James Anthony Bailey and the Ringling Brothers. For the next 80 years they dominated entertainment in America and Europe.

Advanced billing by circus promoters in newspapers and on showbills days and weeks before the show helped to put it front and center in everyone's mind (remember that mass printing capability was new, too). For example, "in 1892 Adam Forepaugh's circus, for one, announced its impending presence in Philadelphia by mummifying an eight-storey building with 4,938 lithographs, in addition to pasting thousands of other posters around the city." When the circus rolled into town, "shops closed their doors, schools cancelled classes, and factories shut down."[54]

The trains arrived, usually at night, with their "stock cars, perhaps with elephant trunks probing outside openings, and a long line of flatcars loaded with red baggage wagons, pole wagons, bandwagons, tableaux, chariots, the steam boiler wagon, and canvas-covered wild-animal cages."[55] They deposited their precious cargo at the circus show grounds and from the ensuing chaos, the free parade magically emerged at about 11:00 a.m. All parades were different but none were boring (Figure 12-2). In America it could include the following.

> Horses, flag bearers, bands on magnificent wagons, allegorical tableaux, clowns, knights in armour, beautiful ladies on steeds, Roman chariots, chimes, bells, a band organ, cage after cage of wild animals (some open to view and others closed to prompt curiosity), cowboys, "Indians," and a long line of highly caparisoned elephants shuffling along trunk-to-tail. The traditional finale to the circus parade was the Pied Piper of the circus, the steam calliope.[56]

In late 19th-century England, George Sanger was the most successful circus entrepreneur. His parade wagons were artistic wonders reminiscent of the pageant wagons of hundreds of years before.

Figure 12-5: Ringling Brothers' circus parade, 1914, showing several tableau wagons (Circus World Museum, Baraboo, Wisconsin, USA).

A typical carriage weighed ten tons and was drawn by four horses in "royal state harness" as part of a grand procession. All the carved woodwork on the carriage was gilded. Sanger's wife, Mlle. Pauline de Vere, sometimes dressed as Britannia and rode on top of a carriage holding a Union Jack shield, a gold trident, and wearing a Greek helmet. The circus lion, Nero, and a lamb sat together at her feet. After this came a string of camels, a herd of elephants, numerous other costumed characters, exotic animals either in cages, or led by their trainers, and of course, the band.[57]

The glory days of the circus parade were short-lived. Ironically, by the middle of the 20th century, technological advances proved their undoing, as well as the undoing of the traditional circus itself. Large, long-haul trucks replaced trains to carry circus hardware and animals. A proliferation of arenas was built for indoor sports such as ice hockey and basketball, which in turn also housed traveling circuses. Television and movies usurped the circus's role as window to the world, turning TV hosts like Ed Sullivan into Ringmasters. Air travel provided increasing access to out-of-the-way places, the very countries that provided the exotic animals that proved so popular with circus audiences. Why see animals—and even exotic peoples—in a circus when one could see them up close and personal in their own habitat? Finally—and probably the real nail in the coffin—was the accelerating disdain welling up in the public conscience for the mistreatment of wild animals. Without animals, the circus became a mere shell of its former self, even though most treated their animals well.

On May 21, 2017, the Ringling Brothers and Barnum & Bailey Circus, the most famous traditional circus in the world, held its final performance in Long Island, New York. One audience member bore witness, "The people in the crowd rose to their feet for a prolonged ovation. The ringmaster cheered back at them, 'You mean the circus isn't antiquated?' The crowd roared. 'You mean you love the circus?' he said. The noise was deafening."[58]

The draw of the circus was obviously—and still is—very powerful, so much so that it has, in the last 40 years, re-invented itself. Gone are the wild animals and freaks. Sadly, gone are the parades. But what has emerged is an evolved version with amazing acrobatics and special effects, original music, incredible costuming, and myth-come-fantasy story lines. Such companies as Canada's Cirque du Soleil have built permanent theaters to house the shows because of their popularity, much like the original traditional circuses of 200 years ago. In fact, they, like others, still travel and have shows under big top tents—but with no parades.

I chose circus parades as a final topic in this book because they were, in their short lifespan, the embodiment of events that anthropologist Don Handelman, whom we met in the Introduction, says "re-present the lived-in world. Their mandate is to engage in the ordering of ideas, people, and things."[59] They—and the traditional circus itself—rose to prominence not only because they provided great entertainment, but especially because they reinforced societal tropes of the day—racism, social hierarchies, white privilege, ethnic stereotypes, sexism and, on the positive side, unambiguous morality and its effects on children.[60] That most of these became the subjects of considerable debate and political demonstrations by the end of the 20th century is in no small measure the reason why the traditional circus and its parade fell from grace. In other words, the circus and circus parades both shaped and mirrored society.

What's Next?

Will parades in the future also mirror and shape society as did circus parades? Will parades of the past be re-invented? Will their life spans be short or will they last hundreds of years? We don't know the answer to any of these questions for sure, and the most likely answer to all of them is a distinctly fuzzy "maybe."

The machinations of society will always lead to an outpouring of expression in some form, and that form may very well be a parade. LGBTQ rights are a prime example. One hundred years ago, to be gay was to break the law. Now, much of the world celebrates it, and they celebrate it with parades, some of which are very large and lucrative to hosting communities, as we saw in Chapter One.

Will the same sort of thing happen to other movements? Almost certainly. The environmental movement is another example similar to gay rights. What has, up to the early 21st century, been the reason for protest marches could easily morph into large, politically acceptable parades, as extreme weather events around the globe serve to reinforce the argument that climate change is anthropogenic or human-caused. Ironically it was the Industrial Revolution that started us on the road to critical levels of atmospheric pollution in the first place, the very same revolution that modernized parades. We can only hope that the experience of viewing and participating in such a parade will be as positive as that of pride parades. Indeed, the trend is already underway with parades such as the Rose Parade occasionally having environmental themes.

Will parades of the past be re-invented? Again, very likely. It would not be a big stretch, for example, to see our increasingly morally ambiguous society move towards the ancient Dionysian processions as part of carnival or pride parades. In fact, something akin to that has already happened in Australia, where pride has merged with carnival. Only history will be the judge of whether it will be a good or bad influence on society.

How tenacious will some of these parades be in terms of staying power? My personal prediction is not very. Pride and the environment can only hold the public's attention for so long, probably until most of what is being demanded—remember they began as protests—is achieved.

Similarly, there is an almost exponential growth in festivals, some of which host parades. Niche festivals now celebrate such diverse offerings as craft beers, cat videos, psychics, celebrity impersonators, and the latest form of dance music, among dozens of others. Realistically, they are not going to last, given both the fickle nature of today's consumer and the low profit margins for event producers. One interesting specimen stands out and that is the Burning Man Festival in Nevada, which has been operating since 1986, a long time in today's terms. It has numerous small parades within its boundaries and is so unbelievably eccentric and creative that this alone may give it staying power.

The other question is whether they will be able to withstand unforeseen disasters such as the global pandemic of 2020–2022, especially the financial fallout.

Technological advances will almost certainly change parades in the future. Artificial intelligence (AI) and the Internet of Things will offer new ways for parade participants to connect with spectators which, as we have seen from the beginning, is the real reason people attend parades. There is no reason why eventually a squad of friendly robots cannot approach spectators along the parade route and call them by name or introduce them to each other. We are close to being able to do this. Maybe floats will be driverless. Maybe spectators' smartphones will be able to control what happens on floats, such as lighting or animation. It's already happening for lighting. Artist Janet Echelman has done just this with her ethereal sculptures mounted high above the ground between buildings. Visitors with smartphones and tablets are able to paint vivid beams of light across the sculpture at a massive scale; small movements made on phones become nearly hundred-foot-long trails on its surface.[61] Other apps also allow audience interaction with performers at concerts.[62]

Several things *are* certain. Humans will continue to want to make live, emotional connections with each other—moving encounters-—and to be wowed by superior performances. Sponsors will continue to want effective messages sent to their target audiences. Parades will continue to fill the bill and societies will continue to be shaped by them.

Chapter Notes

Introduction

1. Zorn (2013).
2. Occasionally the word parade takes on an uglier facade as a verb, connoting people who flagrantly flaunt excess.
3. Vancouver Heritage Foundation (2019).
4. I tend to disagree. That is because by my definition—and I believe it is not an unreasonable definition—a parade would take far less rational thought to execute. In its earliest manifestation it would require no advanced belief in symbols and hence it would be unlikely that any ceremony would be held at either end. I posit that the first parades were probably no more than something resembling a comic march around a campfire in the African bush so that everyone could show off to each other, perhaps as far back as millions of years before we had evolved to our present level of rational thinking. But, of course, I cannot prove it.
5. Ceremony and ritual can be confusing terms, but I like to simply think of rituals as a component of a larger ceremony. For example, the wedding vows are a ritual that is part of the larger wedding ceremony.
6. Handelman (1998: 15–6).
7. I use the terms sponsor and organizer interchangeably in this book, but typically a sponsor would probably hire a person or group/company to do the nitty gritty of organizing the parade.
8. List of largest peaceful gatherings (2020).
9. Sengupta (2019).
10. List of largest peaceful gatherings (2020).
11. INS (1951).
12. Trtworld (2020).
13. Statista (2020); Lipinski (2015).
14. Augsten et al. (2014).
15. Hamilton-Smith et al. (2015: 75).
16. Hamilton-Smith et al. (2015: 75).
17. Doan (2010).
18. Ostrower (2005); Bowdin et al. (2006: 106); Tremblay et al. (2006); Wicks (2000).
19. Engdahl (2015).
20. Jones (2007b).
21. Turner (1982: 44–8); Schechner (2002: 62–3).
22. Ambrosino (2019).

23. Kertzer (1988: 9).
24. Bell (1997).
25. Durkheim (1965).
26. Karecki (2000).
27. Guthrie (2000).
28. Lerner et al. (2015: 799–823).
29. Alcorta & Sosis (2005: 323–359).
30. Redfield (2017: 36–80).
31. Matthews (2016: 40–2); Cameron (2004).
32. Stearns (2007: 111–121).

Chapter One

1. Beeman (1993: 369–393).
2. Turner (1988: 81).
3. Beeman (2010: 118–137).
4. Czikszentmihalyi (1975).
5. Cameron (2013: 157).
6. I have defined entertainment in more detail elsewhere. See Matthews (2016b; 2–3).
7. Karlsson (2020); Fukaya (2012: 191–211).
8. Beard (2007: 13–5).
9. Deutsch (1926: 101–6).
10. Gorlinski (2010).
11. Ta-Kuan (1992: 72–3).
12. Apsaras were believed to be beautiful, supernatural female beings or spirits in Hindu and Buddhist culture. Images of them are prevalent in the temples of Angkor, Cambodia. The Khmer classical dance of Cambodia has taken the figures and incorporated them into dances.
13. Rooney (2005: 170–7).
14. As a comparison, the 1952 Coronation Procession of Queen Elizabeth II had approximately 30,000 men.
15. Ebrey (1999: 33–65).
16. Ebrey (1999: 33–65).
17. Ebrey (1999: 33–65).
18. A *li* is a standard Chinese unit of distance of about a half kilometer.
19. Ebrey (1999: 33–65).
20. Zhou (2017).
21. Balabanlilar (2009: 173–186).
22. A-Z Films (2010).
23. Donzino et al. (2020).
24. Codell (2012).

25. Menpes (1903: 71–98).

26. LGBTQIA2S+ (lesbian, gay, bisexual, transgender, queer/questioning, intersex, asexual, two spirit) is the current term at time of writing, rather than the more general LGBTQ, but the acronym has proven to be a moving target. Also, there were previous protests as early as 1967, but Stonewall is widely credited as the beginning.

27. Allen (2019).

28. Prisco (2019).

29. O'Brien (2004).

30. Haynes (2020).

Chapter Two

1. If one is to believe Curtius Rufus, the historian of Alexander's exploits, in reality he rode into the city in a chariot, not on his horse as shown in the film. Also, a life-size reconstruction of the beautiful Ishtar Gate can be viewed in the Pergamon Museum in Berlin, Germany for those interested.

2. Rufus (2020).

3. Greeley (1995: 94–105); Jones (2007: 112–125).

4. Bell (1997: 138–169).

5. Ellis (2019: 473).

6. Hawkins (2016); Christopherson (2018).

7. Matthews (2016a: 35–9).

8. It is likely that such secular spaces should not be granted the full authority of the term sacred space but instead should be called *quasi-sacred spaces*.

The reason involves two more concepts, consecration and permanence. Consecration is a formal ceremony carried out by God's representative (e.g., a Bishop in Christian churches) that officially dedicates a building—specifically usually a church or cathedral—to divine worship. This, in turn, forbids its use for common or profane purposes. Most religions have similar ceremonies except for Buddhism and Islam. At least for Catholic churches, this ceremony transforms the church into a sacred space forever, which brings us to the concept of permanence. The sacred space cannot be temporarily a profane space. While part of the building (e.g., a separate hall, if there is one) can be temporarily used for secular purposes like bingo or a musical concert, the church itself does not lose its status as sacred space. On the other hand, a profane space such as a school gymnasium can be temporarily used as a church through ceremonial blessing by a priest; however, it loses its status as a sacred space the moment it reverts to a gymnasium. What that means for a sporting place is that even though the ritual activities within it may indeed result in some sort of spiritual or emotional connections as I have defined them in the Introduction, that does not automatically qualify the space to be a sacred one. It does not because first, it has not been consecrated to be a sacred space and second, there is no human who can interpret whether those feelings of spiritual connection are from God or merely a physiological reaction to any number of triggers. Strong national pride resulting from a display of patriotic symbols and flags, sexual lust resulting from risqué costumes, or general euphoria resulting from upbeat music are examples that come to mind. Clearly, a divine power is not at work in all these.

It would follow that a parade route such as the Processional Way in Babylon could be a sacred space, but the argument is not without flaws. Let's think about it. Does it host religious-like rituals? Most certainly it does. Can spiritual connections be made in the space? Quite possibly, yes, because they are real feelings and emotions, but exactly what they are is as yet not certain. Do these answers make it sacred? No, they do not, even temporarily, because the space has not—and probably never will be—consecrated or blessed. At the least it can be considered a general ritual space, but at the most it can be considered no more than a quasi-sacred space.

9. Barrie (1996).

10. Evans & Nichols (2015: 25–51).

11. Morton (2012: 141–165); Schele & Freidel (1990: 364–8); Inomata (2006: 805–842).

12. Davis (2016).

13. Velasco (2020); Lau (2015).

14. Bond (2017).

15. Bond (2017).

16. Marcantonio (2009).

17. Bond (2017).

18. Knapp (2008: 47–59).

19. Joye & Dewitte (2016: 112–125).

20. Hurley (2017).

21. Ricci (2018).

22. Leon Battista Alberti (February 14, 1404–April 25, 1472) was an Italian Renaissance humanist author, artist, architect, poet, priest, linguist, philosopher and cryptographer; he epitomized the Renaissance Man.

23. Green et al. (2017).

24. Wilkinson (2005: 66).

25. In fact, Karnak *is* the largest religious complex in the world.

26. Collins (2020); Livingston (2000).

27. Collins (2020).

28. Collins (2020).

29. Loth (2011).

30. Crystal (2020).

31. Loth (2011).

32. Vopiscus (1932). This passage describes Aurelian's triumph in much more detail.

33. Originally a form of Greek architecture, a stoa is a covered walkway or portico, with columns lining the outside boundary.

34. Steckelberg (2011); Hurley (2017).

35. Macy's Thanksgiving Day Parade (2020).

Chapter Three

1. Boyer (2017).
2. Boyer (2017).
3. Ambady et al. (2000).
4. UBS (2010).
5. Actually, Molloy did this himself before he wrote his original books.
6. Aliakbari & Abdollahi (2013).
7. Ephrat (2016); Slepian et al. (2015: 661–8).
8. Bryson (2015).
9. Howlett et al. (2013: 38–48).
10. Howlett et al. (2015: 105–116).
11. Gillath et al. (2012: 423–430).
12. Bossio (2018); Lukee (2018).
13. Williams (2008).
14. Hagan (2012).
15. Scott-Kemmis (2018).
16. Shukla (2015: 14).
17. Robinson (2018).
18. Ridgway (2016).
19. Wertman (2019).
20. O'Brien (2018).
21. PlanetJanet (2017).
22. Manning (2000: 33–4).
23. Platt & Walker (2019).
24. Robinson (2018).
25. Shukla (2015: 14–15).
26. Weisberger (2016).
27. Krueger (2012: 64–78).
28. Laver (1945: 63–74).
29. Laver (1969).
30. Abler (1999).
31. Fussell (2002: 187).
32. Rusch et al. (2015: 367–373).
33. Krueger (2012).
34. Kelleher (1995).
35. Betts (2015); Suval (2018).
36. Suval (2018).
37. Canadian War Museum (2009).
38. Enloe (2000: 263).
39. Ryan (2014).
40. Ryan (2014).

Chapter Four

1. O'Muirigh (2019).
2. Shah (2016).
3. Matthews (2016b: 257).
4. Croose (2014).
5. Merriam-Webster (2020).
6. Harnett (2014).
7. Newberg (2016).
8. Anthony (2007: 59–82).
9. There is still an unsettled dispute about whether that technology was imported or Indigenous. Whatever the case, so far there has been little evidence of early four-wheeled wagons in that civilization. See Kenoyer (2004: 87–106).
10. Xinhua Net NetWriter (2020).
11. Hamblin (2006: 136).
12. McIntosh (2005: 159).
13. Dunkle (2020).
14. Csapo (2013).
15. *Philadelphus* in ancient Greek translates to something like sibling-loving. Some have taken it to mean that Philadelphus literally loved his sister in keeping with Egyptian tradition, but I doubt this was the case. No children came from them.
16. Rice (1983: 209–10).
17. Athenaeus of Naucratis (1854: 193–203); What was originally written by Kallixeinos was re-recorded from now-lost writings by Athenaeus of Naucratis in Egypt, a Greek rhetorician and grammarian, in the end of the second or beginning of the third century CE, but parts of the original work were missing in Athenaeus. Very little is known about Kallixeinos, including whether he actually lived at the time of the festival. Also, not all scholars agree that the Grand Procession was held at the same time as the Ptolemaieia, or exactly when each was first held. I have taken what seems to be the most prevalent viewpoint, that they were related and held in about February 278 BCE. The League of Islanders stated that the Ptolemaieia was to be equal to an Olympiad.
18. Nysa was the nursemaid of the Greek god of wine, Dionysus. A cubit was an ancient measure of length equal to about 18 inches. Laconia is a historical and administrative region of Greece located on the southeastern part of the Peloponnese peninsula. A thyrsus is an ancient Greek staff or spear tipped with an ornament like a pinecone, carried by Dionysus and his followers.
19. The wagon is 14 cubits long by 8 cubits wide (7 m × 4 m or 23 ft × 6.5 ft) and the statue is 10 cubits high (5 m or 17 ft).
20. The cart or wagon is 20 cubits long by 16 cubits wide (10 m × 8 m or 33 ft × 27 ft) and the wine press onboard is 24 cubits by 15 cubits (12 m × 7.5 m or 40 ft × 25 ft).
21. The statue of Dionysus is 12 cubits high (6 m or 20 ft) and the satyr 5 cubits (2.5 m or 8 ft).
22. The thyrsus is large (90 cubits/45 m/150 ft), as is the spear (60 cubits/30 m/100 ft), but the phallus is enormous (120 cubits long/60 m/200 ft and 6 cubits in circumference/3 m/10 ft). The words "cart" or "chariot" were probably synonyms for four-wheeled wagons as these statues were very large and a basic chariot could not carry them.
23. Although no size was given by Kallixeinos for these statues, they probably would have been at least the same size as other previous statues in the procession, namely four or five meters high (13 to 17 ft). Since they were the culmination of the procession, their height might have been even greater. All statues in the procession would have been brightly painted in a variety of colors. The material of construction was not mentioned but most likely wood, as traditional bronze or marble statues would have been far too heavy to transport in such a procession.

24. Benn (2002: 157).
25. NIWAKA Corporation (2020).
26. Bernabeo (2007: 1100).
27. NIWAKA Corporation (2020).
28. NIWAKA Corporation (2020).
29. Glazier (1997: 222).
30. Krishnan (2020).
31. CENGAGE (2020).
32. Bellinger (1927: 115–21).
33. Kuritz (1988: 139).
34. Kuritz. (1988: 143); McKinnell (2000: 79–104).
35. Kernodle (1989: 225).
36. Kernodle (1989: 237).
37. Pleij & Webb (2001: 7–8).
38. McKinnell (2000).
39. Royal entry (2020).
40. Shearman (1975: 136–154).
41. Knighton & García (1999: 119–163).
42. Zaho (2004: 50).
43. Anglo (1997: 98).
44. Anglo (1997: 102–3).
45. Babelon (1988: 89).
46. Vince (1989: 272).
47. Victoria and Albert Museum (2017).
48. Lincoln (2014).
49. Pentzell (1984: 91).
50. Kuritz (1988: 28).
51. Laurenza et al. (2006: 184–201).

Chapter Five

1. Mansoor (2014).
2. Mansoor (2014).
3. Wakin (1986: 187–8); Huntington (1957: 73).
4. Gabriel & Metz (1992).
5. Xenophon (2013).
6. Hoplites were citizen-soldiers of ancient Greek city-states who were primarily armed with spears and shields.
7. Lonsdale (2007: 38).
8. Lonsdale (2007).
9. Lonsdale (2007: 93).
10. Lee (2015: 125–7).
11. Lee (2015).
12. Lin (2001: 78).
13. Crabtree (2004).
14. philhellene (2010).
15. Valdesolo & DeSteno (2011: 262–66).
16. Lakens & Stel (2011: 1–14).
17. MacDougall & Moore (2005: 1164–73); Hindmarch (2009); Horowitz (2012). The hertz (symbol: Hz) is the derived unit of frequency in the International System of Units (SI) and is defined as one cycle per second. Thus, two steps per second (i.e., a left then a right) is equivalent to 2 Hz or 120 steps per minute. In fact, different parts of the human body have different resonant frequencies and external vibrations at these frequencies can sometimes have strange effects on the body. See references.
18. Moore et al. (1999: 346–361).
19. Milzarski (2018).
20. Goldman (2000: 217–233).
21. Becker-Blease (2004).
22. Most martial music is written in major keys, meaning that even without anything else, the melody alone will sound quite happy and positive. Second, the chordal structure is very simple and is mostly comprised of short passages of melody played on the tonic chord (i.e., the key in which the music is written) interspersed with short passages played on what is known as the dominant chord (i.e., the chord that lies a major fifth or seven half tones above the tonic). It is widely known that this interval, particularly if the music remains on the dominant, causes a desire in our brains for that chord to be resolved back to the tonic. In simple terms, a tension is created when the music strays away from the tonic and the tension is released when the music goes back to the tonic. There are other "passing" chords involved that also add to the tension. Interestingly, one section of the music (called the "trio section") is often played by higher pitched woodwinds such as flutes, clarinets, or piccolos, at lower volume and on what is known as the subdominant chord (i.e., five half tones above the tonic). This tends to make it contrast strongly with the louder, main melodic strains and further sets up a need for the release of tension and a return to the strength of the main melody.
23. Chand & Levitin (2013: 179–193); Lieff (2014).
24. Willimek (2011).
25. The tones that bagpipes produce are full of overtones, which are different frequencies from the fundamental tone. This makes the notes played sound somewhat "larger than life," even though the actual melody is played in unison. More than the melody, though, is the subtle foundation of the music, and that is the drone. By definition, a drone is a continuous musical tone played with no breaks (i.e., the same ancient principle as an Australian didgeridoo). On bagpipes, this tone or tones—depending on the number of drone pipes—is usually the tonic or the tonic and dominant. Because the melody is played over top of this, a constant "longing" is created for the music to resolve and return to the tonic. I believe it is this "longing" feeling that is the reason why so many people say they cannot help crying when they hear bagpipes. Admittedly, though, the classic use of bagpipes at funerals no doubt exacerbates this feeling, as does the timeless image of a lonely piper playing on a foggy Scottish moor.
26. Will & Berg (2007: 55–60).
27. One can say that fear may be an emotional reaction to large army contingents in a parade, and thus a citizenry would buy into the message simply because they feared the consequences of *not* buying in.
28. Kertzer (1988: 77–101).
29. Barron (1991).

30. Ciampaglia (2019).

31. Propaganda in Nazi Germany (2020).

32. The grounds have purposely been preserved in part in order to remind the country of their past. An excellent museum, the Museen der Stadt Nürnberg, sits on the site and covers the entire Nazi experience in great detail.

33. Zeinhefer (2002).

34. This effect was/is the same as used for the Tribute in Light displayed annually at the World Trade Center Memorial in New York City, except that the Tribute only uses 88 lights in total.

35. Cathedral of Light (2020).

36. Triumph of the Will (2020).

37. R. Schwiddessen (personal communication, September 1, 2009).

38. "Walk Softly and Carry a Big Stick" are the famous words that accompany American President Theodore Roosevelt's Big Stick ideology for foreign policy. The concept includes negotiating peacefully—walking softly—while still threatening with the military, carrying the big stick. Experts generally say that this ideology resembles Machiavellian ideals.

39. Cohen (2018).

40. phantuba (2016).

41. Reading Buccaneers Drum & Bugle Corps (2010).

42. Sobczak (2017).

43. Reading Buccaneers Drum & Bugle Corps (2010).

44. Sobczak (2017).

Chapter Six

1. Razzetti (2018).

2. Sherwood (2018).

3. Scham (2008: 23–7).

4. Lucas (2016).

5. Pitts (2008: 49–55); Jacobs (2008).

6. Lima (2011).

7. Kenoyer (2010: 37–58).

8. Logiadou-Platonos (2009).

9. Knossos is very much a real ancient city and Europe's oldest. It is a major tourist attraction today.

10. In the second millennium BCE, Mycenae was one of the major centers of Greek civilization, a military stronghold that dominated much of southern Greece, Crete, the Cyclades, and parts of southwest Anatolia. The period of Greek history from about 1600 BCE to about 1100 BCE is called Mycenaean in reference to Mycenae. In mythology, it is from Mycenae that the king, Agamemnon, set out to bring back Helen, his brother's wife, who had eloped with Paris of Troy. There followed a 10-year war.

11. King & Thompson (1907).

12. The Karnak Temple and surrounding grounds are considered to be the largest religious complex in the world.

13. Lauffray, J. (1979). *Karnak d'Egypte: Domain du divin.* Paris: Centre National de la Recherche Scientifique.

14. Epigraphic Survey. (1994). Reliefs and Inscriptions at Luxor Temple, Vol. 1: The Festival Procession of Opet in the Colonnade Hall, OIP 112. Chicago: The Oriental Institute.

15. Wilkinson, R.H. (2000). *The Complete Temples of Ancient Egypt.* Cairo: The American University in Cairo Press.

16. Allen (1997: 126–7).

17. There can be confusion in names here and in the following paragraphs. The Hittites called their country the Kingdom of Hattusa (Hatti in Akkadian), a name received from the Hattians, an earlier people who inhabited the region until the beginning of the second millennium BC and spoke an unrelated language known as Hattic. Hattusa was also their capital city.

18. Bryce (2002: 189–195).

19. Langgut et al. (2013: 149–175); Drews (1993); Jung & Mehofer (2008: 111–136).

20. The Parthenon or Elgin Marbles are a collection of Classical Greek marble sculptures made under the supervision of the architect and sculptor Phidias and his assistants. They were originally part of the temple of the Parthenon and other buildings on the Acropolis of Athens. They were removed—many say illegally—between 1801 and 1812 by agents of Thomas Bruce, 7th Earl of Elgin. The collection is now on display in the British Museum, in the purpose-built Duveen Gallery. There is an ongoing case for their repatriation.

21. Dunkle (2020).

22. Dunkle (2020).

23. Cartledge (2000).

24. Dionysia (2020, May 7).

25. Schmidt (1995: 1–18); Duff (1992: 55–71).

26. Payne (1962: 211–224).

27. The entrance procession to a Catholic mass is simple but full of symbols. Two servers holding candles lead the procession, walking side by side. An acolyte or another server may hold the processional cross between them, walking with the candle bearers side by side in one line. They are followed by a deacon or other celebrant holding the Gospel Book. The priest is at the end of the procession.

28. Humphrey (1986: 126).

29. Thayer (1940).

30. Latham (2016: 183).

31. Hinduism, the world's oldest religion, is thought to go back four thousand years. I covered a Hindu procession, the Jagannath Rath Yatra, in Chapter Four.

32. The Ark of the Covenant was two stone tablets upon which had been inscribed the Ten Commandments by God and which Moses received on Mt. Sinai during the Jewish exodus from Egypt and search for the promised land of Israel.

33. Coats (n/d).

34. Inauguration of a Torah scroll (2020).

35. Mark (2016).

36. Tong (1996: 49–72).

37. Tong (1996: 49–72).

38. Tong (1996: 49–72).

39. Groom (2016).

40. Hussain (2017).

41. Hussain (2017); Kandy Esala Perahera (2020).

42. Pirenne (1955: 170).

43. The theologian Theodoret of Cyprus (died c. 457) in his Ecclesiastical History Chapter xvii gives what would become the standard version of the finding of the True Cross:

"When the empress beheld the place where the Saviour suffered, she immediately ordered the idolatrous temple, which had been there erected, to be destroyed, and the very earth on which it stood to be removed. When the tomb, which had been so long concealed, was discovered, three crosses were seen buried near the Lord's sepulchre. All held it as certain that one of these crosses was that of our Lord Jesus Christ, and that the other two were those of the thieves who were crucified with Him. Yet they could not discern to which of the three the Body of the Lord had been brought nigh, and which had received the outpouring of His precious Blood. But the wise and holy Macarius, the president of the city, resolved this question in the following manner. He caused a lady of rank, who had been long suffering from disease, to be touched by each of the crosses, with earnest prayer, and thus discerned the virtue residing in that of the Saviour. For the instant this cross was brought near the lady, it expelled the sore disease, and made her whole."

With the Cross were also found the Holy Nails, which Helena took with her back to Constantinople. According to Theodoret, "She had part of the cross of our Saviour conveyed to the palace. The rest was enclosed in a covering of silver and committed to the care of the bishop of the city, whom she exhorted to preserve it carefully, in order that it might be transmitted uninjured to posterity." See True Cross (2020).

44. True Cross (2020).

45. Kaupke (2017).

46. It is even said that the expression "touch wood" may have originated with the true cross although there are also other explanations.

47. Landes (1998).

48. Hillgarth (1986: 19).

49. Klein (2006: 79–99).

50. Broda (2016).

51. Hansen (2017: 305–6).

52. Hansen, 2017: 317).

53. Harner (1977: 46–51).

54. de la Vega (2004: 217–224); Sacsayhuaman was/is a fortress on the outskirts of Cusco, Peru. It was the traditional capital of the Inca Empire.

55. Cudny (2014: 640–656).

Chapter Seven

1. Rauch (2000: 10).

2. Van Gennep (1960: 1–11).

3. Akoma Unity Center (2020).

4. Regrettably, circumcision is still practised on females in some societies.

5. The origins and reasons for circumcision are shrouded in the historical fog of many cultures. In Islam, which is what the Ottomans practiced, the rite was to acknowledge the covenant God made with Abraham, so the circumcision is in itself a sort of blood sacrifice.

6. Atil (1993).

7. Terzioğlu (1995: 84–100).

8. Yerasimos (2009).

9. The Maasai (or Masai) are an ethnic group inhabiting northern, central, and southern Kenya and northern Tanzania.

10. Circumambulation is the act of moving around a sacred object or idol. Circumambulation of temples or deity images is an integral part of Hindu and Buddhist devotional practice and is also present in other religions, including Christianity, Judaism, and Islam. It is a form of procession.

11. Damico (1987); K24 TV (2019).

12. Isaacs (2017).

13. Isaacs (2017).

14. Bedellus comes from the earlier English term beadle, who may have been simply a minor church official. As with so much of timeless ceremonial, it has church origins.

15. University of Glasgow (2021).

16. Maine (1933: 196–7).

17. Johnston (1932).

18. EraGem (2019).

19. Lin & Jirsa (2021).

20. Alexander (2018).

21. TV History (2021).

22. Selin (2016).

23. Liamfoley63 (2020).

24. Parker (2016).

25. Friedman (2014).

26. This is about 18 ft long × 12 ft wide.

27. Kotaridi (1999: 113–120).

28. The "snatching" of Alexander's body and subsequent burial in Egypt is a complex mystery, well worthy of a movie! Much of what happened is linked to the Grand Procession of Ptolemy Philadelphus (Ptolemy I's son) in Alexandria, which is mentioned in Chapter Four; Erskine (2002: 163–179).

29. Sinnema (1992).

30. Ridgley (2020).

31. Sinnema (1992).

32. Frazer (1996: 87).

33. The Coronation service used for Queen Elizabeth II descends directly from that of King Edgar at Bath in 973 CE.

34. Shils & Young (1953: 63–81).

35. Press Secretary to the Queen (2013).

36. Rowse (1953).

37. One can see the parallels between the coronations of Elizabeth I and Charles V in that both sought to settle once and for all the role of the church in politics. In the end, Roman Catholicism was the loser in both cases, thanks to the Reformation, and as will be seen in later chapters, so was any sort of gold standard of morality.

38. Eisenbichler (1999: 430–9).

39. Eisenbichler (1999: 430–9).

40. Heath (2018).

41. Heath (2018).

42. Eisenbichler (1999: 430–9).

43. Kyodo News (a) (2019).

44. Kyodo News (b) (2019).

45. Royal Family (1953).

46. I have called them processions because there is a formal ceremony either preceding or following the procession, although parade is the commonly used term today.

47. Bendat (2012); Eddins (2021).

48. Bendat (2012).

Chapter Eight

1. Calgary (2020).

2. Felske (2008: 74).

3. Calgary Exhibition and Stampede Fonds, M2160/41 (n.d.).

4. Cohen (1985: 50).

5. Connerton (1989: 40).

6. Bell (1997: 127).

7. Calgary Stampede (2019).

8. They are actually divided into 17 sub-phases.

9. Campbell (2008).

10. Schrobsdorff (2011).

11. Brier (1999).

12. Suelzle (2006).

13. Victory Stele of Naram-Sin (2021).

14. Xenophon's writing was done on parchment as opposed to the *carved* language of earlier artifacts such as the stelae and victory scenes described above.

15. See Dakyns (1897: Sec. C.3) who refers to "victims" other than oxen.

16. See Lendering (2010), a translated account of the original description by Quintus Curtius Rufus.

17. Plutarch (n.d.).

18. Taking the current value of silver at approximately $833 USD per kg and an ancient Roman talent equating to 32.3 kg of weight, the present-day value of the 750 vessels of silver coin alone would be more than $60 million USD.

19. The number of vessels filled with gold coin is once again different between Diodorus Siculus and Plutarch. Plutarch states there were *carriers* of gold which was contained in 77 vessels each holding three talents of gold coin. Siculus states 220 carriers only. However, it is likely that the word carriers in each interpretation refers to people, probably about three to carry each vessel which closely matches the numbers. Thus, using Plutarch's figures, today's value of this coin alone would be more than $6 million. The value of the consecrated bowl today would be about $270,000 for the gold alone, let alone the precious stones.

20. The soldiers and spectators along the processional route would have called out the phrase *Io triumphe*, which means "I triumph." Each day's procession would have taken most of the day to pass any given spot. The exact procedures at the end of the celebration are unknown, but based on other triumphs, the many prisoners of war in the procession—possibly tens of thousands, since Paulus captured more than 150,000—would likely have been either executed or sold into slavery. Also, Paulus would have continued up the winding Via Sacra to the top of the Capitoline Hill to the Temple of Jupiter, where he would have made sacrifices to the god of war. It is also likely that there would have been a large feast for the populace of Rome. Most of the booty would have been immediately stored in the state treasury in the adjacent Temple of Saturn.

21. Livius (1905: Vol. 4, Book 31); Livius (1905: Vol. 6, Book 45); Siculus (1947: 87–95); Siculus (1957); Shuckburgh (1962).

22. Lunsford (2004: 11).

23. Versnel (1970: 356ff.) believes it related to the New Year Festival, the purpose of which was to celebrate the return of the victor who was the bearer of good fortune and brought blessings into the city with him. In other words, it had a religious reason. Payne (1962: 9–12) believes it had two reasons—one was as a political tool that reflected the ideals, emotions, ambitions, and mindset of the Roman people, and the other was as an act of propitiation, a gesture to the gods to forgive the crimes of war. This was both political and religious. Kertzer (1988: 29–30) believes it was used as a means to communicate the internal political power structure of Rome, a political reason. Lunsford (2004) believes it depicted how Romans saw themselves and others, in other words a sociological reason. Finally, Beard (2007) basically acknowledges after lengthy analysis that the "why" question is unanswerable.

24. Livy states 120 million sesterces. A sestertius was the equivalent of about 2.5 gm of silver. This translates to about $250 million mentioned using today's value of silver.

25. Hourihan (1997: 1).

26. Krey (1921); Phillips (2015).

27. Hernández (2018); Restall (2018); Prescott (1892). Restall suggests that Moctezuma allowed Cortés to enter Tenochtitlan to keep him and the Spaniards as curiosities, much like the other animals he had in his large menagerie.

28. Sheets (2000).

29. Horne (2007: 45–50).

30. Gee (2019).

31. Studarus (2015).

32. Hernández (2018).

Chapter Nine

1. Ebstein (2020).
2. Levels (2018).
3. Pasadena Tournament of Roses (2020).
4. Code of the City of New Orleans, Louisiana, Chapter 34—Carnival, Mardi Gras (2020).
5. Curran (2020).
6. As with most things concerning morals, it started with the Reformation of the 16th century. Prior to that, there was only one gold standard of morality in the western world: the church and its Judaeo-Christian belief system. At the same time, the church and the state—more often than not an absolute monarchy—were tied at the hip, so to speak. The Reformation started western civilization on the road to humanism and secularism. Humanism is basically the belief that a god is not needed to live a moral life. Secularism basically refers to the separation of church from state. Sometimes the two are combined as secular humanism.
7. Pincott (2014).
8. Pincott (2014).
9. Silverman (2012).
10. Montgomery (2013); Smith (2019).
11. Pincott (2014).
12. Pincott (2014).
13. Klandermans & de Weerd (2000: 71).
14. SPSP (2017).
15. Deeksha (2020).
16. Manstead & Hewstone (1996: 152–6).
17. Klindermans & de Weerd. (2000: 69–74).
18. Reicher (2000: 374–7).
19. Roberts (2020); Van Stekelenburg (2013: 886–905).
20. Jost (2017).
21. Wilkinson (2011: 358–361).
22. McCormack (2018).
23. Dunn (2002).
24. Harvey (1998).
25. Edward Bernays is known as the Father of Public Relations. The term "torches of freedom" was first coined by psychoanalyst A.A. Brill. See Torches of freedom (2021) and Amos & Haglund (2000: 8–9).
26. Gandhi & Dalton (1996: 72).
27. Jack (1994: 240).
28. Branch (1988: 876).
29. White et al. (2013: 667).
30. Bass (2002: 142).
31. Cumberbatch Anderson (2013).
32. Sigal (2013).
33. Bartlett (2013).
34. March on Washington for Jobs and Freedom (2020).
35. Long Bow Group Inc. (1995).
36. Haddad (2021).
37. Brannen et al. (2020).
38. Sugrue (2020).
39. Gay (2018)
40. Gay (2018).
41. At the 1970 celebration, the MC was Ira Einhorn, the self-proclaimed founder of the event. Ironically, he remained true to his beliefs about cleaning up the earth by killing his girlfriend several years later and partially composting her body in a trunk that had also been packed with Styrofoam, air fresheners, and newspapers. See Melina (2011).
42. Brannen et al. (2020).
43. Chenoweth (2020: 69–84).
44. Chenoweth (2020: 69–84).
45. Van Stekelenburg & Klandermans (2013: 886–905).
46. Brannen et al. (2020).
47. Brannen et al. (2020).
48. Brannen et al. (2020).
49. Stekelenburg and Klandermans (2013).
50. Brannen et al. (2020).
51. Stekelenburg and Klandermans (2013).
52. Furedi (2021).

Chapter Ten

1. Bakhtin (1984: 7–8).
2. Langdon (1924).
3. Csapo (2013).
4. A dithyramb was an ancient Greek hymn sung and danced in honor of Dionysus.
5. In Greek mythology, a satyr, also known as a silenos (silenoi is the plural), is a male nature spirit with ears and a tail resembling those of a horse, as well as a permanent, exaggerated erection. Early artistic representations sometimes include horse-like legs, but, by the sixth century BCE, they were more often represented with human legs. Maenads were the female followers of Dionysus and the most significant members of the Thiasus, the god's retinue. Their name literally translates as "raving ones."
6. Csapo (2013).
7. Csapo (2013).
8. Csapo (2013).
9. Ehrenreich (2006: 38).
10. Malm (2018).
11. Lee & Voyles (2019).
12. Walsh (1996: 188–203).
13. James (1963: 182). Note also that the term Mardi Gras came into existence in the Middle Ages and meant Fat Tuesday, referring to Shrove Tuesday, the day before Lent began.
14. Walsh (1996).
15. History.com Editors (2020).
16. James (1963: 175–7).
17. F.E.N.-Vlaanderen (2020).
18. The oldest name that points in the direction of the word carnival is mentioned on an act from the Italian Subiaco from 965 CE as a time indication "carnelevare." In the 13th century we also come across the words "carnisprivialis," "carnis privium," and in an old Liège text the term "quarnivalle." Most attribute the term to the Latin words *caro (flesh)* and *levare* (to remove), referring to the Christian tradition of

abstaining from eating meat on Fridays during Lent (note that it is not a requirement on every day during Lent).

19. Chambers (1903); Harris (2003: 139).

20. Harris (2003: 9).

21. Davis (1975: 99); Petit de Julleville (1885: 199–214).

22. Carpenter (1996: 9–16); Spanish women especially were governed by a strict moral code which at all times except carnival prevented them from even going into bars. See Gilmore (1998).

23. Carpenter (1996).

24. Mardi Gras Unmasked, LLC. (2020).

25. Benotsch et al. (2007: 343–356); Jacobs (2017); Milhausen et al. (2006: 97–106).

26. Froio (2013).

27. Astor (2007).

28. Boodan (2009); Hem-Lee et al. (2019: 40–70).

29. Abbott (1982).

30. Lowrie (2019).

31. Harris (2003: 173).

32. Wünsch (2018).

33. Johnson (2011: 42).

34. Flippo (2020).

35. There are no available studies relating to the exact reasons why people attend carnival in particular. However, some crude studies have been done as to why people attend festivals that found more than 40% of women and more than 80% of men between the ages of 18 and 40 were open to the idea of sex at the festival (i.e., they were probably *expecting* it). See Freeman (2017).

36. Taylor (2018).

37. Gugolati (2018).

38. Gugolati (2018).

39. Forbes-Bell (2020).

40. Soca music is a contemporary Trinidadian style of music. It is now the most popular form of local music associated with the carnival season.

41. Gugolati (2018).

42. Gugolati (2018).

Chapter Eleven

1. Boats have been around since deep in prehistory; ships since ancient times. To clarify the obvious question, boats are considered to be small vessels, with propulsion by humans, wind, or small motors. They usually operate on smaller bodies of water like lakes, rivers, and coastal waters and seldom on the open ocean. Ships ply the oceans and large bodies of inland water. As the saying goes, "a ship can carry a boat but a boat cannot carry a ship." Aircraft, of course, have only been around for barely 100 years.

2. Staff (2020).

3. IMDb (2020).

4. Cartwright (2014).

5. Nichols (2014: 1–8).

6. Nichols (2014: 1–8).

7. Nichols (2014: 1–8).

8. Ridgway (2019).

9. Shewring (2013).

10. Royal Barge Procession (2020).

11. Boyle (2019).

12. Moss (2006: 171–2); River Fencibles were boatmen on the Thames and other southern English towns and cities, who, among their other duties, manned small commercial vessels converted to coastal defense. The HMS *Victory* was Nelson's flagship on which he sailed and was killed at Trafalgar.

13. Heffer (2015).

14. Siculus (1954).

15. Consultancy.uk (2015).

16. Clugston (1984: 26–9).

17. Crawford (2008).

18. Nune (2016).

19. Shelton (2010).

20. Gary (2020).

21. Ford (2001).

22. Gary (2020).

23. Flypast (2020).

24. Department of National Defence (2020).

25. Corbell (2019).

26. Slutsken (2020).

27. In a loop, the control stick is pulled progressively rearward to pitch the nose up and over. The aircraft will complete a 360-degree circle in the vertical plain. The wings remain level throughout the maneuver. In an aileron roll, the aircraft is rolled about its horizontal axis using the ailerons. The aircraft nose stays pointed in the same direction throughout the maneuver. A barrel roll is a combination of pitching up and rolling at the same time. If you imagine a 3D barrel, it's as if the aircraft is flying around the outside of such barrel. In a stall turn, the aircraft does not actually stall. The aircraft is flown directly upward. The aircraft is then yawed, pushing the nose to the side until it is pointing at the ground again. The aircraft is then flown directly down for a short period before pulling out of the dive. If the aircraft is using smoke, the trail looks like an upside-down U. A snap roll is a quick roll, using rudder and back pressure on the stick to force the aircraft to "auto-rotate." A spin can result when an aircraft stalls. The pilot is not in control of the aircraft, it is auto-rolling, auto-yawing and auto-pitching. After a certain number of rotations have been achieved, the pilot can then recover from the spin, using opposite rudder to the direction the aircraft is spinning.

28. Union des Maisons de Champagne (2020).

29. Louis Blériot was the first person to fly solo across the English Channel in 1909. He later went on to build fighter aircraft for WWI with the Société Pour l'Aviation et ses Dérivés (SPAD).

30. Carson (2001).

31. Allison (1999).

32. Carson (2001).

33. Patrouille de France (2020).

34. Barker (2002: 19–20).

35. Onkst (2020).
36. Barker (2002: 11).

Chapter Twelve

1. Love (2008: 196–7).
2. The Age of Revolution was a period from the late 18th to the mid-19th centuries in which a number of significant revolutionary movements occurred in most of Europe and the Americas.... It in turn inspired the French Revolution of 1789, which rapidly spread to the rest of Europe through its wars.
3. Steinbach (2012: 12).
4. It is said that people have been Ireland's largest export. Since 1800, approximately 100 million people have emigrated.
5. American Yawp (2020).
6. McNamara (2020).
7. Snell & Ell (2000: 416–8).
8. The Crisis of Faith was an event in the Victorian era in which much of Europe's middle class began to doubt what was written in the Bible's Book of Genesis as a reliable source for how the universe was created.
9. The Victorian crisis of faith. (2020).
10. Steinbach (2012: 178–80).
11. Hewitt (2012: 9).
12. Hewitt (2012: 720).
13. Hewitt (2012: 627). Sadly, in 2020, only 16% of American adults got their news from newspapers, a decline widely believed to be caused by social media, television, and the internet. See Djordjevic (2021). It would appear that the heyday of newspapers is over.
14. Hills (2015: 27).
15. Hills (2015: 119).
16. Hewitt (2012: 548).
17. Fairchild (1894).
18. Abbott (1982).
19. Vanderbilt (2014).
20. Abbott (1982).
21. The Crystal Palace was a cast iron and plate glass structure, originally built in Hyde Park, London, to house the Great Exhibition of 1851. Designed by Joseph Paxton, the Great Exhibition building was 1851 ft (564 m) long, with an interior height of 128 ft (39 m).
22. Infoplease (2012).
23. Borroz (2009).
24. Bellis (2019).
25. Bellis (2019).
26. CNN (2020).
27. Virginia Asphalt Association (2020).
28. Advamag, Inc. (2020).
29. T. Estes (personal communications, October 2020).
30. Statista (2020).
31. The Aluminum Association (2020).
32. Mayco International (2019).
33. UK Patent office (1857: 255).
34. Khemka (2019).
35. McNeil (1990: 961).
36. CENGAGE (2020).
37. Halacy (1970).
38. Advamag, Inc. (2020).
39. Guinness World Records Limited(b) (2020).
40. Guinness World Records Limited(a) (2020).
41. Hernandez (2017).
42. Phillips (2005); McIntyre (2016).
43. Brooke (2020).
44. Carnivaland (2019).
45. Osborn (2020).
46. Brazil Carnival Shop (2019).
47. Grossman (2014).
48. Fandom (2020).
49. Woods (2019).
50. Gannon (2019).
51. Scarpari (2006).
52. Jando (2020).
53. Saxon (2020).
54. Davis (2002: 1–14).
55. Saxon (2020).
56. Saxon (2020).
57. Victoria and Albert Museum (2020).
58. Nir & Schweber (2017).
59. Handelman (1998: 15–6).
60. Davis (2002: 16–34).
61. Echelman has done this all over the world. Her web site is https://www.echelman.com.
62. There are many such apps, and it's just getting started. Two examples are https://euro-pepmc.org/article/med/32256678 and https://makelight.co.

Bibliography

Abbott, F.A. (1982). *The Quebec Winter Carnival of 1894: The transformation of the city and the festival in the nineteenth century* [Unpublished master's thesis]. University of British Columbia.

Abler, T.S. (1999). *Hinterland warriors and military dress: European empires and exotic uniforms.* Berg.

Advamag. (2021). *Parade float.* How products are made. http://www.madehow.com/Volume-4/Parade-Float.html.

Akoma Unity Center. (2020, March 11). *What are rites of passage and why are they so important?* https://akomaunitycenter.org/what-are-rites-of-passage-and-why-are-they-so-important/.

Alcorta, C.S., & Sosis, R. (2005, Winter). Ritual, emotion, and sacred symbols: The evolution of religion as an adaptive complex. *Human Nature, 16*(4).

Alexander, E. (2018, May 18). Why are we so obsessed with royal weddings? The expert view on the psychology behind the hype. *Bazaar.* https://www.harpersbazaar.com/uk/bazaar-brides/a20135809/why-are-we-so-obsessed-with-royal-weddings-expert-view/.

Aliakbari, M. & Abdollahi, K. (2013, March 1). Does it matter what we wear? A sociolinguistic study of clothing and human values. *International Journal of Linguistics, 5*(2).

Allen, J.P. (1997). The celestial realm. In Silverman, D.P. (Ed.) *Ancient Egypt.* Oxford University Press.

Allen, K. (2019, July 2). About 5 million people attended WorldPride in NYC, mayor says. *abc News.* https://abcnews.go.com/US/million-people-crowed-nyc-worldpride-mayor/story?id=64090338.

Allison, R. (1999). *A short history of aerobatics.* Franklin's Flying Circus & Airshow. https://www.franklinairshow.com/History%20of%20Aerobatics.htm.

The Aluminum Association. (2020). *History of Aluminum.* https://www.aluminum.org/aluminum-advantage/history-aluminum.

Ambady, N., Bernieri, F.J., & Richeson, J.A. (2000). Toward a history of social behavior: Judgmental accuracy from thin slices of the behavioural stream. In Zanna, M.P. (Ed.). *Advances in Experimental Social Psychology, 32.* Academic Press. https://doi.org/10.1016/S0065-2601(00)80006-4.

Ambrosino, B. (2019, May 29). Do humans have a 'religion instinct'? *BBC Future.* https://www.bbc.com/future/article/20190529-do-humans-have-a-religion-instinct.

American Yawp. (2020). *The rise of industrial labor in antebellum America.* United States History I. https://courses.lumenlearning.com/ushistory1americanyawp/chapter/the-rise-of-industrial-labor-in-antebellum-america/.

Amos, A., & Haglund, M. (2000). From social taboo to "torch of freedom": the marketing of cigarettes to women. *Tobacco Control, 9.* http://dx.doi.org/10.1136/tc.9.1.3.

Anglo, S. (1997). *Spectacle, pageantry, and early Tudor policy.* Clarendon Press.

Anthony, D.W. (2007). *The horse, the wheel, and language: How bronze-age riders from the Eurasian steppes shaped the modern world.* Princeton University Press.

Arnold, D., Bell, L., Finnestad, R.B., Haeny, G., & Shafer, B.E. (1997). *Temples of ancient Egypt.* Cornell University Press.

Astor, M. (2007, February 18). Carnival: It's barely about sex. *The Seattle Times.* https://www.seattletimes.com/nation-world/carnival-its-barely-about-sex/.

Athenaeus of Naucratis. (1854). *Athenaeus: The Deipnosophists, 5.* (C.D. Yonge, Trans.) http://www.attalus.org/old/athenaeus5a.html.

Atil, E. (1993). The story of an eighteenth-century Ottoman festival. *Muqarnas, 10.* doi:10.2307/1523184.

Augsten, T., Procopio, P., & Rowan, C. (2014, April 7). *Economic analysis of Toronto World Pride 2014, PLA 1105—Final project.* http://static1.squarespace.com/static/551ebc3ee4b038b5fc34d0b0/t/5521f871e4b04cf2fe2a00e6/1428289649254/FinalEconAnalWorldPride2014.pdf.

Avis, P. (1999). God and the creative imagination: Metaphor, symbol, and myth. In *Religion and theology.* Routledge.

A-Z Films. (2010). Coronation Durbar at Delhi. *Coronation film: Moving images of the British*

Empire. http://www.colonialfilm.org.uk/node/1956.

Babelon, J-P. (1988). Les derniers Valois et Henri IV à Paris. In *Paris et Ses Rois. Le Cadre du Millénaire des Capétiens.*

Bakhtin, M. (1984). *Rabelais and his world.* (H. Iswolsky, Trans.). University Press.

Balabanlilar, L. (2009, April). The emperor Jahangir and the pursuit of pleasure. *Journal of the Royal Asiatic Society Third Series, 19*(2). https://www.jstor.org/stable/27756044.

Barker, D.E. (2002, December). *Zero error margin—Airshow display flying analysed.* Freeworld Publications.

Barrie, T. (1996). *Spiritual path, sacred place: Myth, ritual, and meaning in architecture.* Shambala Publications.

Barron, J. (1991, June 26). A Korean war parade, decades late. *The New York Times.* https://www.nytimes.com/1991/06/26/nyregion/a-korean-war-parade-decades-late.html.

Bartlett, B. (2013, August 9) The 1963 march on Washington changed politics forever. *The Fiscal Times.* https://www.thefiscaltimes.com/Columns/2013/08/09/The-1963-March-on-Washington-Changed-Politics-Forever.

Bass, P.H. (2002). *Like a mighty stream: The march on Washington, August 28, 1963.* Running Press.

Beard, M. (2007). *The Roman triumph.* Harvard University Press.

Becker-Blease, K.A. (2004). Dissociative states through new age and electronic trance music. *Journal of Trauma & Dissociation, 5*(2). https://doi.org/10.1300/J229v05n02_05.

Beeman, W. (1993). The anthropology of theater and spectacle. *Annual Review of Anthropology, 22.*

Beeman, W.O. (2007). The performance hypothesis practicing emotions in protected frames. In Wulff, H. (Ed.), *The Emotions.* Berg Publishers.

Beeman, W.O. (2010). Performance pragmatics, neuroscience and evolution. *Pragmatics and Society 1:1.*

Bell, C. (1997). *Ritual: Perspectives and dimensions.* Oxford University Press.

Bell, L. (1997). The New Kingdom "divine" temple: The example of Luxor. In B.E. Shafer (Ed.), *Temples of ancient Egypt.* Cornell University Press.

Bellinger, M.F. (1927). *A short history of the drama.* Henry Holt and Company.

Bellis, M. (2019, July 20). *The history of trucks from pickups to macks.* ThoughtCo. https://www.thoughtco.com/history-of-trucks-4077036.

Bellis, M. (2019, July 6). *A history of the automobile: The evolution of the car dates all the way back to the 1600s.* ThoughtCo. https://www.thoughtco.com/who-invented-the-car-4059932.

Bendat, J. (2012). *Democracy's big day: The inauguration of our president, 1789–2013.* iUniverse.

Benn, C. (2002). *Daily life in traditional China: The Tang Dynasty.* Greenwood Press.

Benotsch, E.G., Nettles, C.D., Wong, F., Redmann, J., Boschini, J., Pinkerton, S.D., Ragsdale, K., & Mikytuck, J.J. (2007, September). Sexual risk behavior in men attending Mardi Gras celebrations. *Journal of Community Health 32*(5). https://doi.org/10.1007/s10900-007-9054-8.

Bergmann, B., & Kondoleon, C. (1999). *The art of ancient spectacle.* National Gallery of Art.

Bernabeo, P. (2007). *World and its peoples: Eastern and southern Asia—Vol. 8.* Marshall Cavendish.

Betts, H. (2015, March 13). There's a reason women love a man in uniform. *The Telegraph.* http://www.telegraph.co.uk/women/sex/11467328/Theres-a-reason-women-love-a-man-in-uniform.html.

Bianchi, R.S. (1993, July/August). Hunting Alexander's tomb. *Archaeology.*

Bond, M. (2017, June 5). The hidden ways that architecture affects how you feel. *BBC Future.* https://www.bbc.com/future/article/20170605-the-psychology-behind-your-citys-design.

Boodan, A. (2009, February 9). What"s your position? *Trinidad and Tobago Guardian.* https://www.theguardian.com/world/trinidad-and-tobago.

Borroz, T. (2009). *Aug. 14, 1877: Internal combustion's stroke of genius.* Wired. https://www.wired.com/2009/08/dayintech-0814/.

Bossio, G. (2018). Here's *what a man's hairstyle says about his personality.* FashionBeans. https://www.fashionbeans.com/content/heres-what-a-mans-hairstyle-says-about-his-personality/.

Bowdin, G., Allen, J., O'Toole, W., Harris, R., & McDonnell, I. (2006). *Events management.* Elsevier.

Boyer, G.B. (2017, June/July). Dress up. *First things; A monthly journal of religion and public life, 274.*

Boyle, G. (2019, December 13). Royal barge procession completes King's coronation. *Bangkok Post.* https://www.bangkokpost.com/learning/easy/1814604/royal-barge-procession-completes-kings-coronation.

Branch, T. (1988). *Parting the waters: America in the King years 1954–63.* Simon & Schuster.

Brannen, S.J., Haig, C.S., & Schmidt, K. (2020, March). *The age of mass protests: Understanding an escalating global trend.* Center for Strategic and International Studies. https://csis-website-prod.s3.amazonaws.com/s3fs-public/publication/200303_MassProtests_V2.pdf?uL3KRAKjoHfmcnFENNWTXdUbf0Fk0Qke.

Brazil Carnival Shop. (2019, March 21). *History of Rio Carnival floats and adornments.* https://www.brazilcarnivalshop.com/blogs/news/history-of-rio-carnival-floats-and-adornments.

Brier, B. (1999). *The history of ancient Egypt, Part 1 of 4.* The Teaching Company.

Broda, J. (2016). Processions and Aztec state rituals in the landscape of the valley of Mexico. In *Processions in the ancient Americas.* Penn State University Occasional papers in anthropology No. 33.

Brooke, J. (2020). *The flower parades of the Netherlands are a must see.* Flower Power Daily. https://flowerpowerdaily.com/the-flower-parades-of-the-netherlands/.

Bryce, T. (2002). *Life and society in the Hittite world.* Oxford University Press.

Bryson, S. (2015). *The Field of Cloth of Gold.* The Tudor Society. https://www.tudorsociety.com/the-field-of-cloth-of-gold-by-sarah-bryson/.

Calgary. (2020, May 6). In *Wikipedia.* https://en.wikipedia.org/w/index.php?title=Calgary&oldid=955245663.

Calgary Exhibition and Stampede Fonds, M2160/41. (n.d.). *Newsclippings file, 1910–1941.* Glenbow Museum Archives.

Calgary Stampede. (2019). *Parade marshals.* https://www.calgarystampede.com/heritage/parade-marshals.

Cameron, N. (2013). *The cultural development handbook: An A-Z guide to designing successful arts events in the community.* Mimburi Press.

Cameron, R.N. (2004). *New alignments in ritual, ceremony, and celebration* [Unpublished master's thesis]. Griffith University.

Campbell, J. (2008). *The hero with a thousand faces (3rd ed.).* New World Library.

Canadian War Museum. (2009, June 5). *Camouflage: The exhibition.* http://www.warmuseum.ca/media/the-story-of-camouflage-told-at-the-canadian-war-museum-this-summer/.

Carnivaland. (2019). *The ultimate guide to Viareggio Carnival—Featuring the world's best carnival floats!* Carnivaland. https://www.carnivaland.net/viareggio-carnival/.

Carpenter, S. (1996). Women and carnival masking. *Records of early English drama, 21*(2).

Carson, A.J. (2001, October 26). History of aerobatics. *Britannica.* https://www.britannica.com/sports/aerobatics#ref218451.

Cartledge, P. (2000, October). Olympic self-sacrifice. *History Today, 60*(10). https://www.historytoday.com/archive/olympic-self-sacrifice.

Cartwright, M. (2014, March 27). Akrotiri frescoes. *Ancient History Encyclopedia.* https://www.ancient.eu/article/673/akrotiri-frescoes/.

Cathedral of light. (2020, August 30). In *Wikipedia.* https://en.wikipedia.org/w/index.php?title=Cathedral_of_Light&oldid=975825004.

Cavette, C. (2019). Parade float background. *Encyclopedia.com.* https://www.encyclopedia.com/manufacturing/news-wires-white-papers-and-books/parade-float.

CENGAGE. (2020). Medieval liturgy. *Encyclopedia.com.* https://www.encyclopedia.com/humanities/culture-magazines/medieval-liturgy.

CENGAGE. (2020). Parade float. *Encyclopedia.com.* https://www.encyclopedia.com/manufacturing/news-wires-white-papers-and-books/parade-float.

Chambers, E.K. (1903). *The medieval stage. 2 vols.* Oxford University Press.

Chand, M.L., & Levitin, D.J. (2013, April). The neurochemistry of music. *Trends in cognitive sciences, 17*(4). https://doi.org/10.1016/j.tics.2013.02.007.

Chenoweth, E. (2020, July). The future of nonviolent resistance. *Journal of Democracy, 31*(3). https://www.journalofdemocracy.org/articles/the-future-of-nonviolent-resistance-2/.

Christopherson, J. (2018, September 24). *The problem with sacred spaces.* The Exchange. https://www.christianitytoday.com/edstetzer/2018/september/problem-with-sacred-spaces-missio-monday.html.

Chugg, A. (2007). *The quest for the tomb of Alexander the Great.* AMC Publications.

Ciampaglia, C.A. (2019, March 29). *Why were Vietnam War vets treated poorly when they returned?* History. https://www.history.com/news/vietnam-war-veterans-treatment.

Clugston, M. (1984, June 18). The allure of the tall ships. *Maclean's.*

CNN. (2020, January 1). *Before the floats: Carriages of the Rose Parade.* https://www.cnn.com/2016/12/28/us/gallery/tbt-rose-parade/index.html.

Coats, G.W. (n/d). *The ark of the covenant in Joshua: A probe into the history of a tradition.* Lexington Theological Seminary. https://kb.osu.edu/bitstream/handle/1811/58690/HAR_v9_137.pdf.

Code of the City of New Orleans, Louisiana, Chapter 34—Carnival, Mardi Gras. (2020, Mar. 17). https://library.municode.com/la/new_orleans/codes/code_of_ordinances?nodeId=PTIICO_CH34CAMAGR.

Codell, J. (2012, June). On the Delhi Coronation Durbars, 1877, 1903, 1911. In D. Franco (Ed.) *Felluga. BRANCH: Britain, representation and nineteenth-century history. Extension of romanticism and Victorianism on the net.* https://www.branchcollective.org/?ps_articles=julie-codell-on-the-delhi-coronation-durbars-1877–1903–1911.

Cohen, A.P. (1985). *The symbolic construction of community.* Tavistock.

Cohen, E.A. (2018, February 11). The truth about military parades. *The Atlantic.* https://www.theatlantic.com/politics/archive/2018/02/pageantry-military-parades/552953/.

Collins, N. (2020). *Greek architecture (c.900–27*

BCE). Classical Architecture Series. http://www.visual-arts-cork.com/architecture/greek.htm#doric.

Connerton, P. (1989). *How societies remember.* Cambridge University Press.

Consultancy.uk. (2015, August 21). *Nautical event Sail Amsterdam 2015 the biggest ever.* Consultancy.uk. https://www.consultancy.uk/news/2484/nautical-event-sail-amsterdam-2015-the-biggest-ever.

Corbell, S. (2019, September 12). *This is how the 'missing man formation' honors fallen pilots.* We Are the Mighty. https://www.wearethemighty.com/articles/missing-man-formation/.

Crabtree, V. (2004). *Military drill: Its theory and purpose.* The Human Truth Foundation. http://www.vexen.co.uk/military/drill.html#BI_003.

Crawford, M.J. (Ed.). (2008). *The world cruise of the Great White Fleet: Honoring 100 years of global partnership and security.* Naval Historical Center.

Croose, J.F. (2014). *The practices of carnival: Community, culture and place* [Unpublished doctoral dissertation]. University of Exeter.

Crystal, E. (2020). *Roman triumphal arches.* Crystalinks. https://www.crystalinks.com/romanarches.html.

Csapo, E. (2013, February 20). *The Dionysian parade and the poetics of plenitude.* Housman Lecture, Department of Greek and Latin, University College London.

Cudny, W. (2014). The phenomenon of festivals: Their origins, evolution, and classifications. *Anthropos, 109(2).* http://www.jstor.org/stable/43861801.

Cumberbatch Anderson, J. (2017, December 6). *March on Washington 1963: Eyewitnesses to history look back.* Black Voices. https://www.huffingtonpost.ca/entry/march-on-washington-eyewitnesses-to-history-photos_n_3792414?ri18n=true&guccounter=1&guce_referrer=aHR0cHM6Ly93d3cuZ29vZ2xlLmNvNvbS8&guce_referrer_sig=AQAAABCzsjPTKkoUdiAC8aGl18MnPnK6fvkMwroqPa7otuuy3xZfneqZyr7AuRdsPvLJYDGDwHqL1CEPcOpLr4_OrwXvaGh3kt4BTmPA4IGhamuiOxmZGbtl2lwkINM1BDp_1TLdaqb4kxUS24Gz5J3YbKhbbFH5z69l-1uKwrSr2VCi.

Curran, L. (2020). *The rules of Mardi Gras.* New Orleans French Quarter.com. https://www.frenchquarter.com/mardi-gras-rules/.

Czikszentmihalyi, M. (1975). *Beyond boredom and anxiety.* Jossey-Bass.

Dakyns, H.G. (1897). Cyropaedia: The education of Cyrus, book VIII. *The works of Xenophon.* Macmillan and Co. http://ebooks.adelaide.edu.au/x/xenophon/x5cy/.

Damico, J. (1987). *Eunoto ceremony.* Maasai—The Eunoto ceremony. https://www.bluegecko.org/kenya/tribes/maasai/eunoto.htm.

Davis, H.T. (2016). *Alexandria, the golden city, Vol. I - The city of the Ptolemies.* Pickle Partners Publishing.

Davis, J.M. (2002). *The circus age: Culture and society under the American big top.* University of North Carolina Press.

Davis, N.Z. (1975). *Society and culture in early modern France.* Stanford University Press.

Deeksha, S. (2020). *Crowd: Meaning, types and characteristics/psychology.* Psychology Discussion. https://www.psychologydiscussion.net/social-psychology-2/crowd-behaviour/crowd-meaning-types-and-characteristics-psychology/1356.

de la Vega, G. (2004). *The Incas: The royal commentaries of the Inca* (M. Jolas, Trans.). PeruBook.

Department of National Defence. (2020, April 29). *Canadian Forces Snowbirds launch cross-Canada tour.* Royal Canadian Air Force. http://rcaf-arc.forces.gc.ca/en/article-template-standard.page?doc=canadian-forces-snowbirds-launch-cross-canada-tour/k98frkmr.

Deutsch, M. (1926). Caesar's triumphs. *The Classical Weekly, 19*(13).

Dionysia. (2020, May 7). In *Wikipedia.* https://en.wikipedia.org/w/index.php?title=Dionysia&oldid=955303010.

Djordjevic, M. (2021, February 23). *21 extraordinary newspaper statistics you should know about in 2021.* Letter.ly. https://letter.ly/newspaper-statistics/.

Doan, C.L.M. (2010, April 8). *Vancouver 2010.* Catriona Le May Doan, OC. http://catrionalemaydoan.ca/vancouver-2010/.

Donzino, D., Donzino, A., & Fernandez, C. (2020). *Delhi Durbar 1903.* Beau Geste. http://www.beau-geste.com/Durbar1903/index.htm.

Downs, J.F. (1961, December). The origin and spread of riding in the near east and central Asia. *American Anthropologist, 63*(6).

Doyle, N. (1998). *Iconography and the interpretation of ancient Egyptian watercraft* [Unpublished master's thesis]. Texas A&M University.

Drews, R. (1993). *The end of the Bronze Age: Changes in warfare and the catastrophe ca. 1200 BC.* Princeton University Press.

Duff, P.B. (1992, Spring). The march of the divine warrior and the advent of the Greco-Roman king: Mark's account of Jesus' entry into Jerusalem. *Journal of Biblical Literature, 111*(1).

Dunkle, R. (2020). *Religious life.* Brooklyn College Classics Department. http://www.faculty.umb.edu/gary_zabel/Courses/Morals%20and%20Law/M+L/Plato/rligious.htm.

Dunn, A. (2002). *The great rising of 1381: The peasant's revolt and England's failed revolution.* Tempus.

Durkheim, E. (1965). *The elementary forms of religious life.* Free Press.

Ebrey, P. (1999). Taking out the grand carriage: Imperial spectacle and the visual culture of Northern Song Kaifeng. *Asia Major, 12*(1), third series. http://www.jstor.org/stable/41645586.

Ebstein, J. (2020, January). *Expression explained: Rules were meant to be broken because isn't that the point?* Writing cooperative. https://writingcooperative.com/expression-explained-rules-were-meant-to-be-broken-2ea482e3307e.

Eddins, G.Z. (2021). *Americans love a parade: The history of presidential inaugural parades.* Our White House: Looking in, looking out. https://ourwhitehouse.org/presidential-inaugural-parades/.

Ehrenreich, B. (2006). *Dancing in the streets: A history of collective joy.* Henry Holt and Company.

Eisenbichler, K. (1999, December). Charles V in Bologna: The self-fashioning of a man and, a city. *Renaissance Studies, 13*(4), *Special Issue: Civic Self-Fashioning in Renaissance Bologna: historical and scholarly contexts.*

Ellis, N. (1999). *Feasts of light: Celebrations for the seasons of life based on the Egyptian goddess mysteries.* Quest Books.

Ellis, R. (2019, August 10). Sporting space, sacred space: A theology of sporting place. *Religions 2019, 10.*

Engdahl, F.W. (2015, May 13). *Why I wept at the Russian parade.* New eastern outlook. http://journal-neo.org/2015/05/13/why-i-wept-at-the-russian-parade/.

Enloe, C. (2000). *Manoeuvers: The International politics of militarizing women's lives.* University of California Press.

Ephrat, L. (2016, October 23). *The science behind why we dress up.* Quarz.com. https://qz.com/814930/the-science-behind-why-we-dress-up/.

Epigraphic Survey. (1994). *Reliefs and inscriptions at Luxor Temple, Vol. 1: The festival procession of Opet in the colonnade hall, OIP 112.* The Oriental Institute.

EraGem. (2019, July 31). Medieval wedding ceremonies. https://eragem.com/news/medieval-wedding-ceremonies/.

Erskine, A. (2002, October). Life after death: Alexandria and the body of Alexander. In *Greece & Rome, 49*(2).

Evans, S.T., & Nichols, D.L. (2015). Water temples and civil engineering at Teotihuacan, Mexico. In N. Gonlin & K.D. French (Eds.), *Human adaptation in ancient Mesoamerica.* University of Colorado Press.

Fairchild, Jr., G.M. (1894). *A short account of ye Quebec Winter Carnival holden in 1894.* Nabu Press.

Falk, D.A. (2015). *Ritual processional furniture: A material and religious phenomenon in Egypt* [Unpublished doctoral dissertation]. University of Liverpool.

Fandom. (2020). *Largest balloons in the parade.* Macy's Thanksgiving Day parade: 90 parades and counting. https://macysthanksgiving.fandom.com/wiki/Largest_Balloons_in_the_Parade.

Feast of Fools. (2020, March 19). In *Wikipedia.* https://en.wikipedia.org/w/index.php?title=Feast_of_Fools&oldid=946381408.

Felske, L.W. (2008). Calgary's parading culture before 1912. In M. Foran (Ed.), *Icon, brand, myth: The Calgary Stampede.* Athabaska University Press.

F.E.N.-Vlaanderen. (2020). *Wat is carnaval?* https://www.fenvlaanderen.be/carnaval/wat-carnaval.

Flippo, H. (2020). *Fasching and karneval.* The German way & more. https://www.german-way.com/history-and-culture/holidays-and-celebrations/fasching-and-karneval/.

Flypast. (2020, May 12). In *Wikipedia.* https://en.wikipedia.org/w/index.php?title=Flypast&oldid=956338115.

Forbes-Bell, S. (2020, Mar. 3). *Skin, feathers and gems: Psychology and carnival costumes.* Fashion is psychology. https://fashionispsychology.com/skin-feathers-and-gems-psychology-and-carnival-costumes/.

Ford, D. (2001, May). High honor: The origins of the missing man formation. *Air & Space Magazine.* https://www.airspacemag.com/military-aviation/high-honor-2041010/?page=1.

Frazer, J.G. (1996). *The illustrated golden bough: A study in magic and religion.* Labyrinth Publishing.

Freeman, T. (2017, April 13). Here's your actual chance of hooking up at a music festival. *Maxim.* https://www.maxim.com/news/hooking-up-music-festival-study-2017–4.

Friedman, R. (2014, August 20). The primary emotional purposes of a funeral or memorial. *Psychology Today.* https://www.psychologytoday.com/ca/blog/broken-hearts/201408/the-primary-emotional-purposes-funeral-or-memorial.

Froio, N. (2013, February 11). Hyper sexual Carnival atmosphere has a dark side for Rio's women. *Independent.* https://www.independent.co.uk/voices/comment/hyper-sexual-carnival-atmosphere-has-a-dark-side-for-rios-women-8490306.html.

Fukaya, M. (2012, January). Oracular sessions and the installations of priests and officials at the Opet Festival. *Orient, 47.*

Furedi, F. (2021, August 4). *What the 2011 riots revealed about our nation.* Spiked. https://www.spiked-online.com/2021/08/04/what-the-2011-riots-revealed-about-our-nation/.

Fussell, P. (2002). *Uniforms: Why we are what we wear.* Houghton Mifflin.

Gabriel, R.A., & Metz, K.S. (1992). *A short history*

of war: The evolution of warfare and weapons. Strategic Studies Institute, U.S. Army War College. http://www.au.af.mil/au/awc/awcgate/gabrmetz/gabr0004.htm.

Gandhi, M., & Dalton, D. (Ed.). (1996). *Selected political writings.* Hackett Publishing.

Gannon, D. (2019, November 15). *Festive facts and figures about the Macy's Thanksgiving Day parade.* 6sqft. https://www.6sqft.com/festive-facts-and-figures-about-the-macys-thanksgiving-day-parade/.

Gary, D. (2020, May 13). Formation flying. *Encyclopædia Britannica.* https://www.britannica.com/technology/formation-flying.

Gay, R. (2018, January/February). Fifty years ago, protesters took on the Miss America Pageant and electrified the feminist movement. *Smithsonian Magazine.* https://www.smithsonianmag.com/history/fifty-years-ago-protestors-took-on-miss-america-pageant-electrified-feminist-movement-180967504/.

Gee, M. (2019, June 19). The Raptors' victory parade was more than a celebration—It was a glimpse of today's Canada. *The Globe and Mail.* https://www.theglobeandmail.com/canada/toronto/article-the-raptors-finals-run-and-celebration-parade-has-shown-what-a/.

Gillath, O., Bahns, A.J., Ge, F., & Crandall, C.S. (2012, August). Shoes as a source of first impressions. *Journal of Research in Personality, 46*(4).

Gilmore, D.D. (1998). *Carnival and culture: Sex, symbol, and status in Spain.* Yale University Press.

Glazier, S.D. (1997). *Anthropology of religion: A handbook.* Praeger.

Goldman, J.S. (2000). Sonic entrainment. In D. Campbell (Ed.), *Music: Physician for times to come.* The Theosophical Publishing House.

Gorlinski, V. (2010, Jan. 27). Bonampak. *Encyclopedia Britannica.* https://www.britannica.com/place/Bonampak.

Greeley, A.M. (1995). *Sociology and religion: A collection of readings.* HarperCollins College Publishers.

Green, M., Buday, R., & Baranowski, T. (2017, May 1). *Understanding the science and psychology behind buildings.* Common Edge. https://commonedge.org/understanding-the-science-and-psychology-behind-buildings/.

Groom, N. (2016, October 6). Hard act to swallow! Brutal rituals of devotees who force swords, workshop tools and rifles through their own cheeks at Asian vegetarian festival. *Daily Mail.* https://www.dailymail.co.uk/news/article-3825441/Devotees-pierce-cheeks-swords-rifles-Taoist-festival.html.

Grossman, D. (2014, December 1). *Today in history: First flight of a helium airship.* Airships.net. https://www.airships.net/blog/happy-birthday-helium-airships/.

Gugolati, M. (2018). *Pretty Mas': Visuality and performance in Trinidad and Tobago's contemporary carnival, West Indies* [Unpublished doctoral dissertation]. PSL Research University.

Guinness World Records Limited(a). (2020). *Heaviest single chassis parade float.* https://www.guinnessworldrecords.com/world-records/heaviest-single-chassis-parade-float.

Guinness World Records Limited(b). (2020). *Longest single chassis parade float.* https://www.guinnessworldrecords.com/world-records/longest-single-chassis-parade-float.

Guthrie, C. (2000). *Neurology, ritual, and religion: An initial exploration.* Neurotheology. http://www.oocities.org/iona_m/Neurotheology/Neuroritual.html.

Haddad, M. (2021, March 30). Mapping major protests around the world. *Aljazeera.* https://www.aljazeera.com/news/2021/3/30/mapping-major-protests-around-the-world.

Hagan, P. (2012, April 23). The ladies in red who look ready for bed. *Daily Mail (London).* https://www.dailymail.co.uk/news/article-2133683/The-ladies-red-look-ready-bed-Men-think-scarlet-clad-woman-likely-sleep-date.html.

Halacy, D.S. (1970). *Charles Babbage, father of the computer.* Crowell-Collier Press.

Hamblin, W.J. (2006). *Warfare in the ancient near east to 1600 BC: Holy warriors at the dawn of history.* Routledge.

Hamilton-Smith, N., Malloch, M., Ashe, S., Rutherford, A., & Bradford, B. (2015). *Community Impact of Public Processions.* Scottish Government.

Handelman, D. (1998). *Models and mirrors: Towards an anthropology of public events.* Berghahn Books.

Hansen, L.J. (2017). *Aztec human sacrifice as entertainment? The physio-psycho-social rewards of Aztec sacrificial celebrations* [Electronic doctoral dissertation, 1287]. University of Denver. https://digitalcommons.du.edu/etd/1287.

Harner, M. (1977, April). The enigma of Aztec sacrifice. *Natural History, 86*(4).

Harnett, C.E. (2014, May 19). Parade floats sell goodwill and exposure for businesses. *Times Colonist.* https://www.timescolonist.com/business/parade-floats-sell-goodwill-and-exposure-for-businesses-1.1067329.

Harris, M. (2003). *Carnival and other Christian festivals: Folk theology and folk performance.* University of Texas Press.

Harvey, G., & Reid, S. (2001). *The Usborne internet-linked encyclopedia of ancient Egypt.* Usborne Publishing.

Harvey, S. (1998, March). Marching for the vote: Remembering the woman suffrage parade of 1913. *Library of Congress Information Bulletin, 57*(3).

Hawkins, K. (2016, March 3). *Sacred spaces in public places*. Carolina Planning Journal. https://carolinaangles.com/2016/03/03/sacred-spaces-in-public-places/.

Haynes, S. (2020, June 26). What's changed—and what hasn't—in 50 years of Pride Parades. *Time*. https://time.com/5858086/pride-parades-history/.

Heath, R. (2018). The coronation of Charles V. https://www.emperorcharlesv.com/charles-v/emperor-charles-v-coronation/.

Heffer, S. (2015, January 30). The dockers, Churchill, and the war's most shameful secret. *Daily Mail*. https://www.pressreader.com/uk/daily-mail/20150130/282132109852982.

Hem-Lee, S., Hunter, C., & McNab, J. (2019, June). Their story: Carnival, women, sexuality and sex in the Caribbean. *International Journal of Gender and Women's Studies, 7*(1). http://dx.doi.org/10.15640/ijaah.v7n1a5.

Hernandez, J. (2017, January 4). *This 148,000 lb Rose Parade float set a world record and it's a wave pool for dogs*. The Inertia. https://www.theinertia.com/surf/this-148000-lb-rose-parade-float-set-a-world-record-and-its-a-wavepool-for-dogs/.

Hernández, B. (2018, December 18). Guns, germs, and horses brought Cortés victory over the mighty Aztec empire. *National Geographic*. https://www.nationalgeographic.com/history/history-magazine/article/cortes-tenochtitlan?loggedin=true.

Hewitt, M. (2012). *The Victorian world*. Routledge.

Hillgarth, J.N. (1986). *Christianity and paganism, 350–750: The conversion of western Europe*. University of Pennsylvania Press.

Hills, R.L. (2015). *Papermaking in Britain 1488–1988: A short history*. Bloomsbury Publishing.

Hindmarch, S. (2020, October 6). *Resonant frequencies of the body*. Health & Bass. https://www.healthandbass.com/post/resonant-frequencies-of-the-bod.

History.com Editors. (2020, June 28). *Saturnalia*. https://www.history.com/topics/ancient-rome/saturnalia.

Horne, A. (2007). *To lose a battle: France 1940*. Penguin Books.

Horowitz, S.S. (2012, November 20). Could a sonic weapon make your head explode? *Popular Science*. https://www.popsci.com/technology/article/2012–11/acoustic-weapons-book-excerpt/.

Hourihan, M. (1997). *Deconstructing the hero: Literary theory and children's literature*. Routledge.

Howlett, N., Pine, K.L., Cahill, J., Orakçıoğlu, I., & Fletcher B. (2015). Small changes in clothing equal big changes in perception: The interaction between provocativeness and occupational status. *Sex Roles: A Journal of Research. February 2015, 72*(3–4).

Howlett, N., Pine, K.L., Orakçıoğlu, I., & Fletcher, B. (2013). The influence of clothing on first impressions: Rapid and positive responses to minor changes in male attire. *Journal of Fashion Marketing and Management. 2013, 17*(1).

Humphrey, J.H. (1986). *Roman circuses: Arenas for chariot racing*. University of California Press.

Huntington, S.P. (1957). *The soldier and the state*. Random House.

Hurley, A.K. (2017, January 18). A brief history of inauguration parades. *Washington City Paper*. https://washingtoncitypaper.com/article/192641/a-brief-history-of-inauguration-parades/.

Hurley, A.K. (2017, July 14). *This is your brain on architecture*. CityLab. https://getpocket.com/explore/item/this-is-your-brain-on-architecture.

Hussain, T.S. (2017, March 15). *The festival of the tooth: A unique symbol of Sri Lanka*. Culture Trip. https://theculturetrip.com/asia/sri-lanka/articles/the-festival-of-the-tooth-a-unique-symbol-of-sri-lanka/.

IMDb. (2020). *H.M.S. Bounty sails again! (1962)*. https://www.imdb.com/title/tt0265216/.

Inauguration of a Torah scroll. (2020, August 12). In *Wikipedia*. https://en.wikipedia.org/w/index.php?title=Inauguration_of_a_Torah_scroll&oldid=972576657.

Infoplease. (2012). Suburb: History of suburbs. *The Columbia Electronic Encyclopedia* (6th ed.). https://www.infoplease.com/encyclopedia/arts/visual/architecture/suburb/history-of-suburbs.

Inomata, T. (2006, October). Plazas, performers, and spectators: Political theaters of the classic Maya. In *Current Anthropology, 47*(5). https://doi.org/10.1086/506279.

INS. (1951, April 21). *Famous New York City ticker tape parade for MacArthur in 1951*. Timothy Hughes Rare and Early Newspapers. https://web.archive.org/web/20181124134003/http://www.rarenewspapers.com/view/211983?imagelist=1#full-images.

Isaacs, D. (2017, October 4). The graduation ceremony. *Wiley Online Library*. https://onlinelibrary.wiley.com/doi/full/10.1111/jpc.13698.

Jack, H.A. (Ed.). (1994). *The Gandhi reader: A source book of his life and writings*. Grove Press.

Jacobs, J.Q. (2008). *Landscape geometry of the 'cursus' and Stonehenge*. Archaeoblog. http://www.jqjacobs.net/archaeology/stonehenge_cursus.html.

Jacobs, T. (2017, June 14). Studying drunken promiscuity at Mardi Gras. *Pacific Standard*. https://psmag.com/social-justice/studying-drunken-promiscuity-at-mardi-gras-8991.

James, E.O. (1963). *Seasonal feasts and festivals*. Barnes and Noble.

Jando, D. (2020). *Short history of the circus*.

Circopedia. http://www.circopedia.org/ SHORT_HISTORY_OF_THE_CIRCUS.

Johnson, J.H. (2011). *Venice incognito: Masks in the supreme republic.* University of California Press.

Johnston, H.W. (1932). *The private life of the Romans.* Scott, Foresman and Company.

Jones, C.B. (2007b). *Introduction to the study of religion, Part 2 of 2.* The Teaching Company.

Jost, J.T. (2017, April 24). Hitting the streets for science: What motivates protest behavior? *Association for Psychological Science.* https://www.psychologicalscience.org/publications/observer/obsonline/hitting-the-streets-for-science-what-motivates-protest-behavior.html.

Joye, Y., & Dewitte, S. (2016, September). Up speeds you down. Awe-evoking monumental buildings trigger behavioral and perceived freezing. *Journal of Environmental Psychology, 47.*

Jung, R., & Mehofer, M. (2008). A sword of Naue II type from Ugarit and the historical significance of Italian type weaponry in the eastern Mediterranean. *Aegean Archaeology 8.*

K24 TV. (2019, September 30). *"Eunoto" rite of passage for Morans.* https://www.youtube.com/watch?v=GZ_aod9yA48.

Kandy Esala Perahera. (2020, October 29). In *Wikipedia.* https://en.wikipedia.org/w/index.php?title=Kandy_Esala_Perahera&oldid=986040264.

Karecki, M. (2000). Discovering the roots of ritual. *Missionalia: Journal of the South African Missological Society.* http://www.geocities.ws/athens/parthenon/8409/ritual97.htm.

Karlsson, E.L. (2020). *Analysis of the Changes of the Opet Festival Procession: Between the Regents Hatshepsut and Tutankhamun* [Unpublished BA thesis]. Uppsala Universitet, The Institution for Archaeology and Ancient History.

Kaupke, C. (2017, September 14). *This is how we honor the Cross of Christ.* The mystical humanity of Christ. https://www.coraevans.com/blog/article/this-is-how-we-honor-the-cross-of-christ.

Kelleher, K. (1995, September 18). Three cheers for those sexy men in uniform. *Los Angeles Times.*

Kenoyer, J.M. (2004). Wheeled vehicles of the Indus Valley civilization of Pakistan and India. In Fansa, M., & Burmeister, S. (Eds.), *Bad unil wagen: Der ursprung einer Innovation wagen im vorderen Orient und Europa.* Verlagg Philipp von Zabem.

Kenoyer, J.M. (2010). Master of animals and animal masters in the iconography of the Indus tradition. In Counts, D.B., & Arnold, B. (Eds.), *The master of animals in old world iconography.* Archaeolingua Alapìitvaìny.

Kernodle, G.R. (1989). *The theatre in history.* University of Arkansas Press.

Kertzer, D.I. (1988). *Ritual, politics and power.* Yale University Press.

Khemka, P. (2019, February 27). *Plastics in the automotive industry—Which materials will be the winners and losers?* Nexant. https://www.nexant.com/resources/plastics-automotive-industry-which-materials-will-be-winners-and-losers.

King, L.W., & Thompson, R.C. (1907). *The sculptures and inscription of Darius the Great on the rock of Behistûn in Persia: A new collation of the Persian, Susian and Babylonian texts.* Oxford University Press.

Kitchen, K.A. (1982). *Pharaoh triumphant: The life and times of Ramesses II.* Cairo University Press.

Klandermans, B., & de Weerd, M. (2000). Group identification and political protest. In Stryker, S., Owens, T.J., & White, R.W. (Eds.), *Self, identity, and social movements.* University of Minnesota Press.

Klein, C. (2019, November 21). The first Macy's Thanksgiving Day parade. *History.* https://www.history.com/news/the-first-macys-thanksgiving-day-parade

Klein, H.A. (2006). Sacred relics and imperial ceremonies at the great palace of Constantinople. In F.A. Bauer (Hrsg.), *Visualisierungen von herrschaft, BYZAS, 5.*

Knapp, A.B. (2008). Monumental architecture, identity and memory. In *Proceedings of the symposium: Bronze Age architectural traditions in the east Mediterranean: Diffusion and diversity.*

Knighton, T., & García, C. (1999). Ferdinand of Aragon's entry into Valladolid in 1513: The triumph of a Christian king. *Early Music History, 18.*

Kotaridi, A. (1999). Macedonian burial customs and the funeral of Alexander the Great. In *International Congress Alexander the Great: From Macedonia to the Oikoumene Veria.*

Krey, A.C. (1921). *The First Crusade: The accounts of eye-witnesses and participants.* Princeton University Press.

Krishnan, R. (2020, June 24). Jagannath Yatra—a 462-year-old tradition that nearly got cancelled this year. *ThePrint.* https://theprint.in/india/jagannath-yatra-%E2%81%A0-a-462-year-old-tradition-that-nearly-got-cancelled-this-year/447185/.

Krueger, G.P. (2012). Psychological issues in military uniform design. In Sparks, E. (Ed.), *Advances in military textiles and personal equipment.*

Kuritz, P. (1988). *The making of theatre history.* Prentice Hall.

Kyodo News (a). (2019, November 10). *Emperor, empress parade in Tokyo to commemorate enthronement.* https://english.kyodonews.net/news/2019/11/9879bcf30735-emperor-empress-to-parade-in-tokyo-to-commem orate-enthronement.html.

Kyodo News (b). (2019, November 8). *Emperor's enthronement parade inspiring wedding dresses, tours.* https://english.kyodonews. net/news/2019/11/2a4ac3a95cc6-emperors-enthronement-parade-inspiring-wedding-dresses-tours.html.

Lakens, D., & Stel, M. (2011). If they move in sync, they must feel in sync: Movement synchrony leads to attributions of rapport and entitativity. *Social Cognition, 29*(1).

Lakpura™ LLC. (2020). *Kandy Esala Perahera.* https://lakpura.com/kandy-esala-perahera.

Landes, R. (1998). *Relics, apocalypse, and the deceits of history: Ademar of Chabannes, 989–1034.* Harvard University Press.

Langdon, S. (1924, Jan.). The Babylonian and Persian Sacaea. *The Journal of the Royal Asiatic Society of Great Britain and Ireland, 1.* Cambridge University Press.

Langgut, D., Finkelstein, I., & Litt, T. (2013, October). Climate and the late Bronze Collapse: New evidence from the southern Levant, *Journal of Institute of Archaeology of Tel Aviv University, 40*(2).

Latham, J.A. (2016). *Performance, memory, and processions in ancient Rome: The Pompa Circensis from the late republic to late antiquity.* Cambridge University Press.

Lau, G. (2015, June 23). *5 notes on urban boulevards.* Projexity. https://medium.com/pro jexity-blog/5-notes-about-urban-boulevards-7c167da03e7b.

Lauffray, J. (1979). *Karnak d'Egypte: Domain du divin.* Centre National de la Recherche Scientifique.

Laurenza, D., Taddei, M., & Zanon, E. (2006). *Leonardo's machines: Da Vinci's inventions revealed.* David & Charles.

Laver, J. (1945). Fashion and class distinction. *Pilot Papers, 1.*

Laver, J. (1969). *Modesty in dress: An inquiry into the fundamentals of fashion.* Houghton Mifflin.

Lee, S., & Voyles, T.J. (2019). *Join the penis parade.* Now Curation. https://www. nowcuration.com/join-the-penis-parade.

Lee, W.E. (2015). *Waging war: Conflict, culture, and innovation in world history.* Oxford University Press.

Lendering, J. (2010). Alexander the Great enters Babylon. *Livius.Org.* http://www.livius.org/ aj-al/alexander/alexander_t44.html.

Lerner, J.S., Li, Y., Valdesolo, P., & Kassam, K. (2015, January). Emotion and Decision Making. *Annual Review of Psychology, 66.* https://doi. org/10.1146/annurev-psych-010213-115043.

Levels, G. (2018, May 4). *What are rules and why do we need to follow them?* Bring your own science. https://bringyourownscience.com/ rules/.

Liamfoley63. (2020, May 6). May 6, 1954:

Death of Duchess Cecilie of Mecklenburg-Schwerin, Crown Princess of Germany and Prussia. European royal history ~ Exploring the history of European royalty. https:// europeanroyalhistory.wordpress.com/tag/ prince-louis-ferdinand-of-prussia/.

Lieff, J. (2014, March 2). *Music stimulates emotions through specific brain circuits.* http:// jonlieffmd.com/blog/music-stimulates-emotions-through-specific-brain-circuits.

Lima, M.G. (2011, January 18). *Sumerian art: The Warka Vase.* Introduction to the history of art, part 1—From prehistoric art to early Renaissance. http://arthistorypart1.blogspot. ca/2011/01/sumerian-art-warka-vase.html.

Lin & Jirsa. (2021). *Baraati Indian Wedding Tradition.* https://www.linandjirsa.com/ baraat-indian-wedding-tradition/.

Lin, Z. (2001). *Awakened: Qin's terra-cotta army.* Shaanxi Travel and Tourism Press.

Lincoln, M.D. (2014, Apr 2). *Marvelous mechanical bodies in sixteenth-century joyous entries in Antwerp and Vienna.* https:// matthewlincoln.net/2014/04/02/marvelous-mechanical-bodies.html.

Lipinski, J. (2015, Feb. 10). 2014 *Mardi Gras season contributed $465 million to New Orleans economy, study shows.* nola.com. https://www.nola.com/news/business/article_ fb6dee00-4e9b-545c-84af-ddb8e7ffb407. html.

List of largest peaceful gatherings. (2020, May 17). In *Wikipedia.* https://en.wikipedia.org/w/ index.php?title=List_of_largest_peaceful_ gatherings&oldid=957109398.

Livingston, L. (2000, December 12). Egyptian influence on ionic temple architecture. *Special Studies: Directed Research Project.* University of Notre Dame. https://www.saic.edu/~llivin/ research/ionic_architecture/paper.html.

Livius, T. (1905). *The history of Rome, 6*(45). (E. Rhys, Ed.). J.M. Dent & Sons.

Livius, T. (1905). *The history of Rome, 4*(31). (E. Rhys, Ed.). J.M. Dent & Sons.

Logiadou-Platonos, S. (2009). *Knossos: The palace of Minos, A survey of the Minoan civilization.* I. Mathioulakis & Co.

Long Bow Group Inc. (1995). *The gate of heavenly peace.* In collaboration with ITVS. http:// tsquare.tv/film/transcript.html.

Lonsdale, D.J. (2007). *Alexander the Great: Lessons in strategy.* Routledge.

Loth, C. (2011, August 1). *The triumphal arch as a design resource.* Institute of Classical Architecture & Art. https://www.classicist. org/articles/classical-comments-the-triumphal-arch-as-a-design-resource/.

Love, R.S. (2008). *The Enlightenment.* Greenwood Press.

Lowrie, M. (2019, February 13). Quebec City winter carnival vows to improve parade after first event deemed 'total flop.' *Global News.* https://globalnews.ca/news/4958775/

quebec-city-winter-carnival-vows-to-improve-parade-after-first-event-deemed-a-flop/.

Lucas, P.C. (2016). *Almendres stone rows, Portugal*. Neolithic studies. https://www2.stetson.edu/neolithic-studies/stone-rows/almendres-stone-rows-portugal/.

Lukee. (2018, March 14). *Hair psychology: What your hairstyle says about your personality*. addcolo. https://www.addcolo.com/blog/hair-psychology-what-your-hairstyle-says-about-your-personality/.

Lunsford, A.D. (2004). *Romans on parade: Representations of Romanness in the Triumph* [Unpublished doctoral dissertation]. Ohio State University, Department of Greek and Latin.

MacDougall, H.G., & Moore, S.T. (2005, September). Marching to the beat of the same drummer: the spontaneous tempo of human locomotion. *Journal of Applied Physiology, 99*(3).

Macy's Thanksgiving Day Parade. (2020). *Parade route*. Parade trivia. https://macysthanksgiving.fandom.com/wiki/Parade_Route.

Madden, B. (2014, June 19). *The resonant human: The science of how tempo affects us*. Sonic scoop. https://sonicscoop.com/2014/06/19/the-resonant-human-the-science-of-how-tempo-affects-us/.

Maine, B. (1933). *Edward Elgar: His life and works, 2: Works*. G. Bell & Sons.

Malm, S. (2018, February 20). Members only! Penis-themed parades celebrating the god of fertility and lovemaking are held in Greece. *Daily Mail*. https://www.dailymail.co.uk/news/article-5413557/Penis-fertility-festival-held-Greece.html.

Manning, K. (2000). *Rituals, ceremonies, and cultural meaning in higher education*. Bergin and Garvey.

Mansoor, P.R. (2014, Summer). The evolution of military ethos over the ages. *Phi Kappa Phi Forum. 94*(2).

Manstead, A.S.K. & Hewstone, M. (1996). *Blackwell encyclopedia of social psychology*. Blackwell.

Marcantonio, D. (2009, December 28). Natural laws of architecture—The plan. *Marcantonio Architects Blog*. http://blog.marcantonioarchitects.com/natural-laws-of-architecture-the-plan/.

March on Washington for jobs and freedom. (2020, June 14). In *Wikipedia*. https://en.wikipedia.org/w/index.php?title=March_on_Washington_for_Jobs_and_Freedom&oldid=962503458.

Mardi Gras Unmasked, LLC. (2020). *Mardi Gras history*. Mardi Gras traditions. https://mardigrastraditions.com/mardi_gras_history/.

Mark, E. (2016, February 22). Taoism. *Ancient History Encyclopedia*. https://www.ancient.eu/Taoism/.

Matthews, D. (2016a). *Special event production: The process* (2nd ed.). Routledge.

Matthews, D. (2016b). *Special event production: The resources* (2nd ed.). Routledge.

Mayco International. (2019). *What are cars made of? 10 of the top materials used in auto manufacturing*. https://maycointernational.com/blog/what-are-cars-made-of/.

McCormack, L. (2018, January 8). The women's march: Rome. *History Today*. https://www.historytoday.com/history-matters/womens-march-rome.

McIntosh, J.R. (2005). *Ancient Mesopotamia: New perspectives*. ABC-CLIO.

McIntyre, P. (2016, January 7). *The list #0127: Drive a parade float*. Youtube. https://www.youtube.com/watch?v=0DcxnKClGwo.

McKenzie, J., & Moorey, P.R.S. (2007). *The architecture of Alexandria and Egypt, 300 BC–AD 700*. Yale University Press, Pelican History of Art.

McKinnell, J. (2000). The medieval pageant wagons at York: Their orientation and height. *Early Theatre, 3*.

McNamara, R. (2020, August 28). *The colorful history of the St. Patrick's Day parade*. ThoughtCo. https://www.thoughtco.com/history-of-the-st-patricks-day-parade-1773800.

McNeil, I. (1990). *An encyclopedia of the history of technology*. Routledge.

Melina, R. (2011, April 21). Earth Day co-founder killed, composted girlfriend. *Science on NBC News.com*. http://www.nbcnews.com/id/42711922/ns/technology_and_science-science/t/earth-day-co-founder-killed-composted-girlfriend/#.U0h_fV5hzXk.

Menpes, M. (1903). *The Durbar*. Adam and Charles Black.

Merriam-Webster. (2020). *Validate*. https://www.merriam-webster.com/dictionary/validate.

Milhausen, R.R., Reece, M., & Perera, B. (2006, May). A theory-based approach to ynderstanding sexual behavior at Mardi Gras. *The Journal of Sex Research, 43*(2).

Milzarski, E. (2018, May 24). *What science says about the 'marching on bridges' myth*. We are the mighty. https://www.wearethemighty.com/military-life/soldiers-marching-over-bridges-myth/.

Miyamoto, K. (2018, September 2). *5 essential elements every spec script should have*. Screencraft. https://screencraft.org/2018/09/02/5-essential-elements-every-spec-script/.

Montgomery, J. (2013, Jan. 29). Sexual attraction and survival mode. *Psychology Today*. https://www.psychologytoday.com/intl/blog/the-embodied-mind/201301/sexual-attraction-and-survival-mode.

Moore, S.T., Hirasaki, E., Cohen, B., & Raphan, T. (1999, December). Effect of viewing distance on the generation of vertical eye movements during locomotion. *Experimental Brain Research, 129*(3).

Morton, S.G. (2012). Ritual Procession and the creation of civitas among the ancient Maya: A case study from Naachtun, Guatemala. *Canadian Journal of Archaeology, 36*(1).

Morton, V. (2019, June 6). Youtube bans 'Triumph of the Will,' allows Soviet Communist films. *The Washington Times.* https://www. washingtontimes.com/news/2019/jun/6/ youtube-bans-leni-riefenstahls-triumph-will-under-/.

Moss, M. (2006, February). Nelson's grand national obsequies. *English Historical Review, CXXI*(490).

Newberg, M. (2016, January 2). What's a $250,000 Rose Parade float really worth? *CNBC.* https://www.cnbc.com/2016/01/02/ rose-parade-is-a-great-roi-companies-say. html.

Nichols, J. (2014). *John Nichols's The progresses and public processions of Queen Elizabeth: Volume V: Appendices, bibliographies, and index.* Oxford University Press.

Nir, S.M., & Schweber, N. (2017, May 21). After 146 years, Ringling Brothers Circus takes its final bow. *The New York Times.* https://www. nytimes.com/2017/05/21/nyregion/ringling-brothers-circus-takes-final-bow.html.

NIWAKA Corporation. (2020). *Gion Matsuri.* Discover Kyoto. https://www. discoverkyoto.com/event-calendar/july/ gion-festival-yasaka-shrine-downtown/.

Nune, S. (2016, February 9). *International Fleet Review 2016 concluded in Visakhapatnam.* Jagran Josh. https://www.jagranjosh.com/ current-affairs/international-fleet-review-2016-concluded-in-visakhapatnam-1454 939069-1.

O'Brien, B. (2018, August 25). *Buddhist monks' robes.* Learn Religions. https://www. learnreligions.com/the-buddhas-robe-p2-4123187.

O'Brien, J. (2004, June 4). *Changing the subject.* Echo NYC. https://web.archive.org/ web/20040604124424/http://www.echonyc. com/~women/Issue17/art-obrien.html.

O'Muirigh, D. (2019, November 5). *Guinness stout and Guinness World Records: What's the connection?* IB4UD. https://www. irelandbeforeyoudie.com/guinness-stout-and-guinness-world-records-whats-the-connection/.

Onkst, D.H. (2020). *Air shows—An international phenomenon.* U.S. Centennial of Flight Commission. https://www.centennialofflight. net/essay/Social/airshows/SH20.htm.

Osborn, C. (2020, *February* 21). Rio's Carnival floats put drama and comedy in motion. *The World.* https://www.pri.org/ stories/2020-02-21/rio-s-carnival-floats-put-drama-and-comedy-motion.

Ostrower, F. (2005). *Motivations matter: Findings and practical implications of a national survey of cultural participation.* The Urban Institute.

Parker, G. (2016). *A look behind the most extravagant wedding ever.* Money Inc. https:// moneyinc.com/the-most-extravagant-wedding-ever/.

Pasadena Tournament of Roses. (2020). *Rose parade participants.* https://tourna mentofroses.com/events/about-rose-parade/#participants.

Patrouille de France. (2020). *Les prémices de la voltige.* Patrouille de France. https://www. patrouilledefrance.fr/histoire/.

Payne, R. (1962). *Rome triumphant: How the empire celebrated its victories.* Barnes & Noble.

Pentzell, R.J. (1984) The staging of religious drama in Europe in the later Middle Ages: Texts and documents in English translation (P. Meredith & J.E. Tailby, Eds.). *Comparative Drama 18*(4) Article 6. https://scholarworks. wmich.edu/compdr/vol18/iss4/6.

Petit de Julleville, L. (1885). *Les comédiens en France au moyen âge.* Slatkine Reprints, 1968.

phantuba. (2016). *Inspirational quotes— drumcorps.* Reddit. https://www.reddit. com/r/drumcorps/comments/3sy69i/ inspirational_quotes/.

philhellene. (2010, December 11). *Ancient Greek military drills.* Historum. https:// historum.com/threads/ancient-greek-military-drills.18511/.

Phillips, J. (2005, February 1). Ever wonder who's inside a parade float? *Car and Driver.* https:// www.caranddriver.com/features/a18202216/ ever-wonder-whos-inside-a-parade-float/.

Phillips, J. (2015, May 5). The crusades: A complete history. *History Today, 65.* https:// www.historytoday.com/archive/feature/ crusades-complete-history.

Pincott, J.E. (2014, November 4). Are these rules worth breaking? *Psychology Today.* https://www.psychologytoday. com/us/articles/201411/are-these-rules-worth-breaking.

Pirenne, H. (1955). *A history of Europe: From the invasions to the XVI century.* University Books.

Pitts, M. (2008, January/February). The henge builders. *Archaeology.*

PlanetJanet. (2017, March 30). *Laos' Luang Prabang: Colorful monk's alms procession is a must see.* https://www.planetjanettravels.com/ laos-luang-prabang-colorful-monks-alms-procession-a-must-see/.

Platt, R.E., & Walker, L.H. (2019). Regalia remembered: Exploring the history and symbolic significance of higher education academic costume. *American Educational History Journal, 46*(1–2).

Pleij, H., & Webb, D. (2001). *Dreaming of*

Cockaigne: Medieval fantasies of the perfect life. Columbia University Press.

Plutarch. (n.d.). The life of Paulus. In *The parallel lives.*

Plutarch. (1910). *Plutarch's lives. English edition by Sir Thomas North in ten volumes, 3.* J.M. Dent.

Polybius. (1962). *Histories* (E.S. Shuckburg, Trans.). Macmillan. (Original work published 1889).

Prescott, W.H. (1892). *History of the conquest of Mexico, with a preliminary view of the ancient Mexican civilization, and the life of the conqueror, Hernando Cortés, Vol. III.* David McKay.

Press Secretary to the Queen. (2013). *50 facts about the Queen's coronation.* https://www.royal.uk/50-facts-about-queens-coronation-0.

Prisco, J. (2019, June 7). A colorful history of the rainbow flag. *CNN Style.* https://www.cnn.com/style/article/pride-rainbow-flag-design-history/index.html.

Propaganda in Nazi Germany. (2020, September 11). In *Wikipedia.* https://en.wikipedia.org/w/index.php?title=Propaganda_in_Nazi_Germany&oldid=976462983.

Ramsay, W. (1875). Triumphus. *A dictionary of Greek and Roman antiquities.* John Murray.

Rauch, A. (2000). *The hieroglyph of tradition: Freud, Benjamin, Gadamer, Novalis, Kant.* Fairleigh Dickinson University Press.

Razzetti, G. (2018, Sep. 18). How to overcome the fear of change. *Psychology Today.* https://www.psychologytoday.com/ca/blog/the-adaptive-mind/201809/how-overcome-the-fear-change.

Reading Buccaneers Drum & Bugle Corps. (2010). *Quotes.* https://readingbuccaneers.wordpress.com/.

Redfield, A. (2017). An analysis of the experiences and integration of transpersonal phenomena induced by electronic dance music events. *International Journal of Transpersonal Studies, 36*(1).

Reicher, S. (2000). In Kazdin, A.E. (Ed.), *Encyclopedia of psychology.* American Psychological Association.

Restall, M. (2018). *When Moctezuma met Cortés: The true story of the meeting that changed history.* HarperCollins.

Ricci, N. (2018). *The psychological impact of architectural design* [Unpublished Senior Thesis]. Claremont McKenna College. https://scholarship.claremont.edu/cgi/viewcontent.cgi?article=2850&context=cmc_theses.

Rice, E.E. (1983). *The grand procession of Ptolemy Philadelphus.* Oxford University Press.

Ridgley, P. (2020). *Wellington's death: Lying in state and funeral procession.* The Waterloo Association. https://www.waterlooassociation.org.uk/2019/04/12/wellingtons-death-lying-in-state-and-funeral-procession/.

Ridgway, C. (2016). 28 April 1603—*Elizabeth I's funeral.* The Tudor Society. https://www.tudorsociety.com/28-april-1603-elizabeth-funeral/.

Ridgway, C. (2019, May 29). *20 May 1533—Queen Anne Boleyn's coronation river procession.* The Anne Boleyn files. https://www.theanneboleynfiles.com/29-may-1533-queen-anne-boleyns-coronation-river-procession/.

Roberts, N.F. (2020, May 29). Psychological research explains why people protest. *Forbes.* https://www.forbes.com/sites/nicolefisher/2020/05/29/the-psychology-of-protests-reveals-why-americans-are-ready-for-action/?sh=1c64c039bbbb.

Robinson, A. (2018). Indigenous regalia in Canada. *The Canadian Encyclopedia.* https://www.thecanadianencyclopedia.ca/en/article/indigenous-regalia-in-canada.

Rooney, D. (2005). *Angkor: An introduction to the temples* (4th ed.). W.W. Norton & Company.

Rowse, A.L. (1953, May 5). The coronation of Queen Elizabeth. *History Today, 3*(5). https://www.historytoday.com/archive/coronation-queen-elizabeth.

Royal barge procession. (2020, October 11). In *Wikipedia.* https://en.wikipedia.org/w/index.php?title=Royal_Barge_Procession&oldid=983010202

Royal entry. (2020, June 29). In *Wikipedia.* https://en.wikipedia.org/w/index.php?title=Royal_entry&oldid=965156094.

Royal Family. (1953, June 2). *The Queen's coronation oath, 1953.* The royal family. https://www.royal.uk/coronation-oath-2-june-1953.

Rufus, Q.C. (2020, July 14). Curtius Rufus on Alexander entering Babylon. In (J. Yardley, Trans.) *History of Alexander the Great of Macedonia, Section 5.1.17–33.* Livius.org. https://www.livius.org/sources/content/curtius-rufus/alexander-the-great-enters-babylon/.

Rusch, H., Leunissen, J.M., & van Vugt, M. (2015, September). Historical and experimental evidence of sexual selection for war heroism. *Evolution and Human Behavior, 36*(5).

Ryan, K.M. (2014, December 1). Uniform matters: Fashion design in World War II women's recruitment. *Journal of American Culture, 37*(4).

Saunders, N.J. (2006). *Alexander's tomb: The two-thousand year obsession to find the lost conquerer.* Basic Books.

Saxon, A.H. (2020). Circus. *Britannica.* https://www.britannica.com/art/circus-theatrical-entertainment/General-characteristics.

Scarpari, M. (2006). *Ancient China: Chinese civilization from the origins to the Tang Dynasty.* VMB Publishers.

Scham, S. (2008, November/December). The world's first temple. *Archaeology.*

Schechner, R. (2002). *Performance studies: An introduction.* Routledge.

Schele, L., & Freidel, D. (1990). *A forest of kings: The untold story of the ancient Maya.* William Morrow and Company.

Schmidt, T.E. (1995). Mark 15.16–32: The crucifixion narrative and the Roman triumphal procession. *New Testament Studies, 4.*

Schrobsdorff, S. (2011, August 19). The hero with a thousand faces. *Time.* https://entertainment.time.com/2011/08/30/all-time-100-best-nonfiction-books/slide/the-hero-with-a-thousand-faces-by-joseph-campbell/.

Scott-Kemmis, J. (2018). *Business clothing: Color psychology and your business clothing.* Empowered by color. https://www.empower-yourself-with-color-psychology.com/business-clothing.html.

Selin, S. (2016). *The marriage of Napoleon and Marie Louise.* Imagining the bounds of history. https://shannonselin.com/2016/04/marriage-napoleon-marie-louise/.

Sengupta, H. (2019, January 26). Why the Kumbh Mela is an economic blessing. *Fortune India.* https://www.fortuneindia.com/polemicist/why-the-kumbh-mela-is-an-economic-blessing/102900.

Shafer, B.E. (1997). Temples, priests, and rituals: An overview. In B.E. Shafer (Ed.), *Temples of Ancient Egypt.* Cornell University Press.

Shah, V. (2016, May 8). *Theatre, performance and society.* ThoughtEconomics. https://thoughteconomics.com/theatre-performance-and-society/.

Shearman, J. (1975). The Florentine entrata of Leo X, 1515. *Journal of the Warburg and Courtauld Institutes.*

Sheets, G.R. (2000). *The grand review: The Civil War continues to shape America.* Bold Print.

Shelton, I. (2010, June 6). Victoria welcomes the world: Six nations, 8,000 sailors to take part in navy's centennial fleet review. *Times Colonist.* https://www.timescolonist.com/news/victoria-welcomes-the-world-six-nations-8-000-sailors-to-take-part-in-navy-s-centennial-fleet-review-1.7122.

Sherwood, H. (2018, August 27). Religion: Why faith is becoming more and more popular. *The Guardian.* https://www.theguardian.com/news/2018/aug/27/religion-why-is-faith-growing-and-what-happens-next.

Shewring, M. (Ed.) (2013). *Waterborne pageants and festivities in the Renaissance: Essays in honour of J.R. Mulryne.* Taylor & Francis.

Shils, E., and Young, M. (1953, December). The meaning of the coronation. *The Sociological Review, 15*(3).

Shukla, P. (2015). *Costume: Performing identities through dress.* University Press.

Siculus, D. (1947). *The library of history of Diodorus Siculus, IX.* Loeb Classical Library Edition. http://penelope.uchicago.edu/Thayer/E/Roman/Texts/Diodorus_Siculus/18B*.html#26.

Siculus, D. (1954). *The library of history of Diodorus Siculus, X.* Loeb Classical Library Edition. https://penelope.uchicago.edu/Thayer/E/Roman/Texts/Diodorus_Siculus/20D*.html.

Siculus, D. (1957). *The library of history of Diodorus Siculus, XI*(XXXI). Loeb Classical Library Edition. http://penelope.uchicago.edu/Thayer/E/Roman/Texts/Diodorus_Siculus/31A*.html.

Sigal, C. (2013, Aug. 24). Remembering my time at the 1963 March on Washington. *The Guardian.* https://www.theguardian.com/commentisfree/2013/aug/24/march-on-washington-anniversary-martin-luther-king.

Silverman, R.E. (2012, Aug. 6). Wrongdoers feel a 'cheater's high.' *The Wall Street Journal.* https://blogs.wsj.com/atwork/2012/08/06/wrongdoers-feel-a-cheaters-high/.

Singh, S.D. (1989). *Ancient indian warfare: With special reference to the Vedic Period.* Motilal Banarsidass Publishers.

Sinnema, P.W. (1992, Spring). Mourning and merchandising: Wellington's London funeral and the case of the Illustrated London News. *Nineteenth-Century Prose, 26*(1).

Slepian, M.L., Ferber, S.N., Gold, J.M., & Rutchick, A.M. (2015). The cognitive consequences of formal clothing. *Social Psychological and Personality Science, 6*(6).

Slutsken, H. (2020, September 15). Why passenger jets could soon be flying in formation. *CNN Travel.* https://www.cnn.com/travel/article/airbus-formation-flight/index.html.

Smith, K. (2019, May 22). *Why anxiety can be a huge turn-on: The paradoxical psychology of the erotic mind.* Start it up. https://medium.com/swlh/why-anxiety-can-be-a-huge-turn-on-the-paradoxical-psychology-of-the-erotic-mind-2a33f76b4072.

Snell, K.D.M., & Ell, P.S. (2000). *Rival Jerusalems: The geography of Victorian religion.* Cambridge University Press.

Sobczak, A. (2017, September 28). *I asked 35 people why they love marching band.* Odyssey. https://www.theodysseyonline.com/asked-35-people-why-they-love-marching-band.

SPSP. (2017, December 17). *Entitled people don't follow instructions because they see them as "unfair."* http://spsp.org/news-center/press-releases/entitled-people-instructions-unfair.

Staff. (2020, September 6). Several vessels sink during Trump supporters' boat parade in Texas. *Associated Press.* https://globalnews.ca/news/7318867/trump-supporters-boat-parade-texas/.

Statista. (2020). *Passenger car construction material—comparison of 1975 and 2005.* Vehicles and Road traffic. https://www.statista.com/statistics/275305/passenger-car-materials/.

Statista. (2020). *Revenue of the tourism and*

services sector during Carnival in Brazil from 2012 to 2020. https://www.statista.com/statistics/974580/carnival-revenue-brazil/.

Stearns, P.N. (2007). *A brief history of the world: Part 2 of 3*. The Teaching Company.

Steckelberg, A. (2011, January 18). Mapping the inauguration and parade. *The Washington Post*. https://www.washingtonpost.com/graphics/local/2017-inauguration-map/.

Steinbach, S.L. (2012). *Understanding the Victorians: Politics, culture, and society in nineteenth century Britain*. Routledge.

Studarus, L. (2015, October 6). Why we love flawed heroes. *Relevant Magazine*. https://relevantmagazine.com/culture/why-we-love-flawed-heroes/.

Suelzle, B.P. (2006, November). An evaluation of two recent theories concerning the Narmer Palette. *Eras, 8*.

Sugrue, T.J. (2020, June 11). 2020 is not 1968: To understand today's protests, you must look further back. *National Geographic*. https://www.nationalgeographic.com/history/article/2020-not-1968.

Suval, L. (2013). *Men in uniform and women's psyches*. Psych Central. https://psychcentral.com/blog/archives/2013/01/27/men-in-uniform-and-womens-psyches/.

Ta-Kuan, C. (1992). *The customs of Cambodia, 2*. The Siam Society.

Taylor, C. (2018, April 29). *Trinidad carnival: the birth & evolution*. Discover Trinidad & Tobago. https://www.discovertnt.com/articles/Trinidad/The-Birth-Evolution-of-Trinidad-Carnival/109/3/32#axzz4ZRlw7vuI.

Teeter, E., & Brewer, D.J. (2004). Religion in the lives of the ancient Egyptians. *Fathom Archive*. University of Chicago Digital Collections. http://fathom.lib.uchicago.edu/1/777777190168/.

Terzioğlu, D. (1995). The imperial circumcision festival of 1582: An interpretation. *Muqarnas, 12*.

Thayer, B. (1940). The Roman antiquities of Dionysius of Halicarnassus. *Loeb Classical Library Edition, IV*. http://penelope.uchicago.edu/Thayer/E/Roman/Texts/Dionysius_of_Halicarnassus/7C*.html.

Thorp, R.L. (1988). *Son of heaven: Imperial arts of China*. Son of Heaven Press.

Tong, C.H. (1996). The festival of the nine emperor gods in Malaysia: Myth, ritual, and symbol. *Asian Folklore Studies, 55*.

Torches of freedom. (2021, August 2). In *Wikipedia*. https://en.wikipedia.org/w/index.php?title=Torches_of_Freedom&oldid=1036688755.

Tremblay, P., Boyle, A., Rigby, H., & Haydon, J. (2006). *Darwin Festival 2004: a trial of the national events evaluation kit*. CRC for Sustainable Tourism.

Triumph of the will. (2020, September 9). In *Wikipedia*. https://en.wikipedia.org/w/index.php?title=Triumph_of_the_Will&oldid=977535075

Trtworld. (2020, Feb. 27). *How important is the Umrah pilgrimage for the Saudi economy?* https://www.trtworld.com/middle-east/how-important-is-the-umrah-pilgrimage-for-the-saudi-economy-34163.

True Cross. (2020, May 2). In *Wikipedia*. https://en.wikipedia.org/w/index.php?title=True_Cross&oldid=954400398.

Turner, V. (1982). *From ritual to theater: The human seriousness of play*. PAJ Publications.

Turner, V. (1988). *The anthropology of performance*. PAJ Publications.

TV History. (2021). *Number of TV households in America 1950–1978*. The American Century. https://americancentury.omeka.wlu.edu/items/show/136.

UBS. (2010). *Dresscode UBS à l'attention des collaborateurs PKB*. https://www.scribd.com/fullscreen/45325094?access_key=key-296jtldidj6kp3hdiyn0.

UK Patent office. (1857). *Patents for inventions*.

Union des Maisons de Champagne. (2020). *1909—Premier meeting d'aviation en Champagne*. Grandes Marques & Maisons de Champagne. https://maisons-champagne.com/fr/encyclopedies/berceau-mondial-de-l-aviation/1909-1er-meeting-d-aviation-en-champagne/article/synthese-histoire.

University of Glasgow. (2021). *History of graduation*. The University of Glasgow Story. https://universitystory.gla.ac.uk/history-of-graduation/.

Valdesolo, P., & DeSteno, D. (2011). Synchrony and the social tuning of compassion. *Emotion, 11*(2). American Psychological Association.

Vancouver Heritage Foundation. (2019). *It's a parade!* Places that matter. https://www.vancouverheritagefoundation.org/place-that-matters/its-a-parade/.

Vanderbilt, P. (2014, April 3). *When did passenger trains begin to run between New York City and Montreal?* Railroad History. https://penneyvanderbilt.wordpress.com/2014/04/03/when-did-passenger-trains-begin-to-run-between-new-york-city-and-montreal/.

Van Gennep, A. (1960). *The rites of passage*. Routledge.

Van Stekelenburg, J., & Klandermans, B. (2013, September). The social psychology of protest. *Current Sociology Review, 61*.

Vedantam, S. (2017, April 18). *Researchers examine the psychology of protest movements*. Hidden Brain. https://www.npr.org/2017/04/18/524473948/researchers-examine-the-psychology-of-protest-movements.

Velasco, D. (2020). *Boulevards and parkways*. Seattle Open Space 2100. https://nacto.org/wp-content/uploads/2015/04/boulevards_parkways_velasco.pdf.

Versnel, H.S. (1970). *Triumphus: An inquiry into the origin, development and meaning of the Roman Triumph*. E.J. Brill.

Victoria and Albert Museum. (2017). *The ommegang in Brussels on 31 May 1615: The triumph of Archduchess Isabella, historical context note*. http://collections.vam.ac.uk/item/O18973/the-ommegang-in-brussels-on-painting-alsloot-denys-van/.

Victoria and Albert Museum. (2020). *The story of Circus*. https://www.vam.ac.uk/articles/the-story-of-circus.

The Victorian crisis of faith. (2020). In *British Wiki*. https://sites.udel.edu/britlitwiki/the-victorian-crisis-of-faith/.

Victory stele of Naram-Sin. (2021, April 23). In *Wikipedia*. https://en.wikipedia.org/w/index.php?title=Victory_Stele_of_Naram-Sin&oldid=1019546494

Vince, R.W. (1989). *A companion to the medieval theatre*. Greenwood Press

Virginia Asphalt Association. (2020). *The history of asphalt*. https://vaasphalt.org/the-history-of-asphalt/.

Vopiscus, F. (1932). The life of Aurelian, part 2. *Historia Augusta*. Loeb Classical Library. http://penelope.uchicago.edu/Thayer/E/Roman/Texts/Historia_Augusta/Aurelian/2*.html.

Wakin, M.M. (1986). *War, morality, and the military profession*. Westview Press.

Walsh, P. (1996). Making a drama out of a crisis: Livy on the Bacchanalia. *Greece & Rome, 43*(2).

Weisberger, M. (2016, October 26). *Getting in character: The psychology behind cosplay*. Live Science. https://www.livescience.com/56641-why-people-cosplay.html.

Wertman, J. (2019, April 28). *April 28, 1603—Funeral of Elizabeth I*. https://janetwertman.com/2019/04/28/april-28-1603-funeral-of-elizabeth-i/.

White, D.G., Bay, M., & Martin, W.E. Jr (2013). *Freedom on my mind: African Americans and the new century, 2000-present*. St. Martin's.

Wicks, B.E. (Sep/Oct 2000). *"Eventing" and other festival trends*. http://www.lib.niu.edu/2000/ip000916.html.

Wilkinson, R.H. (2005). *The complete temples of ancient Egypt*. The American University of Cairo Press.

Wilkinson, T. (2011). *The rise and fall of ancient Egypt: The history of a civilization from 3000 BC to Cleopatra*. Bloomsbury Publishing.

Will, U., & Berg, E. (2007, August 31). Brain wave synchronization and entrainment to periodic acoustic stimuli. *Neuroscience Letters, 424*(1).

Williams, S. (2008, July 17). *Ref, you must be colour blind—We're the team playing in red so we have to win; Colour bias is a huge factor, claims research*. Wales Online. https://www.walesonline.co.uk/news/wales-news/ref-you-must-colour-blind-2164866.

Willimek, D. & B. (2011). *Music and emotions: Research on the theory of musical equilibration (die strebetendenz-theorie)*. http://www.willimekmusic.de/music-and-emotions.pdf.

Woods, L. (2019, November 28). How much does a float in Macy's Thanksgiving Day Parade cost? *CBS News*. https://www.cbsnews.com/news/thanksgiving-day-2019-parade-float-costs/.

Wünsch, S. (2018, February 2). A kiss for your tie? Why Carnival kicks off with gender power games. *Deutsche Welle*. https://www.dw.com/en/a-kiss-for-your-tie-why-carnival-kicks-off-with-gender-power-games/a-19022057.

Xenophon. (2013, January 15). Anabasis. In Dakyns, H.G. (Trans.), *The project Gutenberg ebook of Anabasis, VI*(V). https://www.gutenberg.org/files/1170/1170-h/1170-h.htm#link2H_4_0050.

Xinhua Net NetWriter. (2020, January 19). Central China discovers earliest wheel ruts. *Chinese Archaeology*. http://kaogu.cssn.cn/ywb/news/new_discoveries_1/202001/t20200119_5081197.shtml.

Yerasimos, S. (2009). *The imperial procession: Recreating a world's order*. WebCite. https://www.webcitation.org/query?url=http://www.geocities.com/surnamei_vehbi/yerasimos.html&date=2009–10–25+22:34:18.

Zaho, M.A. (2004). *Imago triumphalis: The function and significance of triumphal imagery for Italian Renaissance rulers*. P. Lang.

Zeinhefer, S. (2002). *Die reichsparteitage der NSDAP in Nürnberg*. Verlag Nürnberger Presse.

Zhou, S. (2017). *Visualizing power, Studies of how information of imperial power in Qing China was communicated in the eighteenth century, through visual representation of printed processions* [Unpublished master's thesis]. University of Dublin, Trinity College.

Zorn, E. (2013, March 13). I hate a parade! *Chicago Tribune*. https://www.chicagotribune.com/news/ct-xpm-2013–03–15-ct-oped-0315-zorn-20130315-story.html

Index